MW01505998

BY UNITED MEN OF HONOR

FIT 2 FIGHT

ARE YOU ARMORED UP?

VISIONARY AUTHORS

ALLEN L. THORNE & KEN A. HOBBS II

Published by World Publishing and Productions
PO Box 8722, Jupiter, FL 33468
Worldpublishingandproductions.com

ISBN: 978-1-957111-41-4
Library of Congress Control Number: 2024921669

Scripture quotations marked ASV are taken from the American Standard Version. Public Domain.

Scripture quotations marked *ESV® Bible are taken from (The Holy Bible, English Standard Version®),* Copyright ©2001 by Crossway, a publishing ministry of Good News Publishers. Used by permission. All rights reserved.

Scripture quotations marked KJV are taken from the King James Version. Public Domain.

Scripture quotations marked NASB are taken from the New American Standard Bible®, Copyright ©1960, 1962, 1963, 1968, 1971, 1972, 1973, 1975, 1977, 1995 by the Lockman Foundation. Used by permission.

Scripture quotations marked NIV are taken from THE HOLY BIBLE, NEW INTERNATIONAL VERSION®, NIV® Copyright ©1973, 1978, 1984, 2011 by Biblica, Inc.® Used by permission. All rights reserved worldwide.

Scripture quotations marked NKJV are taken from the New King James Version®. Copyright ©1982 by Thomas Nelson. Used by permission. All rights reserved.

Scripture quotations marked NLT are taken from the *Holy Bible,* New Living Translation, copyright ©1996, 2004, 2015 by Tyndale House Foundation. Used by permission of Tyndale House Publishers, Inc., Carol Stream, Illinois 60188. All rights reserved.

Scripture quotations marked NRSV are taken from the New Revised Standard Version Bible, copyright ©1989 National Council of the Churches of Christ in the United States of America. Used by permission. All rights reserved worldwide.

Scripture quotations marked TPT are from The Passion Translation®. Copyright ©2017, 2018, 2020 by Passion & Fire Ministries, Inc. Used by permission. All rights reserved. ThePassionTranslation.com.

CONTENTS

INTRODUCTION

You are about to get a glimpse into some of the battles so many men struggle with and fight through. Sometimes we lose, and sometimes we win. But often, our stories go unseen and untold. The valiant authors in this book have written to let you in on *their* stories of warfare, to tell you how they fought to overcome, and to teach you what weapons they used—or learned they should have used—to become victorious. These men have become transparent and vulnerable—they are United Men of Honor, warriors, leaders, and heroes willing to share their messages of hope and faith. As the enemy does his best to take men out and off mission, we may ask where all the mighty men have gone. The answer is that so many have been taken down by the enemy because they were not armored up to be *Fit 2 Fight*.

Men of God—our families, communities, and countries need us to be on guard and vigilant men of courage who are battle-ready warriors. We must prepare to lead and overcome evil with courage. We are called to be conquerors, not wounded casualties of mental, emotional, physical, and spiritual warfare. This book has been written to share insight and guidance on how you can become *Fit 2 Fight,* prepared to win the battle for our souls and lives. Together, we can save many from heartbreak and protect families from disaster.

What does it mean to be *Fit 2 Fight* and to armor up?

If you ask a soldier, "Are you fit to fight?" they will know you are asking them if they are mentally, emotionally, and physically ready for action; you are asking if they are trained and prepared for the fight, up for the challenge, or even fit for war.

Being *Fit 2 Fight* refers to being in a state of readiness and capable of engaging in warfare or combat operations. It means an individual, squad, or team is equipped, trained, and ready to perform effectively in combat. This can include many factors, such as:

1. Having the necessary weapons, gear, and protections—being armored up.

2. Being mentally, emotionally, physically, and spiritually prepared for the demands of combat.

3. Having completed relevant training and drills in order to be fully prepared.

4. Understanding and being prepared to follow orders, plans, and coordination.

To prepare to be *Fit 2 Fight,* we must operate with our eyes wide open, our minds fixed on God, and our spirits tuned to the voice of the Lord. Claiming victory in our battles is at stake. Although our struggles might look different, preparation is always the key! Being prepared ahead of time, being *Fit 2 Fight,* is the best plan of attack. Like a good football strategy, our best defense is a strong offense. And to be warfare ready, we must make sure we not only have our armor on but that it's in good condition and we know how to use it. Yes, Christians have spiritual armor! That armor is described in detail in Ephesians 6:10-17 and is referred to many times in the chapters of this book.

As you read, hear the hearts of these authors, become a part of our United Men of Honor battalion, and prepare to fight with us through the battles of life as part of God's squad. No man fights alone! The mission is the man.

May your life be filled with purpose as you use this book as a guide to find your heart again. There is a battle to fight, a beauty to rescue, and an adventure to live. Together, let's get fully equipped to live the life God has for us, using these stories of hope, guidance, and coaching as inspiration to win the war on men and save families.

Will you pray with me?

God, ready me for battle. Fit me with the full armor specific to the fight. Go before me in strength and guard me from behind with Your power. Keep my mind on Your Word and focused on You instead of my circumstances. Fight for me as I remain Fit 2 Fight and armored up, Lord.

In Jesus' name, I pray. Amen.

ALLEN L. THORNE

Allen L. Thorne is a grateful follower of Jesus Christ, our Lord. He earned his ministerial leadership degree from Southeastern University and enjoys speaking, writing, and sharing the Lord's truth as the Spirit guides him.

Allen is the faithful pastoral teaching author of *Reviving Recovery: Unbound,* a growing Spirit-led recovery ministry newly planted in South Florida. Amid sobriety's freedom, Allen values God's "teachable moments" as the Spirit enhances his ministerial, personal, and professional gifts. As a grateful leader in the Band of Brothers Bootcamps, he shares Christ's freedom from a pliable heart.

Allen lives in Stuart, Florida, with his beloved wife, Stacy Jo, their darling daughters, pampered Shi Tzu pups, and calico cat. Allen and Stacy serve together at Stuart's Revive Church, enjoying the free-flowing Word and Spirit Truth, leading believers to experience their own personal relationship with the Lord.

Allen embraces God's divine perspective while standing firm in Christ and fighting from victory! Email Allen at *revivingrecovery@gmail.com*

Trusting Truth

By Allen L. Thorne

> *You, O Lord, will not withhold Your compassion from me. Your lovingkindness and Your Truth will continually preserve me.*
> (Psalm 40:11 NASB)

Thirty years of my thoughts and decisions nearly led me to death. I was broken and burdened with abandonment's unworthiness and self-sufficiency's weariness slathered in addiction's never-ending pursuit of "more." I choked down satan's detrimental lies as fast as he could feed them to me while I ran as far away from God as possible. However, when I stopped running long enough to listen, God showed me that my only hope to fulfill His purpose is found in His capital "T" Truth—Jesus Christ. His Truth reveals that the *Spirit of truth...will guide you into all the truth* (John 16:13 NASB). The Holy Spirit encourages, enlightens, and empowers my vulnerable embrace of Jesus' objective Truth. Only His Truth transforms from the inside out and empowers the fulfillment of the purpose for which He created us in His image.

As finite creations under our infinite Creator Father God, we discover Truth from Deuteronomy and into and through the Gospels and the Epistles, which teach that we are emotive creations wired for loving connections with God and each other. His love resounds to the point of God sending

Jesus to show His love for us in that whoever believed in the One in whom He sent would be saved. Our blood-bought belonging in Christ reconciles us back to the Father.

However, somewhere along the way, we may *experience* detrimental challenges that skew our divinely intended identity. Such detriment presents satanic lies that appear more true amid the hurtful circumstances. From a spiritual perspective, it is not the experience alone that skews our belief structure; instead, it is the lies we believe, such as insecure unworthiness, that we carry away from previous experiences that cause long-term harm and challenges.

The believed lie can be used against us by the satanic enemy of our souls and become buried under fear and shame, while its false belief wreaks havoc on our impressionable souls. Harbored lie-based beliefs affected my emotions, thoughts, and behaviors. Inappropriate behavior, thoughts, and sideways emotions were never the challenge but only the resultant symptom of the believed lies underneath it all. The lies that I was not worthy of love and belonging, a blackened past can never be escaped, and a pure heart would never be mine blocked my purpose for as long as I allowed them to be strongholds in me. However, through *new* Holy Spirit-guided experiences, Jesus met me where I was and traded these lies for His Truth. His Truth heals from the inside out. Friends, when Truth fuels our emotions and thoughts, our actions align and abide accordingly. As Jesus said, *"If you continue in My word, then you are truly My disciples, and you will know the truth, and the truth will set you free"* (John 8:32 NASB).

So, maybe you're thinking, *Do you really believe all that?*

I do! I am certain of all the above because I *experienced* it. God's only Son and His Holy Spirit shone Their Truth through darkness. They called and led me back to my *Truth Identity*. I am *Fit 2 Fight* because I choose to embrace vulnerability with the Holy Spirit, faithfully face fear, and accept Jesus Christ's Truth. As such, I receive the Spirit's answer to the Why-am-I-here question. Let me tell you how.

For me to have such a message to share, you can surmise there must be a mess back there somewhere. Let's start there.

I am the oldest of three boys who lived in a fearfully violent home operated under our three-tour Vietnam vet father's reign. Sometime between 1977 and '78, Dad's dominant reign decided that we were going to start going to church. Now, I'm not certain if Dad chased the woman into the church, but in due time, he surely chased and followed her out of the church. It didn't take too long for him to run off with my Sunday school teacher and leave Mom and us far behind him. (For a more detailed angle of these early years and the ensuing forgiveness, check out our last United Men of Honor anthology, *Navigating Your Storm*). The early violence, paternal neglect, and abandonment perpetuated poverty's scarcity mindset and love and belonging's painful absence. Such damage fed me lies that I would never be good enough and never have enough. The satanic father of lies seemingly said, "Life has no sunny side, kid. This pain and darkness are all you get, boy. God don't love you. What a load of crap! I have something for you, though. Look at it shine! Feels good, right? Go ahead, take all you want. It'll make it all alright. Take it! Hold it real tight, boy. I have plenty for you. Yeah, I got what you need."

My addiction cover-up started early with food, pornography, and alcohol. These were later accompanied by drugs, promiscuity, and an unhealthy desire to prove that I was good enough to be liked, accepted, and loved. The aforementioned believed lies caused the pain that fueled the emotions and thoughts that resulted in such addictive and compulsive behaviors. After nearly three abusive decades, I sought recovery and got sober. I worked on a solid plan and addressed many challenges along the way. However, even as I remained sober, the believed lies remained because conventional recovery is largely a cognitive series of behavior-focused exercises. My initial recovery skimmed the surface and buffed up the outside a bit. However, it wasn't until the Lord invited me to go deeper into an inner healing experience that the Holy Spirit finally revealed the buried lies, and Jesus Himself addressed them.

To set the stage for the vision, you should know that when Dad left, he was gone—no visits, financial help, or property upkeep assistance. He was gone as in not to be seen at all for quite some time. So, as the oldest, at 9-10 years old, I was Mom's big helper. The bulk of the chores—such as lawn mowing and burning the trash we couldn't afford to have taken away—became my responsibility. Because I hated handling the trash and could only burn so much at a time, it would pile up in the garage bay corner. It was emphatically unpleasant, to say the least. So, where am I going with this? I am so glad you asked!

I was seven years sober, "leading" a local Christ-centered recovery program in 2020. However, even as I had worked a solid program and was approved for "leadership," I was still emotionally triggered in our home. One day, the in-fighting in our house was so heinously detrimental that it scared me—that was the low point that led me to a series of inner healing sessions. However, I was so bound up in self-sufficient logic, fear, and shame that I didn't experience a breakthrough until the third session. Anger and rage ensued because I felt lonely, overwhelmed, unappreciated, and disrespected. Rage turned into a despairingly deep sadness.

As I sat with the session facilitator, I embraced these emotions, and we prayerfully inquired the Holy Spirit about what He had to show me concerning my rage and despair. During the first two sessions, which appeared unsuccessful to me, I was taken back to where I grew up. I saw the eight-year-old me standing in front of the huge trash pile in the first bay of the three-bay garage. The boy was sad and afraid. He was overwhelmed and alone. He knew nothing of connected belonging as he was poor and pushed away by the other kids. He just wanted to belong. Even though his mother's love for him and his brothers could never be denied, the dismally dark circumstances often clouded her love's brilliance.

"So," the facilitator said, "where is Jesus in this scene? What does Jesus have to say about the sadness, fear, and disconnection?"

I thought to myself, *Jesus, where are you?*

The garage scene was dark and gray, but the second and third bays on my left were clouded and blurry, as if to say that day's focus resided in the first bay. Then, a figure moving from the far opposing corner of the third bay appeared. He strode through the accumulated junk as if nothing was there. He was tall and wore a white robe. He was coming right for me, and as He broke the second bay's blurry boundary, He stood next to me as I wept. It was Jesus standing with me in the gray. Not saying a word, He touched my right cheek, wiped my tears, and walked past me out the garage's side door, turning left. As He walked away, He said nothing, but I heard the Spirit's whisper say, "Follow Me." I was stunned by His peaceful authority as I stood there and looked out the garage's rear windows. I saw Him walk past the first and second windows, but He did not pass the third. When I couldn't see Him, I ran out the side door and followed His steps around the back of the garage, and there He sat.

He was sitting on the large log I would sit on while I burned the trash. He motioned me toward Him and invited me to sit with Him. As I sat on His lap, He held me close; the boy in my vision and my current adult were overtaken by uncontrollable sobbing. Jesus held me until the bawling subsided and listened when I told Him of the unworthiness I felt for my own father's love. He listened while I explained through the sobs that I was such a disappointment because I couldn't keep up with the chores and schoolwork. He listened while I revealed myself as a failure.

As we rose, He knelt to my level. He put His hands on my shoulders, looked me in the eyes, and said, "No more." At that point, I knew I had an opportunity to turn it all over to Him and allow Him to bear the pain's burden for me. The prophet Isaiah foretells His plan when he scribes, *However, it was our sicknesses that He Himself bore, And our pains that He carried* (Isaiah 53:4a NASB).

Jesus then asked me if I wanted to release the fear, sadness, and inadequacies to Him. Of course, I agreed. The chaotic attributes appeared as trash that He received and heaped on the existing pile in the garage. He then embraced me, stating that I belong to Him and He has always been and will always be with me. He filled me with His hope for new tomorrows and strength to endure upcoming challenges. He filled me with the confidence that I am not ever alone and our best days together were yet to come. We walked together back toward the garage's side door. He stopped, looked over His left shoulder, and took off like a flash! All I saw were silver streaks through the field to the neighbor's property. I somehow knew where He had gone and felt overridden with shame.

I was swiftly transported to a storage building where the neighbor girl and I used to look at pornographic magazines. The building door was absent; a dark void appeared through the doorway. As I stood next to Jesus, He put His hand on my shoulder and said, "This is not love, and this is not what I have for you, son." He called me son! A wave of joy and peace washed over me that words cannot explain. *He called me son!* Any bit of pre-existing shame was taken from me in that moment and replaced with a fulfillment of His love and belonging. My precious Savior, Christ Jesus, calls me His own! Moreover, His love letter tells me that, in Him, *[I am] a chosen people, a royal priesthood, a holy nation, a people for God's own possession* (1 Peter 2:9a NASB). Therefore, *[I] may proclaim the excellencies of Him who called...[me] out of darkness into His marvelous light* (1 Peter 2:9b NASB). Praise Him!

From there, we went back to the garage's side door. I followed Him inside, and we stood in the first bay. The heaping trash pile was gone, and the first bay was spotless. I felt light and free but was a little befuddled as to why the other two bays with all of Dad's left-behind junk were still dark and blurry. I asked Him why, and He told me that the mess doesn't belong to me, and that He has it handled when Dad is ready.

Fit 2 Fight: Are You Armored Up?

Dad passed the next year, in 2021. Thanks to Jesus and the absolute power of forgiveness, we developed a great relationship with each other, but more importantly, we both gained strong relationships with Jesus. The Apostle John accentuates how in his initial Epistle when he scribes, *If we confess our sins, He is faithful and righteous so that He will forgive us of our sins and cleanse us from ALL unrighteousness* (1 John 1:9 NASB, emphasis added). Friends, when God cleanses us from ALL unrighteousness, how much of the burden is left for us to carry? OH YEAH! ZERO! When we decide to release our junk to Him who came to carry the burden, He takes it ALL! Praise His holy and powerful name!

At the end of that third session, the facilitator and I went back to test the triggers from the initial argumentative scene with my wife and me. To Christ's authoritative credit, He had replaced my rage with His peace, my sadness with happiness and understanding—which is still being refined into joy by the Holy Spirit of Truth, and my fear with a deeper faith in the One who stood by me and called me His own. Praise Him!

Our 2023 Ohio visit provided additional healing proof when I had an opportunity to return to the house and property where I had grown up. I couldn't access the house, but I was permitted to walk the property, which was unkept and overgrown. The house showed clear evidence that spirits of fear, shame, doubt, and despair still resided there. I strode through the property, stood by the garage's side door, and moved around between the second and third windows where Jesus assuredly held me. I could not help but smile, remembering how He healed me from the inside out during that third session. What had seemed so large when I was a child now appeared small.

Where once was a row of three apple trees across the backyard, now there were only two. I noticed the concave ground where the first of three trees once stood. The missing tree had shaded my childhood sandbox and supported my tire swing. Ahhh, so many memories came rushing back then and continue to do so now as I write here today. Standing in the concaved yard and looking up at the house that bore so much sorrowful strife and fear, I felt a peace that surpassed all understanding. I was drawn to my knees in absolute gratitude for all Jesus has seen me through and how His restorative healing ensues.

It was almost time for me to go. I walked up to the house and stood under that towering maple tree that once supported Mom's clothesline. To my left was the dilapidated basement doors I used to hide under. To my right was the old well cover I used to sit on, wondering what was down in that hole while I listened to Mom sing along to those old country tunes chiming from her kitchen clock radio. Right ahead of me was the porch where Jesus and I sat during a different session when He told me why Dad was the way he was back then. Compassion and forgiveness were born after that one. His Truth never ceases to amaze me.

I drove away that day entirely at peace because, as Isaiah prophesied, Jesus ensured His prophetic fulfillment. The Truth affirms, *"The Spirit of the Lord is upon Me, Because He has anointed Me to bring good news to the poor. He has sent Me to proclaim release to captives, And recovery of sight to the blind, To set free those who are oppressed, To proclaim the favorable year of the Lord"* (Luke 4:18-19 NASB). Praise Him!

Friends, our entire worldview, including our emotions, thoughts, and actions, derive from what we believe. As such, whether we choose to believe a lie or the Truth determines how we function.

So, what do you believe?

For me, faith in Christ opened doors to God's higher and greater perspective. Helpless became helpful, prideful became humble, and His victory crucified the victim. When I stopped and listened, He led me to be open to His divine perspective. Only the Holy Spirit exposes believed lies while Jesus fills me with His Truth. He introduced me to my purposeful *Truth Identity* in Him!

Folks, I'm not special. I am just a guy who stopped believing satan's lies and shifted my gaze to the One whose life is the light for us all. I am *Fit 2 Fight* because I trust His Truth, Way, and Life to guide me for the rest of my days. I am *Fit 2 Fight* because my Creator calls me His own.

Our first moves toward freedom are cultivating a pliable heart for the Lord, openness to His divine perspective, and a willingness to embrace new or renewed beliefs so that the Spirit's renewing of our hearts and minds may transform us!

We are not the sum of our failures!

We are children of the One, True, and Living God!

I encourage you to believe and trust His Truth and be *Fit 2 Fight!*

And again, I say, Praise Him!

Fit 2 Fight Hurt

By Ken A. Hobbs II

Many men have abandoned their relationship with God. Others have been called to serve Him but refused because they have been hurt. And in many instances, wayward individuals have allowed pain to crush their lives and take them off mission.

There is a large spectrum of hurts, including emotional, physical, and circumstantial—which includes things like dealing with people or losing a friend or relationship. Hurt can stem from changes in our lives, broken hearts or painful relationships, lost hope, aging, deaths, sickness, and other events that can encompass our minds and cause wounds.

It takes a radical step of faith to overcome hurt before it consumes you. Many believers have been conquered by hurt when they have allowed their flesh to get in the way and were not equipped for the battle. This one powerful word, hurt, can quickly overcome us. So, we must be on guard to war against worry, envy, anger, retaliation, and evil responses. Hurt can cause us to fall prey to these actions and reactions. So, what is the solution to a man's hurting heart? As men, we are often protective and guarded against being vulnerable when dealing with hurts. Do you think you could trust your hurting heart to someone who can help you?

God is our perfect solution—He never makes a mistake. Someone who makes no mistakes and who loves and cares about you is always with you. Only God can oversee every heart supernaturally. God provides truth in His Word for us to hear when the world feeds us lies. One of those truths is that God loves us so much that He sent His only Son, Jesus, to heal us from our hurts. His perfect love is all-encompassing. When one of His sons is hurting, He knows it. When one of His sons is feeling pain, He feels it. He cares. God is a God of wisdom and understanding; He is just and will always take action to protect His children and start healing our wounds.

> If any of you lack wisdom, let him ask God, who gives generously to all without reproach, and it will be given him.
> (James 1:5 ESV)

The first step in allowing God to humble your heart is to trust Him and His wisdom, knowing He will guide you. The more you know Him, the more you will be open to trusting Him.

> Keep trusting in the Lord and do what is right in his eyes. Fix your heart on the promises of God, and you will dwell in the land, feasting on his faithfulness.
> (Psalm 37:3 TPT)

Please give your heart and all that comes with it to God. Put on the helmet of salvation, allowing Him to wash your mind and hurts. All your past sins will be covered with the healing power He so generously gives to us when we fully accept His grace and forgiveness. If you are dealing with pain, recognize that the pain you experience from your past is not sinful. To blame victims for their pain is a sin against the wounded, the brokenhearted, and the oppressed. It is a sin against God Himself, whose heart is with those who are hurt. Hurt hurts God, and He comes close to those who are brokenhearted; He confirms that in Psalm 34:18. Please read and hold the following scriptures close if you are dealing with tremendous hurt.

Even when bad things happen to the good and godly
ones, the Lord will save them and not let them
be defeated by what they face.
(Psalm 34:19 TPT)

My beloved son, I pray for a greater release of God's grace,
love, and total well-being to flow into your life from
God our Father and from our Lord Jesus Christ!
(2 Timothy 1:2 TPT)

. . . .

KEN A. HOBBS II

Ken A. Hobbs II is a Christ follower, devoting his life to impacting others in para-church ministries, missions, and his business, where he leads a marketplace ministry. He founded United Men of Honor—leading, coaching, and empowering men to lead with integrity and faith in their homes, businesses, and communities. www.unitedmenofhonor.com. His previous two books, *United Men of Honor: Overcoming Adversity through Faith* and *Navigating Your Storm: By United Men of Honor*, are Amazon #1 best-sellers.

Ken is an executive team leader and serves on the Leadership Team of Band of Brothers. He is strongly passionate about the Bootcamps and believes they are needed in this world so that men do not have to fight their struggles alone. www.BandofBrothersFL.com

As a Senior Vice President/Financial Coach Multiple Brokerage owner and operator for www.PRImerica.com/kenhobbs2, Ken has impacted communities nationwide with business-building, coaching/training, personal financial coaching, and services for over 30 years.

Ken supports his wife, Kimberly, co-CEO of Women World Leaders and World Publishing and Productions, www.WomenWorldLeaders.com. He also supports Kerus Global Education, African Orphan Care Project and Anti-trafficking/trauma training as an Advisory Board member. www.kerusglobal.org

Ken is a father, stepfather, husband, brother, and uncle who passionately loves his family and friends.

Prepare for the Blindside

By Ken A. Hobbs II

As I was driving down the road with my wife, I listened to a voicemail that came in unexpectedly; it was from my father. As I played back his voice message, something seemed off. My dad—the rock in my earthly life, my mentor, my business leader, and the pastor of my church growing up—had called me. *Was he drunk?*

I had missed the phone call, but as my wife and I listened to my father's message, we both agreed he sounded intoxicated. *But how could this be?*

We played his message back over and over, knowing that my dad didn't drink whatsoever. *What is going on?* The message didn't make sense but wouldn't leave my mind either. Later, when I questioned him about it, my stepmom and father brushed it off, saying it was a joke.

But, it wasn't any joke!

Fast forward some years ahead, this unforgettable message was not a prank or my dad messing with us, which I thought was the case at the time, but one of the worst battles I will ever fight. Getting blindsided can make you rise up or run away. Some of the most challenging times in my life have centered around loved ones battling against mental, physical, or emotional attacks from our enemy, but nothing surprises God. He calls us to be (Romans 8:37

NIV). Still, it was so hard walking every day through this battle that turned out to be a long goodbye to my father.

How could I know that one of the strongest men in my entire world would eventually be diagnosed with dementia and early-onset Alzheimer's? Initially, I had no guidance or advice on handling the emotional impact this disease would have on me, let alone on him. But the enormity of the storm would soon come, and the dramatic changes to his health, brain, and lifestyle would begin to sabotage his earthly being. My dad would battle internal enemies that caused such devastation.

Even now that this struggle is over, I still find it difficult to understand how I endured such hardship. I saw the devastating effects on my stepmother and brothers—especially my brother, Kevin, as he and I walked it together. It was difficult for my wife and I to face because of such extreme emotions. But God walked with us and had prepared us for this fight of our lifetime. He equipped us to be *Fit 2 Fight!*

As I began to watch my stepmom engage in her battle to care for my dad, I was yet to realize the combat that would pull me in as the oldest son and also the one who would carry on the family business and ministries. My dad lived his life and fought so hard to leave something impressionable and sustainable for his family. In what seemed to be a flash, I had no choice but to armor up! I had to become *Fit 2 Fight* against one of the most devastating diseases a person can face as I watched my loved one suffer. The agonizing moments warped my reality and any sense of how I could help my father through the worst battle of "his" life. But this was indeed what I needed to do. My biggest weapon would be my shield of faith in God. He alone is Who armored me up for the battle I would fight to help my father. God helped us "Stand Firm..."

As the symptoms started emerging, when my dad and I were at the office together, I would pay special attention to him—listening to him speak and watching as he led his team with strength, dignity, and honor, just as he always had. At first, nothing seemed too different. Yet, as his disease progressed, peculiar things began happening. He would slur his words, stutter, and stammer for phrases he had previously known by heart. He also began to shuffle around, and sometimes, I would need to step in and hold him up.

"Oh God, how do I handle what is happening?"

I adjusted quickly to heading to the front of the room to clarify the words he spoke that didn't make sense. His lack of ability to facilitate the financial information he once taught people as a coach and inspirational teacher was declining. And random behaviors began emerging. Standing up in front of a room of people, the once staunch, knowledgeable, and confident leader of our family business who knew his content like the back of his hand and had maintained all his licenses for years was now experiencing extreme memory issues. Those challenges, coupled with emotional and physical shifts from the disease, made it so hard to stand by as he declined.

At first, I tried to cover for my dad, who had once taken care of me and taught me so much of what I know. I would jump up to his rescue, then patiently walk him through the teaching part of the meeting, hoping nobody would realize something was dramatically wrong. However, over time, the extreme shifts in demeanor and lack of confidence he displayed became evident to all watching. We had to face the truth and share the news with all his teammates who were taking notice. These changes were not getting better; in fact, I knew deep inside they'd only be getting worse. It was only a matter of time before people would soon be looking to me for all of their help and guidance. *How could I do this? How would I watch my father slip away from reality without letting him lose his dignity as a man of honor, a true man who loved and served God his entire life?* Let me say here. It about broke me. BUT GOD!

Let me give you some context. My father, I am his namesake, was not a perfect man, but he was truly a forgiven and repentant man. As I wrote about in United Men of Honor: Overcoming Adversity Through Faith, our first book, my dad was highly convicted and passionate about his beliefs, ministry, business, and family. He was purpose-driven, almost to a fault. He was highly responsible and had great integrity as he built churches, helped raise four children, took care of his widowed mother, fathered the fatherless, was a husband to his wife for over 50 years, and coached finances to thousands. My dad led and built ten financial brokerages + teams, ran and led small groups, and loved and served on the leadership team for the Band of Brothers Florida Bootcamps. His favorite role was to be the most amazing Pop Pop to his ten grandchildren. Knowing all this was why it was so hard to walk through this traumatic journey and rely on the Lord through it all.

If God had not equipped me to become *Fit 2 Fight* in the way He did, I surely would have drowned in the emotional and physical distress of watching my father die a slow death mentally and physically.

My family and friends went through denial, anger, bargaining with God, and depression. I knew I had no choice but to gird up the strength to stand, exactly how my father taught me. I would need to do what he would expect of me, even knowing his decline was imminent. My task became harder and harder as I tried to get my dad to the office, taking him for "outings" when he was becoming housebound. I would go to his house and pick him up in an effort to change his routine environment and keep him from becoming stifled, which also allowed my stepmom some time to rest and recover. My dad went from going to lunches with me, able to eat adult food on his own, to me helping feed him as he needed. Eventually, I fed him baby food as he could barely swallow. He needed my help in every way as I took him on each outing. Many times, we'd just go for ice cream and call it a day.

My dad went from using the toilet on his own to times I'd need to change him and then put adult diapers on him. He would be so embarrassed. That was one of the hardest things I had to do for my own father, a man of such dignity. But I looked to God for my strength to handle the extreme accidents that came out, and yes, those did often happen. When they did, I would clean him up to the best of my ability and not let him know what and how I was feeling. I just loved on him and told him, "Don't worry, Dad. We've got this."

You might be wondering where I received my arsenal of strategies to fight this battle, watching my strong father crumble before my eyes, bringing me to my knees in tears and pain. IT WAS GOD, I tell you. ONLY GOD!

I relied on God's Word, and according to the phrase, "full armor of God," from Ephesians 6:11,13-17. I suited myself up. I repeatedly centered my thoughts to armor up accordingly, and then I *would sit before God,* remembering that His Word is true. I relied on my faith in God and His promises. Everything my dad had taught me from the Word of God as I was growing up, I put into action. I was now using the strengths and values instilled in me "from" him, "on" him.

> Put on all of God's armor so that you will be able to stand firm against all strategies of devil...Therefore, put on every piece of God's armor so you will be able to resist the enemy in the time of evil. Then after the battle you will still be standing firm. Stand your ground, putting on the belt of truth and the body armor of God's righteousness. For shoes, put on the peace that comes from the Good News so that you will be fully prepared.
> In addition to all of these, hold up the shield of faith to stop the fiery arrows of the devil. Put on salvation as your helmet, and take the sword of the Spirit, which is the word of God.
> (Ephesians 6:11,13-17 NLT)

In 2013, my dad, brother, and I attended the first Band of Brothers Florida Bootcamp. There, we learned the importance of "standing firm" and what it means to put on the full armor of God. We carry a coin that shows a warrior and lists all the armor God has given to equip us for life's battles.

Now, that coin is given to participants when they complete Bootcamp. "Coin Up" brothers!!!! I carried my coin daily throughout this season of my dad's illness to remind me where my strength came from. And I still carry it today.

Daily, I used the armor of God in many different situations.

I put on the belt of truth, securing myself with the complete belief in God's truth and power, understanding that what I saw happening in front of me were continual lies that the enemy was throwing at me. Lies like, "How could God be real when your father gave his whole life to a God who would allow this to happen to him???" I stood strong, knowing that God's Word is truth, and those who truly worship God worship Him in Spirit and in truth, just as I watched my father do for so many years!

> Jesus replied..."For God is Spirit, so those who worship Him must worship in spirit and truth."
> (John 4:21, 24 NLT)

Besides the belt of truth, I needed to wear the breastplate of righteousness! I knew my dad had a right relationship with God, so God's righteousness was part of his character and also had been ingrained in me. I held fast to that righteousness as I went on doctor visits with my dad. We would go to different places to receive help for degenerative disease maintenance, providing us ample opportunities to share with others. Sharing the gospel message of Jesus and our strong faith brought both my father and me joy, especially in times of hurt and pain. People would marvel at how we were getting through such a difficult crisis together as a family. Not only did I get to use this breastplate of righteousness as an opportunity to share, but so did my brothers, stepmom, and the rest of our family, as we were all raised to talk about Jesus and what He has done for us.

Another necessary part of my armor was my shoes—the peace that comes from knowing the good news of Jesus Christ. I put my shoes on daily to boldly proclaim Christ's message and overcome the enemy. When I was tired and weary from the mental and emotional strain of trying to balance business, ministry, and family stresses, I'd put on my shoes yet another time, proclaiming Jesus has defeated the enemy. Then, I would head out the door to serve another day. God always provided great opportunities to share my dad's pastoral messages, and there were times I'd get to share some of the vivid skits he used to do. My favorite enactment my dad did once was that of the "Defeat the Devil" campaign! He taught this lesson in the Winn Dixie parking lot in front of crowds of people. He had his friend from church dress in a devil's costume and fly in on a helicopter that landed in the center of the parking lot. Dad was preaching and sharing the gospel, binding the devil, quoting scripture, and sharing with the crowds how to use God's armor to stand firm and defeat the devil!!!!

Besides my dad teaching me to fight the enemy from the pulpit, he taught me how to proclaim the good news everywhere we went. The voice he instilled in me is a big part of what helped me get through this time of struggle. Sharing Jesus was always joyful and a blessing with my father, and it certainly got me through this hardship. Dad was mainly joyful through his trial. He loved to sing the hymns every day. His caregiver and I would sing with him and sometimes sing for him when he couldn't voice the words.

As I actively grabbed my shield of faith and placed it over the fear I faced each day as I saw my father decline, I would let my faith rise up and put a smile on my face when I went to pick up Dad. I would greet him and smile, saying, "Dad, today we are heading out to conquer again. Let's do it together." Then, I would help my stepmom get him ready and gather up all the things needed to take him to the office. With heads held high in dignity, we'd head out the door and into the car, with smiles for yet another day as we struggled to do life.

Sometimes, the car rides would be extremely difficult because he wouldn't know where we were going even though I kindly retold him many times during the short ride. Often, he wouldn't be able to "hold it," if you know what I mean, and he would have accidents in the car. That was very hard. When my fear set in that I wouldn't be able to handle this much longer, my shield of faith rose up in defense and said, "You can do this for your dad." I always seemed to get stronger after hearing God's voice.

As I put on my helmet of salvation, I had to renew my mind regularly each time I saw my father. Especially as the end was drawing closer. What is this life that we live? How quickly it comes to an end. From strength to weakness, our lives decline at a rapid pace; seeing this happen before my eyes with my father was sometimes more than I thought I could handle. Despite seeing him lying in a hospital bed in the bedroom of his home, no longer able to speak but only stare, I knew my dad was still inside the shell of his body. So I would renew my mind, confident of the life he had in Christ, knowing he wore the helmet of salvation. My dad was a solid example of what it meant to constantly wash the bad and discouraging thoughts out of our brains and wear a smile. He always portrayed confidence in his salvation and eternal destination. Let me tell you, knowing beyond a doubt that my dad never took off the helmet of salvation was the ONLY thing that got me through my struggles of seeing him slowly dying in a hospital bed in his bedroom!

In the moments before my dad took his last breath, I was standing at his bedside, wielding the sword of the Spirit. I recited and sang God's Word out loud, using the offensive weapon God gave us to attack the enemy. I knew the devil thought he was going to take my father away in death, but thank God that through Jesus Christ, death has been swallowed up in victory.

I will never forget watching my dad move beyond this earth and go to be with Jesus. God had equipped me through this entire battle by guiding me over and over again to wear His full armor. In every situation I encountered through Dad's dementia struggle, not only did I armor up as the little boy who learned from his father and grandfather, "When the going gets tough, Ken, armor up for battle and stay *FIT 2 FIGHT.*"

My dad proved he was indeed armored up not only as he suffered from Alzheimer's, but throughout his life as he continually exemplified being *Fit 2 Fight*. When his most challenging battle came, he didn't need to prepare. He was ready! Having learned so much from the peace he exhibited despite his difficulties in the flesh, my dad's lifetime lessons taught me to be ready always. So I was equipped and prepared to fight the spiritual battles like a warrior on my knees before our Almighty God.

My father is with our Lord and his father today. We didn't say "goodbye"; we said "see you soon"—just not yet. I know that for him in heaven, he will blink his eyes, and I will be there. That gives me peace for his absence.

Your battle may be different than mine. You may not deal with a family member's illness—but in some way, you will face a difficult challenge directed at your own life. Learning from someone else's example and testimony is a gift we should never take for granted.

I had a father who loved, lived, and exemplified Jesus—especially in the last part of his life. But that didn't prevent him from the reality of facing a battle. I pray this story will impress upon your heart that you might be called into battle at any moment. Are you fit to fight? Do you wear the armor that God has given you?

God equips each one of us if we remember to say yes to Him and get dressed each day with the armor He has provided. Put on the whole armor of God, as the Bible teaches, and prepare to fight all the battles of your life fully equipped for any blindside.

Armor Up with Praise

By Allen L. Thorne

From the rising of the sun to its setting,
The name of the Lord is to be praised!
(Psalm 113:3 NASB)

Every move we make through these challenging days requires a decisive choice. Will we choose to gaze at the current challenge ceaselessly, or will we decide to look consistently to the One who can make a difference?

Are you the difference maker? Yeah, no, neither am I! It's possible, however, that we get caught up in the mire's confusion and lose sight of who's in control. Even as we attempt to focus forward faithfully, we can easily become entangled.

So, what if in the middle of the warfare we stopped and recognized things for what they are? What if we took a few steps back, a few deep breaths, and actively decided to *rid ourselves of every obstacle and the sin which so easily entangles us,...looking only at Jesus, the originator and perfecter of our faith* (Hebrews 12:1-2 NASB)? What would happen when, in the middle of the storm, we decided to *consider Him who has endured such hostility by sinners against Himself, so that we will not grow weary and lose heart* (Hebrews 3 NASB)?

When we deeply consider Jesus' sacrifice and triumph, our faith can rise over even fearful situations (anger, anxiety, depression, doubt) as our praise for Him ensues! Praising God in the storm shifts our perspective. More than that, daily praising God develops our relationship with Him and advances our faith, taking it from ourselves to our God as we begin to recognize He is the only authentic difference-maker.

> *Not to us, O Lord, not to us, But to Your name give glory,*
> *Because of Your mercy, because of Your truth.*
> (Psalm 115:1 NASB)

Friends, as we understand that our confession in Christ as Savior King over our lives does not ensure smooth and flawless living, we also must believe, walk enduringly with Him by faith, and come to understand that it is His divine insight, power, and authority that guides us through current challenges. It is *only* our Triune Godhead: God the Father, Christ the Son, and the Holy Spirit who enlighten and empower us to be *Fit 2 Fight* the battles before us!

So, amid Their guidance, what are we learning through the challenge? Do we find ourselves complaining about the challenging circumstances, or are we actively seeking a godly situational perspective? The difference between the two is a total game-changer! Complaining keeps us bound in fear and locked down by our limited, finite perspective. In contrast, seeking the Lord's perspective kicks down the doors of limitation and lets the Light of the world pour in and destroy doubt and fear's darkness.

> *In him was life, and that life was the light of all mankind. The light*
> *shines in the darkness, and the darkness has not overcome it.*
> (John 1:4-5 NIV)

Our challenging circumstances do not often cause us to praise cheerfully. However, when we decide to do what we haven't previously done, we discover a newness we may have been unaware of. I appreciate the Apostle Paul's perspective in His first Epistle to his church in Thessalonica. He declares, *Rejoice always, pray continually, give thanks in all circumstances; for this is God's will for you in Christ Jesus* (1 Thessalonians 5:16-18 NIV).

In this verse, Paul issues three essential moves to action to enhance our faith and empower our fighting fitness. He tells us first to *rejoice always*. Always? That's what the man said. Remember, we are all works in progress. So, let's progress forward, shall we?

Is the medical report unfavorable? Praise Him!

Are your finances appearing less than hopeful? Praise Him!

Are your professional expectations not landing where you wanted? Praise Him!

Are your life expectations not being met? We encourage you to stop and praise Him for the challenge.

Second, Paul teaches we must *pray without ceasing*. Ask Him, sit quietly, and listen to His perspective.

Finally, Paul tells us, *in everything, give thanks*. Profitable words here are, "Thank You, for this challenge, Lord, what are You showing me here? What is my teachable moment here, Lord?"

Again, stop, sit quietly, and listen. He'll speak. He's just waiting for us to start the conversation while we seek His relational *face* over His provisional *hand*.

Praise Him with worthy recognition, friends!

> The Lord is my strength and shield; My heart trusts in Him
> and I am helped; Therefore my heart triumphs,
> And with my song I shall thank Him.
> (Psalm 28:7 NASB)

Our fighting fitness is in His Truth. Armor up and praise Him!

. . . .

DR. BRUCE HEBEL

Dr. Bruce Hebel (ThM, DD) is an international speaker with a compelling message that is revolutionizing the hearts of people from all walks of life. Raised in a pastor's home and educated to pastor the local church, Bruce is now following God's call to the Church-at-large. Backed by over 30 years experience leading churches, all of his training has led to this: helping people experience the freedom of the gospel through forgiveness. His passion is pointing people to *"Christ in you, the hope of glory."*

A graduate of Dallas Theological Seminary, Bruce is President of ReGenerating Life Ministries. Along with his wife, Toni, he is co-author of *Forgiving Forward: Unleashing the Forgiveness Revolution.* Bruce and Toni have been married since 1979. They have been blessed with three adult children and are the proud grandparents of six grandchildren.

Forged *Through* Forgiveness

By Dr. Bruce Hebel

In 2009, after 30 years of pastoral ministry in local churches, God led my wife Toni and me to launch Forgiving Forward, a ministry dedicated to helping people experience the freedom of the Gospel through the power of forgiveness. Since that time, we have taught the Forgiving Forward message to churches of all sizes around the world, from mega-churches to small groups. We've seen marriages restored, families reunited, churches unified, addictions ended, and hearts renewed. A pastor friend once told me, "Bruce, Forgiving Forward is truly an Ephesians 3:20-21, above-and-beyond-your-imagination type of ministry!" No one I know would have predicted nor could we ever have dreamed of the impact the Forgiving Forward message would have in people's lives. To understand why, you need to know our back story.

I was born into a pastor's home. My parents modeled walking with Jesus for me from the moment I discovered the planet. At 5½, I understood that I needed a Savior. Because I was so young, my parents spent several weeks making sure I understood the Gospel; once satisfied, they led me to receive Christ. My baptism must have been a comical sight. My dad wore big waders when he baptized people during a church service, but when he baptized me, he had to raise his toes up on one foot so I could stand tip-toed on them just to keep my head above water!

While I don't remember the details of many sermons that my dad preached while I grew up, I do remember one. On a Sunday evening in my ninth year, Dad was teaching on Joshua's final charge to the nation of Israel in Joshua 24, and he challenged the congregation to "Choose for yourself who you will serve, but for me and my house, we will serve the Lord."

At that moment, I felt a clear call in my spirit: "I'm talking to you, Bruce. I'm calling you to serve Me just like I called your dad. I know you are young, but I am calling you to give your life to serve Me and My Church. Will you choose Me tonight?"

I went to the altar and surrendered my life to pastoral ministry. While I didn't fully know what that meant at the time, I never wavered from that commitment. My first official role was as our church worship leader when I was 15, and I have been pursuing ministry ever since.

After graduating high school, I went to Bible college, where I met my wife, Toni. The church Toni and I attended together hosted Dr. Bruce Wilkinson at the Sunday morning service. That morning, he taught on the "Prayer of Jabez" from 1 Chronicles 4:9-11. Jabez was an honorable man who asked God to bless him, enlarge his influence, keep His hand on him, and protect him from evil. Toni and I were engaged at the time and actively planning our future together. We were so moved by the message that we went to the altar, surrendered our future together to God, and asked that He would use us in such an extraordinary way that everyone would know that He did it. We then began praying the Prayer of Jabez together daily.

A month later, we broke off our engagement. We now know that was the beginning of our training for Forgiving Forward.

Later that summer, after God had worked in both of our hearts, Toni and I were reconciled and married five months after our originally planned wedding day. We finished college and went to Dallas Theological Seminary for further training and mentoring. While at DTS, some of the most significant spiritual leaders on the planet poured into us. We entered into full-time ministry together with great hope for a Jabez-sized ministry. Then we got wounded! Deeply! Multiple times, in multiple ways, in multiple places, over multiple years! We suffered deep hurts and very difficult circumstances that left our whole family wounded, both individually and collectively.

In one situation, I was deeply wounded by a betrayal at a church where I worked. It was a very dark and painful time for me and our family. At the lowest point in my life, when I thought all hope was gone, God miraculously rescued us by taking us to a new place and giving us a fresh start. The deliverance was quite remarkable, and the timing was amazing. Yet, in the middle of what we saw as vindication, I neglected to truly forgive from my heart the man who wounded me. Oh, I gave lip service to forgiving him, but what I really did was stuff the wound deep inside me.

Through an unexpected encounter a few years later, the wound I thought was behind me was quietly reopened. The bitterness began to ooze out, but I didn't notice. To make matters worse, current church happenings where I served reminded me of a previous betrayal. Looking back at it now, I can see I was being tormented by the memories of the past wound that distorted my perception of the present reality. I became defensive and self-protective. My decisions and reactions as a leader were affected. My relationships suffered. I didn't share my struggle with anyone, not even my wife. That should have been a clue to me because Toni and I have always been very open with each other.

God used a sabbatical, a counselor, a three-day personal retreat, and a book on forgiveness to set me free. In a borrowed lake house in Alabama, I realized I had not truly forgiven the man from the previous church. During a time of personal confession, God revealed the wounds deep in my heart. This was one of those bittersweet times with the Lord. (Bitter because God showed me the ugliness of my flesh; sweet because He showed me the beauty of

His grace.) Then my Heavenly Father reminded me of a letter I wrote to the man who had hurt me, telling him I had forgiven him. My tortured mind rationalized the letter as being conciliatory and magnanimous, but in reality, it was accusatory and vengeful. I didn't like what I heard God tell me, but I knew He was right. I had not truly forgiven what he had done from my heart.

I heard God ask me a few questions: "Is this man's sin against you any worse than what I have forgiven you for? If I forgave you, who are you not to forgive him? Do you not realize that I love him just as much as I love you?"

With my heart broken, I stood rebuked—I had to forgive him.

As I confessed my sin of unforgiveness to God and forgave the man for the specific things that he had done to hurt me and my family, my heart was transformed and set free. It was like a dam had broken as peace flooded the whole house. I began to sing worship songs at the top of my lungs as my heart, once filled with torment, was now filled with praise! As I was worshipping, God gently convicted me that I needed to ask this man's forgiveness for the judgmental letter. While that was one of the most difficult confessions I have ever had to make, it was also one of the most freeing. I am now at peace with all of it.

When I returned home, I shared my experience with Toni and helped her forgive the same man for what he had done to hurt her. We then gathered our kids together. Pastors' kids often suffer collateral damage from what happens to their parents. Our kids had suffered greatly through the years, including being uprooted and having to leave their home and friends because of what had happened. I shared my lake house experience, and then we helped them forgive the people in our past who had hurt them. We spent 11 hours in one day forgiving, including burning incriminating documents and deleting emails related to what we forgave. These acts of cleansing led each of us to give and receive forgiveness for how we had hurt each other over the years. Our entire family was set free that day through forgiveness.

We were all forever changed and healed.

Three weeks later, Toni and I made the 400-mile trek from Atlanta to Paducah, Kentucky, to help my parents with a bathroom remodeling project. (Okay, for those who know me, Toni did the faux painting, and I did my best Tim-The-Tool-Man-Taylor imitation.) Dad and I had maintained a great relationship over the years. No "father wounds" for me. (Maybe there were a couple of bruises but no real wounds.) I am blessed.

At this point, Dad had retired after serving churches for over 50 years. Since I followed in his footsteps and became a pastor, we always found plenty to discuss. I greatly respected him, and he always made sure I knew how proud he was of me. He had walked with us through all our pain and struggles in ministry. So, of course, my story of forgiveness became a topic of conversation during our visit with my folks as we caught up between coats of paint.

On our last morning there, Mom was out running an errand. Toni and I sat at the table after breakfast, sipping coffee and tea and chatting with Dad. He typically was pretty upbeat despite struggling with heart disease and diabetes. But on this particular day, he was kvetching about a couple of people. He wasn't saying anything really mean, but bitterness leaked out of his words. He couldn't see it, but we could. It was obvious. These wounds were eating him alive.

At this point, I heard a voice inside my spirit say, "Speak into your Father about unforgiveness." It wasn't an audible voice, but it was very clear. I immediately went into a high-speed debate in my head. It went something like this:

"Lord, you know he is my Dad, right?"

"I know. I was there when both of you were born. Speak into his life!"

"But sons do not correct their parents," I said.

"They do if I tell them to. Speak into him!"

"Well, if I knew it was really You, Lord, I would. How do I know it's You?"

"You know it's Me. Quit stalling and speak into your Dad's heart. It will be alright."

"This may upset him," I responded.

"Who do you prefer to be upset with you, him or Me?"

"Good point!" I replied.

"Just trust Me."

"OK Lord, here goes..."

Swallowing hard, I said, "Papa, you know I love you, and you can do whatever you wish with this. I hope I don't make you mad, but it sounds to me like you are bitter at Don and John. You've been friends with Don for over fifty years. I'm sure he did not mean to hurt you, and he probably doesn't even know that he did. You've known John for over thirty-five years. He was like a son to you, and Carla (his wife) was like my third sister. I think it might be time to forgive and let them off the hook. You can do what you want to, but that's what I sense I am supposed to say to you." And then I braced for his response.

What happened next was remarkable.

Without any hesitation, my 76-year-old father immediately responded by saying, "Son, I stand rebuked. You are right. I need to forgive both of them. Will you pray with me?"

Papa then left his kitchen chair and kneeled with his face to the floor. As we prayed together, tears welled up in his eyes. He repented of his unforgiveness and forgave both of his friends from his heart. As soon as he finished, I noticed his countenance had changed, and his spirit was at peace. It took great effort for him to stand up from that praying posture, but as he did, he wrapped his arms around me—weeping and thanking me. We embraced for quite some time. Papa was free!

Within a month, God gave us a graduate-level exam in forgiveness when we were deeply wounded and betrayed at the church I was pastoring. Although it was very painful, we chose to forgive quickly and walked in freedom through the situation. We eventually planted a small church; the first four messages were on forgiveness.

God did amazing things through that little church with *incredible breakthroughs* in the lives of people who came through there. I say "through there" because people would come broken and wounded, we would teach them how to forgive, and then they would go and be reconciled to the church where they came from. We were like a MASH unit for wounded souls.

In our second year as a church, God reconnected us with Dr. Bruce Wilkinson. We hosted him for a series of teachings for a new book he was writing. After sharing our story with him over lunch one day, he looked at us and said, "All you have been through in ministry has not been your ministry. It has been training for your true ministry. Unforgiveness is the number one problem in the church today. You need to leave the local church and go to the big Church to teach it how to forgive, and you need to write a book on forgiveness. But don't just take my word for it, go ask one of your mentors and see if he confirms this."

I made an appointment for breakfast with Pastor Tom Rowe, who is a mentor and father figure to me. The day was March 19, 2009. I shared with him what Bruce was suggesting. Tom chuckled and said, "God told me three years ago that this is what you were going to do. He also told me to wait to confirm it until you came to me."

After we finished our breakfast, I went home and told Toni what Tom said. We got on our knees in our special prayer spot on our living room floor, and

I began to pray. As I was praying, Toni saw the number "30" flash before her mind and thought, *What is this about?*

She sensed God say, "I trained Jesus 30 years before I sent Him into His public ministry."

When I finished praying, Toni asked, "When was it that we first heard Bruce Wilkinson teach on the prayer of Jabez, and we asked God to use us in such an extraordinary way that we wouldn't get the credit?"

I went to my office, found my notes, and discovered it was March 19, 1979! Thirty years to the day, God confirmed the ministry of Forgiving Forward.

From that day on, our lives have never been the same as God continues to answer our Jabez prayer. We moved away from pastoring a local church and began crafting the Forgiving Forward message. We developed a seminar format and presented it to churches. We wrote the book and published it in 2011, and it has since been translated into Hebrew, Arabic, Spanish, Korean, and Russian. We released the Forgiving Forward Home Edition DVD Series in 2012, which has been completed by thousands of people, including incarcerated individuals in over 20 prisons. We have taught hundreds of thousands of people in live events in over a dozen countries. Toni and I have personally coached well over a thousand people and have also trained others as forgiveness coaches. The Forgiving Forward Freedom Center opened in the fall of 2020. The updated version of the video course was released in 2022, and the expanded Second Edition of the book came out in 2024.

"'For I know the plans that I have for you,' declares the Lord,
'plans for welfare and not for calamity,
to give you a future and a hope.'"
(Jeremiah 29:11 NASB1995)

God has a good plan for each of us, and He alone knows the end from the beginning. With His plan in mind, He begins to work on us, often using pain and heartache in order to craft us into what He wants us to be. God permits what He could prevent in order to bring about His greater glory and our greater good. He also prevents what He could permit for the same reason. What He wants from us is simply to trust Him in the process.

The only way to learn how to forgive is to have something to forgive. Knowing this, God allowed us to go through all that we went through, as deeply as we went through it, so we could speak authentically about forgiveness to multitudes of people around the planet.

If Toni and I had known what we would have had to endure for our Jabez prayer to be fulfilled, we might not have prayed it. Yet, looking back, we could not be more grateful that God called us and trained us to share the message of Forgiving Forward with the world. The suffering we endured does not compare to the joy we have when we help someone experience the freedom of the Gospel through the power of forgiveness.

MIKE TOBEY

Mike Tobey is the Executive Director of The Heaven Guy Ministry based in North Palm Beach, Florida. His precious wife Kathy went home to heaven in October of 2019 and has been the inspiration for the ministry.

Mike has been in Christian ministry for over 40 years, serving as a pastor, teacher, author, and motivational speaker. He is a former Spring Training Chaplain for the St. Louis Cardinals and has been a Law Enforcement Chaplain and Trainer since 2010. He is also the official Chaplaincy Trainer for the Zambian Government in Africa.

Mike is passionate about bringing as many people as possible to heaven and encouraging God's people to become more heaven-minded. The Heaven Guy Ministry is a 501c3 organization recording over 8,000 decisions for Christ with a global reach of over 190 countries and territories.

www.TheHeavenGuy.org

Set your minds on things above, not on earthly things (Colossians 3:2 NIV).

LOVE NEVER FAILS

By Mike Tobey

If you have ever loved deeply and lost your loved one, you know the pain and heartache I felt when my wife and I received the life-changing news that she had Stage 4 colon cancer. Together and with unconditional love, we persevered for many months and experienced an almost fairy tale ending of her life.

In her final days, my wife had a very special request for me. As I've endeavored to deal with her loss for the last five years and honor her in every way, God has miraculously been fulfilling her request. Amazingly, it has changed not only my life but the lives of tens of thousands of others. I'm proud to share my story with you.

A BLESSED RELATIONSHIP

My wife, Kathy, and I had a beautiful relationship. We were best friends and, in every sense of the word, inseparable. I used to tell her our relationship was what love stories and fairytales were made of. She would say that our souls were knit together like Jonathan and David's were in the Bible. We would regularly think one another's thoughts and finish each other's sentences. She often said we were "just the same person in different bodies." And then we would start laughing. One of the keys to our beautiful marriage was simply how we viewed and valued each other. I always considered her above me, in a higher place than myself, and I'm sure she saw me the same way. Our actions toward one another always stemmed from our respect for each other.

Kathy and I both enjoyed the outdoors, and we loved to travel. We had made plans for the future, adventurous plans, plans of buying an RV, and traveling across the country visiting national and state parks. Our desire was to share the love of Jesus everywhere we went, dotting our way across the mountains and countryside, enjoying the beauties of God's creation and our American homeland. Kathy envisioned building relationships with other campers, talking and laughing around the campfires. She lit up as she spoke of praying for others, believing God would show up in power and with His presence. Kathy understood we were a team and believed God would use us to share His love and message with many as we traveled.

GROUNDING FAITH

When things didn't seem like they could get much better, Kathy began experiencing some unusual pains internally. At first, she didn't seem too concerned, but when they persisted, she found a local naturopathic doctor and explained her recent pains and discomfort. He said she was probably experiencing pelvic floor disorder; he had seen this before and assured her it was nothing to worry about. He gave her several natural products and told her to take it easy. Kathy did as the doctor prescribed, but the pain continued and became more frequent and with greater intensity.

We eventually decided to get another opinion and visited a highly recommended medical doctor. After he ran a CT scan, we waited in the lobby for the results. Minutes later, our lives changed forever. When the doctor and his assistant entered the room together, their faces said it all. The doctor told us that Kathy had a large tumor in her colon and that she would need to be admitted to the hospital for immediate care. He called one of the top physicians from the hospital close by, who came right over. Things seemed to get worse from that moment forward, at least medically speaking.

My beautiful other half was diagnosed with Stage 4 colon cancer. The physician informed us that the location of the tumor made it far too risky to attempt to remove it; Kathy would not survive surgery to remove it.

This was a major shock to us. My bride was just 54 years young. And she looked even younger.

After a few days, the shock began to wear off, and the reality of this devastating life change started to settle in.

Kathy's first response was one of faith. Along with researching medical journals and articles for possible cancer cures, she spent her precious time reading and studying God's Word and listening to faith-building messages—always operating in faith just as she had done her whole life.

For those first few months, Kathy believed God would heal her—either through an inexplicable miracle or scientifically through the medical field. She still wanted to accomplish so much and had dreams that had not yet been fulfilled.

She watched and listened to countless videos and audio recordings on healing and faith. She meditated on the scriptures nonstop, focusing on every scripture she could find on healing.

It was amazing how she always kept a smile on her face through the trial. She never complained, and I never once heard her question why God was allowing her to go through this.

ANTICIPATING HEAVEN

One day, after Kathy had been through about four months of chemo, I remembered a book I had been given years before titled *Heaven* by Randy Alcorn. I mentioned it to Kathy, and she just lit up, saying, "Oh Michael, I want you to start reading that book to me every day!"

The book had a major impact on both of us. Not only did it add to our strong faith, but it also seemed to take the edge off her staunchly held conviction that God would heal her. The subtle shift was noticeable over the next few months as she fed her desire to learn more and more about heaven. I could see a remarkable and unmistakable peace and a calmness growing in her—as if her face reflected the beauties and joys of heaven that her spirit was somehow anticipating.

Months later, I showed our pastor a photo of her reading *Heaven.* When he looked at it, he said, "She looks like someone getting ready for a long journey, and they're reading the travel brochure." He couldn't have said it better. That really was what she was doing. She was learning as much as she could about where she would someday be going—possibly soon.

Although she was standing in faith and hope for healing, she eventually did come to a place of complete surrender and yielded the outcome to the Father. She knew that He knew best.

As we contemplated heaven, a frequent conversation Kathy and I had was about where we planned to meet once we both got there. The first time I asked her where she wanted us to rendezvous, she smiled and said, "The Judah Gate... the Praise Gate," referring to the scripture in Revelation 21:12, which says, *On the gates were written the names of the twelve tribes of Israel* (NIV). She told me that the name Judah was the word for Praise in the Hebrew scriptures. After that, we had many happy discussions about what it will be like when we finally meet again at the entrance to the beautiful city, the New Jerusalem. It was one of the last things we talked about in this life.

SEEING WITH CLARITY

On Kathy's last day in the hospital, just 2 1/2 weeks before she passed on to heaven, we were looking out the window from the cancer ward on the fourth floor. I asked her if the sunrise looked different to her.

She said, "Everything looks different." She said that clarity had come, and she was seeing things in a way she had never seen before.

Knowing things were about to change once she came home from the hospital, I said to her these special words—words that would ultimately shape my future and the lives of thousands of people around the world.

"Kathy, if the Lord takes you home, which it looks like He may, what do you want me to do?"

I slipped the phone onto the bed and began recording. She didn't hesitate and said, "Michael, I want you to do everything possible to bring as many people as you can to heaven."

That was her heart's desire. I believe she was beginning to get a heavenly perspective even before she got there. After walking with Christ for almost 40 years, she had come to a special place of intimacy with Him and desired nothing more than to please Him.

PEACE AND STRENGTH

The hospital finally discharged Kathy, and we came home a few hours later. The hospice nurse arrived shortly after, and she and the other nurses rotated 12-hour shifts, staying with my wife every hour. Although Kathy had significantly changed from the weight loss, chemo treatments, and strains of cancer, her face shone like the face of an angel. You could almost feel the light of God's presence when you were near her.

One very special moment occurred just a couple of days before Kathy's passing. Her favorite nurse and I were standing at the foot of her bed in our Florida room overlooking the water. Kathy had not moved at all in over a day. She had already come to the point where she could no longer see me, but I was told she could hear me when she was awake. So, I leaned over the bed and greeted her, saying, "Hi, Honey. It's Mike."

As the nurse and I were watching her, we noticed her lips begin to move. She appeared to softly mouth the letter L.

The nurse perked up and said, "Ask her to do it again."

So, I did. And Kathy visibly mouthed the letter L again.

Then the nurse grabbed my arm and said, "I know what she is saying. She is saying, 'I love you.'"

So I quickly said, "Kathy, if you are saying, 'I love you,' would you please do it one more time?"

And again, as clear as day, she pushed the letter L out for the third time. I leaned over the bed and told her how much I loved her, too!

With her medical expertise, the nurse observed that Kathy's action had taken unbelievable physical and mental strength. Then the nurse turned to me and said, "She really loves you!"

Our pastor and his wife came over that evening and prayed over Kathy. By the next evening, my beautiful bride had passed peacefully on to glory.

TRUSTING GOD IN ALL THINGS

When I am asked how we were able to deal with Kathy's cancer, I usually share how we were determined never to be discouraged, look at the negative, or doubt the goodness of God. We kept our minds locked onto the promises in God's Word. Our strategy was never to give fear or doubt a chance. When we were tempted in those areas, we would quickly lean on each other and turn to God's Word to steady us in His truth. We kept our minds in heavenly places and consistently discussed the joys ahead of us.

I share these things because they had everything to do with how I responded after my wife's passing. Her faith and trust in the Lord have surely carried over to me. She confidently knew where she was going and that she and I would be reunited in heaven—at the very least, as best friends, like we were here.

Those first few days and weeks after Kathy's passing were tough. My heart continuously ached as I thought about her morning, noon, and night. The loss of my best friend and closest companion was difficult beyond words. Like so many others who have been through the loss of a loved one, I turned to the promises and hope found in the Bible.

I continued studying the scriptures about heaven and reading "heaven books." I wanted to learn as much as I could about where she was. As of this writing, I have purchased or been given over 90 books on heaven. I haven't read all of them yet, but I'm getting there. I have found that the books fell neatly into two categories. About half of them I consider "academic books," and the other half are more "experiential books."

The academic books focus almost entirely on what the Bible teaches about heaven, examining scripture quotes and giving personal interpretations. They were written by men like Billy Graham, C.S. Lewis, Greg Laurie, and David Jeremiah, to name a few.

The other group of books, the experiential type, were written by people who had been declared clinically dead after a severe auto or plane crash or the like, or maybe they had flat-lined on the operating table during surgery. These were people like Capt. Dale Black, Jim Woodford, and Dr. Mary Neal which had amazing stories. John Burke's book, *Imagine Heaven,* a compilation of the stories of many who have had similar death experiences, has been a great resource.

The stories I've read have varied greatly, but the more I read, the more I found commonalities between the experiences. No two were ever the same, but there were some things that many who had died saw, heard, or felt that rang true to me. I found them very encouraging, especially when I considered that Kathy might be seeing and experiencing some of these very things.

One scripture that has really encouraged me is 1 Corinthians 2:9-10— *"Eye has not seen, nor ear heard, nor has entered into the heart of man the things which God has prepared for those who love Him. But God has revealed them to us by His Spirit"* (NKJV). The word "them" here clearly refers to "the things" just mentioned. In other words, the very things we would be incapable of imagining in our own minds may be revealed to us with the Holy Spirit's inspiration.

This opened my mind to the possibility that some of the accounts I'd been reading may be accurate and believable. It brought joy to my heart, increased my faith, and even brought me comfort and hope at the thought of being reunited with Kathy. As you can imagine, keeping my mind as much as possible on the things of heaven has greatly helped me stay in a place of hope, peace, and even joy.

Another great verse along these lines is found in the book of Colossians, chapter 3, verse 2. After he returned from his visit to heaven, the apostle Paul wrote, *Set your minds on things above, not on earthly things* (NIV). Paul had seen such amazing things in heaven that later, he was able to endure unbelievable hardships on earth, knowing what he would be returning to one day.

BECOMING THE HEAVEN GUY

I knew early on that I needed to find a way to fill the void from Kathy's passing and cope with my feelings of loss. I wanted to keep her close to my heart and in my thoughts while fulfilling her last wish— "Michael, I want you to do everything possible to bring as many people as you can to heaven."

Inspired by my love for her and newfound passion for heaven, I birthed a new ministry called "The Heaven Guy." This ministry has given me focus and purpose in my life as it has grown and touched so many lives around the world.

Our team created a six-minute salvation video featuring 12 international students, each from a different country, sharing the gospel of Christ in their own language. The video is followed by a compelling salvation prayer and concludes with a heartfelt welcome into God's family for the new believer.

We then developed a colorful website to host the videos, complete with a discipleship section called Roadmap to Heaven, covering the fundamentals of the faith, and an evangelistic training section called Fishers of Men. And with God's help and inspiration, I've written and included multiple messages focused on heaven.

To attract people to the website with its video and trainings, we also developed Heaven Cards—colorful, uniquely designed plastic cards printed with inspiring thoughts or scriptures. Each card has a unique QR code on the back directing people to our website: TheHeavenGuy.org.

The Heaven Cards are an exceptional tool for initiating conversations or just giving as gifts. Our website has now been viewed by hundreds of thousands of people from over 190 countries and territories worldwide, and in just three short years, the ministry has seen over 8,000 decisions for Christ.

Kathy's dream of her and I ministering together as a team is fully coming to pass with me as the boots on the ground and her watching and cheering me on from heaven (Hebrews 12:1).

Friend, if you would like the assurance of going to heaven when you pass from this life, please watch our life-changing video at www.TheHeavenGuy. org. This is the most important decision you will ever make. And it is the most rewarding. It is forever. I pray you and I will meet in heaven someday, and in that glorious place, you will share your story with me.

Despite the heartbreak of losing Kathy's presence on this earth, God has used the love my wife and I had for each other for His glory. Trusting Him, surrendering wholeheartedly to His perfect will, and simply believing His promises concerning heaven have led me to an amazing path that only He could have orchestrated.

I know my precious Kathy will be waiting for me at the beautiful Praise Gate. I can almost hear her saying, "You did it, Honey. I was cheering you on all the way.

Armor Up to See Miracles

By Ken A. Hobbs II

Miracles show us God's power and help us to believe in Him. Our eyes can behold all kinds of miracles if we are open and equipped to see them. Some miracles reflect supernatural acts of creation, and others go against the laws of nature—like when Jesus walked on water. Some miracles involve healing, even demonstrating divine power over death, and others showcase God's miraculous power over plant and animal life—as in Balaam's donkey noted in Numbers 22. In the Bible, we read about miracles over material things, such as when Jesus multiplied the loaves and fishes in Matthew 14. But miracles are not just in the past; they are also happening all around us today—we just need to know how to look for them.

Nothing is impossible for God!
(Jeremiah 32:27)

You may be asking God for a miracle today. When we cannot see our way ahead, we must trust God. Our Lord is sovereign over the seemingly insurmountable mountains, raging oceans, and violent storms that appear to battle and attack us. Throughout the Bible, miraculous stories show us what God can and will do if we are armored up and *Fit 2 Fight*.

Miracles are the extraordinary measures God reveals when we are close to Him. Miracles remind us that God does not depend on the elements of nature or our abilities to do the impossible. God can do anything.

Sometimes we come to a place in our lives where it seems everything we have is about to run out. What do we do? These are the times we must trust the

Lord, go to our war room on our knees in prayer, and armor up in faith. The Lord provides all we need for our battles. The Apostle James tells us, *Draw near to God and He will draw near to you* (James 4:8 NKJV). So, draw closer to Him who loves and understands you the most.

During our times of battle, when we call on God and stand *Fit 2 Fight,* He provides miraculous intervention—either in front of our eyes or behind the scenes. Either way, we can trust God is working. His response may not make sense to us, or He may require us to do things that are not convenient for us—that is when we must respond with faith and obedience as we cry out to Him for wisdom.

> *If anyone longs to be wise, ask God for wisdom, and He will give it!*
> (James 1:5 TPT)

This is a truth from God's Word—a promise that He will not hold back from you.

> *No word from God will ever fail.*
> (Luke 1:37 NIV)

If you ask for it, God will give you His wisdom to make decisions that can lead to miracles and deliverance. God promises that He will not hold His wisdom back from anyone who asks and is in what I call the "blessing zone"—that place where you stand *Fit 2 Fight* and armored up as you walk in His will.

When you seek God's presence and request Him to intervene in your situation, miracles will happen. God has the ability and power over all creation to work a miracle for you. Pray. Believe by faith. Get fully equipped spiritually. Seek His wisdom. And wait on God, standing ready for His miracles. God will show up and show off!

> *Then we cried out, "Lord, help us! Rescue us!" and He did! God stilled the storm, calmed the waves, and he hushed the hurricane winds to only a whisper. We were so relieved, so glad as he guided us safely to harbor in a quiet haven.*
> (Psalm 107:28-30 TPT)

Our God can and will do the same for you when you ask and stand ready for your miracle.

. . . .

Junior Saint-Val

Junior Saint-Val resides in West Palm Beach, Florida, with his amazing wife, Mandie, and their two beautiful boys, JR & Avery. They are honored to be a part of the incredible move of God at Recovery Church.

Junior worked in business in his 20s and started down a path of addiction to drugs and alcohol. In 2013, God delivered him from his addiction. Junior now believes his pain is his ministry! He and his family are on a mission to see addicts and alcoholics find freedom from their bondage of addiction.

Junior has the privilege of being the National Coach for Recovery Church Movement and being the Teaching Pastor at Journey Church. Additionally, he has served as the Discipleship Pastor, Groups Pastor, and Kids Pastor at Journey Church for several years.

Junior is passionate about seeing lives transformed to live and love like Jesus. The Saint-Val family truly believes that there will be a Recovery Church in every city in America and beyond.

WORTHLESS WELLS

By Junior Saint-Val

What are you looking for?

This is a question I've asked myself often, a question that I believe everyone is asking in different ways. Some are asking, "What's my purpose?" "Should I move, or should I stay in this state?" "Should I marry this person or that person, or should I stay single?" "Should I choose this profession or that one?"

We are all asking questions because we are all looking for answers. What is the answer you are looking for? My hope is that as I share my story, you will find the answer to your question. I venture to guess what you are truly looking for is quite common and that many of us are looking for the same thing! I believe that at the end of this story, you will find the answer to your Big Question!

My name is Junior Saint-Val, and yes, Junior is my real name. I am the youngest of five children, raised by a single mother. We didn't really have anything growing up, but my mom tried her best. At an early age, I found out that my dad left because he didn't want to have another kid; the kid he didn't want was me. I felt rejected by the father I've never met and know nothing about. When I was four, my mom remarried to the man I got to know and love and considered to be my father.

My mother moved to America when I was seven, but my father chose to stay in France. When I was ten, I was so excited to go to France for the summer to stay with my oldest brother. My dad told me that when I got to France, we would hang out all the time. He said we would get ice cream and have so much fun—I couldn't wait. I flew thousands of miles and stayed with my brother for two months. My father didn't come to visit me one time. Man, I felt so rejected by him. I haven't heard from him since.

So much rejection in my childhood left me feeling unworthy of love. I felt like I wasn't good enough, which led me to seek acceptance. I just wanted somebody to like me, Anyone. I believe we all have a desire to be loved and accepted for who we are. Sadly, when we are not, we go looking for love in all the wrong places.

I entered high school with a longing to fit in. I wanted to be one of the cool kids, but I simply wasn't. A sitcom on TV called *Family Matters* had a character that I could relate to. Yep, I was Steve Urkel—the complete opposite of cool. I used to love watching the show because Steve Urkel was a scientist who created this machine he would walk into that would transform him into Stefan Urquelle. For those who have never seen the show, Stefan was cool! He dressed cool, looked cool, talked cool, walked cool—everything he did was cool. And man, did I want to be Stefan. The only problem was that I was Urkel. And I wasn't smart enough to create a machine that could make me cool.

One day, some kids offered me alcohol. I knew that I wasn't old enough to drink and that it was wrong, but they seemed to want to be my friends. Rejected people just want to be accepted, so I went for it. I finally understood why people join gangs; it's not necessarily because they want to do bad things; they just want to fit in, be accepted, and be a part of a group.

I remember taking that first drink; it was liquid courage! That day, I may have still looked like Urkel, but I felt like Stefan Urquelle. And to an addict, what we feel matters. I had finally found my solution; alcohol was my answer. It was the thing that I ran to when I was mad, sad, glad, anxious, fearful—you name the emotion, alcohol became my answer. Then, I came to see that what we run to for comfort in one season (alcohol, drugs, bad relationships, sex, gambling, watching things you shouldn't watch, comfort foods, fill in the blank) can become our prison in the next season!

I've learned that it's a thirst trap. None of those things will ever truly satisfy. They will always leave us craving more. Jesus teaches us about this in a story where He is sitting with a woman at the well and says to her, *"Everyone who drinks this water will be thirsty again"* (John 4:13 NIV). If we start drinking alcohol to fill that void, it will never be enough; we will just keep drinking more and more until we no longer have control of it, and it has control of us. As my friend Rick likes to say, "First you take a drink, then the drink takes a drink, then the drink takes you!"

You've never seen a kid eat sugar and say, "This is the best thing ever. I'm never having sugar again!" Instead, they say, "I want MORE!" It is the same with us if we run to anything but Jesus to fill that void. When we drink from the worthless wells that the world has to offer, we are always thirsty. BUT JESUS told the woman at the well, *"But whoever drinks the water I give will never thirst"* (John 4:14 NIV).

I didn't know this verse at that point in my life, so I just kept chasing worthless wells, hoping to quench my thirst. When I graduated from high school, I asked myself, "Who do people in the world love?" I so wanted to be loved, and I realized that people love people with money. So, I set out on a mission to make a lot of it! I believed that if I had enough money, people would love me like they love celebrities.

Then, I befriended some millionaires. I liked the Porsches, BMWs, Mercedes, and Hummers they drove much more than the borrowed, broken-down old Honda I was driving. They traded the markets and told me that if I did what they said, I would make a lot of money. So, I became a commodities broker and learned my new friends' good habits of selling and making money. However, I also picked up their bad habits of drinking, partying, and doing a lot of drugs. At 29 years old, I finally had all the things I had believed would fulfill me and make me happy in life. I had the cars, blinged-out watches, Gucci and Versace glasses, an awesome bachelor pad, and plenty of money in my pocket. I was taking vacations and was often at the club V.I.P, NO I.D., I did it real B.I.G. But I was empty!

I had everything I thought I wanted, and I was very depressed! WHAT!?! For my whole life, I thought those things were the answers. How could I be so depressed? I began drinking more and doing more drugs to numb the pain and fell deeper and deeper into addiction.

I was miserable! I wondered, *What's the point of all this anyway? I wake up, drink, deal with other people's problems, deal with my problems, watch the news and see how much hate and brokenness we have in the world, drink more, do drugs, go to sleep, and do the same thing all over again.*

> "Everything is meaningless...completely meaningless."
> (Ecclesiastes 1:2 NLT)

At that point, I was drinking a bottle of Jack, a bottle of Rosé, and washing it down with six beers daily. I wanted to end my life. The interesting thing is, when I was growing up, I always said that we didn't really have anything. Now, at 29, I realized I did have something when I was young—I had hope that one day, when I got all those things, I would be happy. My hope was in the wrong things. I realized hope's power because I was hopeless when my worthless well was full. I realized I would rather have hope and nothing else than have everything else and be hopeless. The trouble was I had no idea where to find hope.

I decided to check myself into a treatment center. They gave me a lot of Klonopin when I came in because they said if they didn't detox me, I would have a seizure and die because of how much I was drinking. After a week, I was off the Klonopin completely, and I felt great. It was the first time in years that I had gone days without drugs or alcohol.

One day, my friend said, "Hey, Junior, let's go to church today, Brother. After two weeks, you're allowed to go to church."

To which I replied, "Nah, God doesn't want anything to do with me!"

The sad fact is I really believed that—because they called God "Father." My earthly father and two other stepfathers didn't want anything to do with me. Every male role model in my life had left me. Now you're saying that there is a Father in heaven who is perfect and wants something to do with this broken man who's sitting in rehab? I didn't buy it.

He asked me again, "Come on, man, church is awesome. You should really come."

I replied, "Ok, let me clean myself up a bit. Let me get my life together. Then I'll go."

I believed that I needed to get my life together before going to church. That's like saying, "Let me get fit, then I'll go to the gym!" It's backward. You go to the gym to get fit, and you go to church so God can clean you up. But I didn't know that. I bought the lie that I could clean myself up. A lie can seem like the truth when you don't know the truth. That's why Jesus said, *"Then you will know the truth, and the truth will set you free"* (John 8:32 NIV). At that time, I didn't know the truth.

The third time, my friend invited me to church, saying, "There's real coffee at church!"

I love coffee, so I went.

We arrived at a fancy West Palm Beach church in a 15-passenger "druggy buggy." I remember thinking people were probably judging us. That's how insecure I was. I grabbed my cup of coffee and heard the story of the prodigal son mixed in with the story of the adulterous woman from John, chapter 8.

In the story, a woman was caught in the act of adultery, and the Pharisees wanted to trap Jesus. They brought the woman to Jesus and said to Him, *"This woman has been caught in the very act of committing adultery. Now in the Law, Moses commanded us to stone such women; what then do You say?"* (John 8:4-5 NASB). They knew that if Jesus stoned her, He would look vicious, but if He didn't, He would be breaking the Law. They thought they had Him for sure.

But Jesus, in His brilliance, stooped down and wrote in the dust. Then He said, *"Let any one of you who is without sin be the first to throw a stone at her"* (John 8:7 NIV).

The Bible tells us that, one by one, the oldest to youngest walked away. What I love about the story is that there was One there without sin, and His name was Jesus. The One Who had the right to throw a stone didn't. That day, God told me that He is not my accuser; He is my defender.

I heard a gospel that I had never heard before. All my life, I thought God was perfect and that He was accusing me because I was not. But the truth is, He isn't our accuser. He is our defender; Satan is the accuser. That day, everything changed for me.

I completed treatment, moved to a halfway house, and started inviting everyone to church. I wanted people to experience this God that I just experienced. Ever since that day, I've been on fire for God.

God called me to move to Charlotte, North Carolina, for ministry training, and I became a pastor. I met my lovely wife, Mandie, and we have three beautiful children together. What's remarkable about that is that when I was 26 years old, doctors told me that I couldn't have children. God really does have the last say.

Today, life is amazing. I have a personal relationship with God, a beautiful family, and I get to do what I love—plant churches for addicts and alcoholics. God has brought me into this incredible organization called the Recovery Church Movement. We've planted seventy Recovery Churches in twenty-five states! Our goal is to plant a Recovery Church in every city in America and beyond because addiction kills. Accidental overdose is the number one cause of death for people under 50. People are dying without knowing Jesus, and it burdens us. Alcoholics Anonymous and The 12-Steps were designed to lead people to Jesus. The founders of AA were going to call it "The James Gang" based on the book of James in the Bible. Alcoholics Anonymous' step three states, "Made a decision to turn our will and our lives over to the care of God as we understood Him." I believe that is one of the most misunderstood steps in the 12 steps, especially for people who resent God because someone misrepresented Him. What is meant by "as we understood Him"—notice the capital H—is that when understanding God as the founders did—meaning Jesus—rarely has a person who has thoroughly followed the AA path failed. The founders did not say, "as y'all understand him," they said, "as WE understood HIM." They found the God of the Bible. The Lord's prayer that we pray at the end of every AA meeting is actually the prayer Jesus prayed. To find true freedom and joy, we need a relationship with the Father, which comes through Jesus Christ. Such contextual comprehension allows one to come in and start the journey with the hope of actually finding the one true God in the process.

There are over 60,000 AA meetings in America. In each one of those meetings, everyone is looking for God. We realized that we know who God is, and we want to make Him known to others. My personal experience has taught me that we need Jesus, and for the real alcoholic or addict, we need a program of recovery. Recovery Church has become a bridge between the

12-Step fellowships and the church. We aren't trying to replace either one but are trying to bridge the gap between them. We realize there is a stigma in AA towards the church. There's also a stigma in the church towards AA. We believe both entities are called to work together. The 12-Steps were designed to lead people to Jesus. Jesus leads us to the Father, cleanses us, and gives us the fruit of the Spirit.

Today, I no longer chase worthless wells. I have realized that what I was looking for was out of this world. Growing up, we didn't have money, so I thought money would bring peace. It wasn't money I was chasing; it was peace. I also thought that money could bring me joy. I thought that if I had money, I could have a lot of fun. I wasn't chasing money; I was chasing joy. Growing up, I felt insignificant. I thought money would make me significant so people would love me. I wasn't chasing money. I was chasing love.

Today, I realize that when I was chasing those things in the world, I never caught them. The world can't offer me what the world can't give me. Galatians 5:22 tells us that the fruit of the Spirit is love, joy, and peace. That whole time, I was really chasing the fruit of the Spirit—which can only be given by the Spirit.

Years ago, I heard in an AA meeting that we are all born with this void inside us. That void is meant for God's Spirit. When we try to fill it with alcohol, drugs, gambling, sex, or relationships, we still feel empty. That void was put there by God so that we would long for Him. The only thing that will fit that void perfectly is His Spirit.

Jesus tells us in Matthew 6:33, *"Seek the Kingdom of God above all else, and live righteously, and he will give you everything you need"* (NLT). If we seek the things, we'll miss the kingdom. But if we seek the kingdom, He'll give us the desires of our hearts. Things have never been an issue for God. He just knows that if we're still looking for the things to fulfill us, they never will.

So, what are you looking for? Can it really be found in this world?

My experience has taught me that Christ truly is enough, and if we seek Him wholeheartedly, He will give us everything we need. I pray you will seek Him with everything you have and find the same love, joy, and peace that millions have found in Him. He is the answer to all of life's questions.

Thank you for letting me share.

BILL MCGRANE

Bill McGrane is recognized as one of the world's foremost experts on personal coaching and restoring marriages. It wasn't always this way. McGrane Global Centers began with the questions: why do people hurt so much, and what can be done about it?

Bill grew up with parents who had low self-esteem, which affected him deeply. A speech impediment made school difficult and led to low confidence and people-pleasing behaviors. His first marriage ended in divorce, and he faced financial issues, prompting a quest to find his true self and purpose.

His breakthrough came when he discovered how to believe in himself and gain genuine confidence. This led him to help others resolve their issues and thrive in their relationships and careers. After extensive research, he developed the SEE process to help people transform their marriages into fulfilling partnerships.

With 47 years of experience, Bill offers group and individual coaching. He continues to lead McGrane Global Centers, sharing his expertise and best-selling books. Explore mcgrane.com and receive a free eBook gift.

What Everyone Hungers For—TUL!

By Bill McGrane

Have you ever thought about what is most important to you? What would you say most people you care about are looking for in their lives? I believe it's love. Total Unconditional Love.

Total Unconditional Love, or TUL as I like to call it, is Christ's love that flows *to* us from Him and *through* us to others. It's a simple concept with far-reaching effects.

The "T" in TUL stands for TOTAL.

Only by God's grace and power can we, as flawed humans, love in totality. Jesus Himself showed us how. Hebrews 10:14 tells us that one sacrifice by Jesus was actually powerful enough to perfect those who received the free gift of salvation. Total means complete, done, irreversible! When we accept His sacrificial work and are willing to change our minds, nothing else is needed for our salvation.

Paul tells us we are a new creation through Jesus Christ's blood. We died with Him, and we rose with Him as a new creature. He says we are perfect in Him. He has already done and offered us everything we need—even the full inheritance that Christ got from His Father.

For in Christ all the fullness of the Deity lives in bodily form, and in Christ you have been brought to fullness. He is the head over every power and authority.
(Colossians 2: 9-10 NIV)

Jesus has already done the work required for us to yield to TUL! Our minds and our actions are just catching up to Him.

Do you remember the feeling of being totally sure, positive, and convicted of something you really believed in as a child?

As a child and young adult, I didn't feel totally sure of anything, including who I really was. My identity was being formed by who others told me I was. I knew there were missing pieces in my life. Two questions haunted me for years. First, I questioned why I hurt so much. Second, I wondered where the painful hole in my soul came from and what I could do about it.

My parents tried to love me the way they had been loved. In their own ways, though, they had low self-esteem because of their life journey and background, which they passed on to me.

Growing up, money was tight. I was afraid of my father because of his anger. And I fought with my siblings, who teased me and relentlessly criticized me, singing a song, "It's a Shame, it's a Shame for BJ McGrane." I was clumsy, so my family called me "Hands" McGrane.

I felt rejected. And I was so fearful of my father's anger I would hide under the table when I could hear him come home. Seeing my lack of confidence, my mother tried to help by having me say affirmations as I jumped up our stairs, one step and affirmation at a time.

At times I felt the absence of Total Unconditional Love from my parents and siblings, even though I knew they cared for me.

My peers also rejected me because I felt different and didn't fit in. I had low self-esteem.

Have you ever felt like a nobody wanting to be a somebody?

I was a people-pleaser, looking to be accepted, liked, and loved. I didn't do well in grade school. It didn't help that I had a speech impediment—I couldn't pronounce my Ss or Ts. I felt bad about myself and decided to watch the smartest kid in my class and mimic or imitate their actions. If they put their hand on their face, I put my hand on my face. If they crossed their legs, I would cross my legs. If they took notes, I took notes—but I had no clue what they were taking notes on. The next time my grades came out, they had gone down even further.

Everybody wants to be somebody, but most of us learned the quickest way to be a somebody is to make others feel like they are a nobody. That is an endless cycle. The person targeted by the person wishing to be a somebody begins to feel like a nobody too, so they find somebody else to treat like a nobody so they can be the somebody they always wanted to be. The cycle continues until someone realizes that a real somebody always treats themselves and others like a somebody!

My journey with Jesus started early in my life. My parents raised me to have a personal relationship with the Lord. At age 15, my father invited me to attend a silent spiritual retreat that taught me to be quiet and hear the Lord, which I attended for 25 years. In the small chapel was a picture of Jesus with His hands outstretched. John 7:37-38 was written below it.

> "If any man thirst, let him come unto me and drink.
> He that believeth on me, as the scripture hath said,
> out of his belly shall flow rivers of living water."
> (John 7:37-38 KJV)

This became one of my favorite scriptures that has helped shape me as a Christian. It has been a visual reminder of the powerful blessing that comes when we lay down all our burdens and surrender to His will for us.

Another journey led me to marry Sonia. I was looking for the total package when I married her. Years went by, and we had our two children, Laura and John. My career as a personal and professional development coach was going great. Unfortunately, my marriage wasn't totally what I thought it would be, and I had to make the tough decision to end it after 13 years, which was one of the hardest decisions of my life.

I remember laying on the floor with my hands outstretched, crying, saying. "Dear Lord, help me to know what next step you want me to take in my life."

The answer came that I needed to end my marriage for myself, my wife, and my children's sake.

Even though I didn't believe in divorce and had wanted for years to work things out with my wife, I knew this was the best choice for all concerned. That's when I learned that God's love is not only total but that it is also unconditional.

Have you ever heard God speak to you?

When I was 25, I was walking down a street and heard the Lord say, "I'm going to give you the people, systems and procedures, infrastructure, and finances to heal the emotional wounds of the world."

I said, "Who, me?"

The answer I got back was, "Don't sweat the details. I'll take care of the rest."

That's the journey that I've been on since then.

The "U" of TUL stands for UNCONDITIONAL.

Have you ever felt loved unconditionally? Unfortunately, most people experience the opposite, conditional love. I love you IF you think, feel, or behave the way I want you to. You're my friend WHEN (fill in the blank). You're a godly person IF. You are a valued employee WHEN you toe the line. You are a great leader IF you follow the rules.

"Conditional" refers to something that is dependent on certain conditions or requirements.

"Unconditional" refers to something that is absolute, not contingent upon any conditions or requirements.

If we believe what we do determines who we are, we cannot live in or give unconditional love. We will constantly feel less than perfect, therefore unlovable, and we will only be equipped to offer conditional love to others. If who I believe I am is based on how I perform, or if I judge myself on who others want me to be or tell me I am, then I do not recognize and appreciate who God says I am. We all have a choice to base our worth on past experiences, wounds, and the response of others or to base our worth unconditionally on who God says we are—His beloved children.

I learned early to pray, ask, and look for confirmation when making life-impacting decisions.

Over the next several months after my divorce, God's confirmation of His unconditional love for me came through. I felt a calm and peace I knew could come only from God. I discovered the power of unconditional love in the most painful time. We find out who we really are and what is important through tough times.

God will never leave a void in your life. When we seek Him and ask earnestly, He will always come through. Maybe not in the way you think it should be, however, because God's ways are always higher and greater than our ways (Isaiah 55:8-9).

"L" is for LOVE, for which everyone hungers.

We can only love because Christ first loved us. And when we realize how deeply we are loved, that same love can flow out of us.

Just think—Jesus Christ willingly left the holy throne of heaven because He loves YOU. He left perfect peace, perfect love, and perfect unity with the Father to become the flesh. He took on the sin and emotional pain of every man, woman, and child who would ever live just so that we could live and reign with Him in heaven. He came so that He could give us everything that was given to Him by God the Father, including His inheritance.

After my divorce, I was not looking for someone else to marry. In my mind, I was going to be a single father and be the best me I could be. But God! God had plans for me, just like He has plans for you.

Without notice, someone appeared to offer me TUL. It did not take long for us to know that we were meant to be together, and Linda became my wife. With her two children and my two children, we embarked on the journey of blending our families together. This was not easy because of the hurt and pain of separation her son Jay, daughter Heidi, and my daughter Laura and son John went through. However, when your heart is open to love, it opens room for more love and giving accordingly.

As the years went by, Linda and my life together had ups and downs, like everyone's. For example, I got a call one day from my daughter, Laura. Crying, she said, "I just punched John in the stomach, and they had to take him to the hospital."

This created a God moment where they discovered that my son John had Wilms tumor—a rare kidney cancer. Fortunately, they were able to remove it, saving future issues down the road in his life.

God is so good. John's surgery went well, and today, he is healthy and married to the love of his life, Allison.

Additionally, one of the most life-changing experiences was discovering that Linda had kidney disease. She began dialysis and eventually needed a kidney to replace the two that were failing. However, when love is present, all things are possible.

The Lord's loving grace told me to write an article concerning her ailment and post it in our local community magazine. His certain instruction led to answered prayers just months before as Linda's organs were shutting down and she was close to death. Our blessing, Michael, read the article and informed us that the Lord told him to give this stranger one of his kidneys. That is Total Unconditional Love. The Lord's TUL flowed to Michael and then *through* him to my wife.

> You intended to harm me, but God intended it for good to accomplish what is now being done, the saving of many lives.
> (Genesis 50:20 NIV)

Learning to embrace God's love is what life is all about. Allowing God to love us helps us learn to love and accept ourselves, warts and all. And accepting healthy love makes it possible for us to share Total Unconditional Love with others.

At this stage of my life, it is such a wonderful, freeing feeling to receive and give Total Unconditional Love.

How can we walk and talk in TUL? We need to write this on our eyelids and read it until we believe it: *God's Word says I'm complete in Him.*

Let your prayer be: *God, help me to believe that I am complete so that I no longer reach to inferior things to fill me when You have already filled me with everything You have. The Holy Spirit convinces me of who I am. I am dependent on You, Holy Spirit, to teach me to yield to Your truth and trust that Your presence is in me now.*

Friends, believing we are worthy because we worked hard, stayed strong, or accomplished tasks produces superficial, self-righteousness. Hence, we accomplish nothing for the kingdom of God. God is more than capable of handling things on His own. What He wants from us is our Total Unconditional Love for Him and our brothers and sisters.

The Apostle Paul recognizes through life's growth challenges that love is the pinnacle. Paul writes, *And now these three remain: faith, hope, and love. But the greatest of these is love* (1 Corinthians 13:13 NIV). Love is the greatest of the three because, without love, authentic faith and hope aren't possible.

God doesn't base His love for us on our deeds. We are already complete in Christ. If we've given our lives to Him, He has seated us at His right hand, and the same Spirit that raised Christ from the dead already lives in us.

> *God raised us up with Christ and seated us with him in the heavenly realms in Christ Jesus.*
> (Ephesians 2:6 NIV)

> *"If you love me, keep my commands. And I will ask the Father, and he will give you another advocate to help you and be with you forever— the Spirit of truth...He lives with you and will be in you."*
> (John 14:15-17 NIV)

We don't need to look to people, relationships, substances, or titles to complete us.

As we accept God's TUL for us, He empowers and teaches us to love those around us not for what they can do for us but because we know what He has already done for us. God's Total Unconditional Love will overflow out of us and allow us to offer TUL to others.

But we cannot exude unconditional love if we do not accept our identity in Christ.

If we're not walking in unconditional love, it is because we do not fully appreciate what God has already accomplished. Do we believe it? Do we believe that the same Spirit that brought Christ from the tomb lives in us? He completes us! When we accept His reality, we live from the kingdom place inside us!

So, how can we walk and talk in TUL? One way is to use TUL language. As you think and speak, so you are. You can practice living who God made you to be by blanketing yourself and others in affirming words.

> *The tongue has the power of life and death,*
> *and those who love it will eat its fruit.*
> (Proverbs 18:21 NIV)

A stem is the beginning of a sentence that you fill in the rest with a variety of words. Fill in the rest of these words with answers about yourself. Then, do the same thing, thinking of those you care about.

I respect you for...

I admire how you can...

I delight in...

I like...

I congratulate...

I cherish...

I applaud...

I appreciate...

I thank you for...

I love...

Why do we so often wait until a person is gone before we tell them how much we love them? Make a commitment now to never allow a moment to go by when you can be an affirming encouragement to yourself and others. Isn't that what God wants us to do and be? Jesus affirms, *"A new commandment I give you: Love one another. As I have loved you, so you must love one another. By this, everyone will know that you are my disciples if you love one another"* (John 13: 34-35 NIV).

You were made to walk in TUL.

Conditional love requires some kind of finite exchange, whereas unconditional love is seen as infinite and measureless.

Unconditional love is irrespective of our own feelings or will. It is God's love flowing through you because He resides in you, and you reside in Him.

Unconditional love separates an individual from their behavior. Imagine acquiring a new puppy. The puppy is cute and playful, and the owner's heart swells with love for this new family member. Then, the puppy urinates on the floor. The owner does not stop loving the puppy but works to modify the puppy's behavior through training and education.

We can love the essence of every person. Though their behavior may be a little (or way) out of alignment, love the person anyway. Even though you may not like someone's behavior, you can determine to love them as Christ loves you. Accept that they are doing the best they can based on their awareness.

When you are feeling judgmental, here are three practical steps that can help you acquire Total Unconditional Love:

1. Recognize and accept that nobody's behavior is ever perfect.

2. Ask questions.

3. Be open to understanding and learning.

Total Unconditional Love is so important to me that I asked myself what empowering anchor I could incorporate into my life. The answer came: make it your license plate for your car. So now my license plate says TUL.

TUL is what I want to receive and it is what I want to give to others.

Now, I pass that mantle on to you to receive God's gift of TUL; receive it in yourself and challenge yourself to offer Total Unconditional Love to others.

No matter our life stage, TUL is the peace and reward God has always wanted for us and the gift He wants us to share. Only you can choose to receive and embrace TUL and offer it to others. The greatest gift we can give is Total Unconditional Love, and now, through my journey and your journey, you can pass it on to those you love, to those you work with, to your family, your community, and even the world you live in.

The hunger you have always had in your life can be fulfilled by receiving and giving TUL.

Commit to the experience. Enjoy it. And watch what happens!

FIT 2 FIGHT FOR VICTORY

By Ken A. Hobbs II

As men of honor, we face different battles and temptations. But God has overcome the world, and we are promised victory through our faith. We can find many places in the Bible where God gives His people victory over battles. Victory is a gift. *We thank God for giving us the victory as conquerors through our Lord Jesus, the Anointed One* (1Corintians 15:57 TPT).

We can all rise above our circumstances and be victorious with God on our side to fight our battles. We are more than conquerors in Christ (Romans 8:37 NIV) and can claim victory over any challenge that comes our way because *He who is in you is greater than he who is in the world* (1 John 4:4 NKJV).

If you are facing some of life's most challenging situations—possibly a "thorn in the flesh," so to speak—you can claim victory over your circumstances, not by your own might or power, but by the power of the Holy Spirit, who will accomplish God's will (Zechariah 4:6). Being victorious in a situation is not a matter of education, progress, or even a feeling. It is a matter of faith!

> *For whatever is born of God overcomes the world, And this is the victory that has overcome the world—our faith.*
> (1 John 5:4-5)

You can become an overcomer and claim victory. Only God can deliver you from the battle you are fighting. Faith is the victory that overcomes the world.

In our weakness, God gives us His strength. Through difficult and painful times, we can find God's grace. He has already told us, *"My grace is sufficient for you, for My strength is made perfect in our weakness"* (2 Corinthians 12:9 NKJV).

You can live a victorious life through Jesus Christ, our Lord and Savior.

Remember: In the end, God wins!

. . . .

STEVE SOLOMON

Steve Solomon came to the faith in November 1991. He attended a Christian Business Men's Connection (CBMC) Luncheon in 1994 and almost immediately began Operation Timothy with Steve Estler, who is still a mentor. Steve served the CBMC South Florida Leadership Team from 1997 until 2005, then rejoined in 2015. On July 1, 2018, he answered God's calling and became the Area Director, where he continues to serve.

Steve attended The City University of New York, Herbert Lehman College, attaining a bachelor's in Mass Communications in 1976. Upon graduating, he worked in retail management for ten years before starting a sales career that lasted until 2018. Steve's sales career included Brandt Money Processing Systems (1986-1997), BellSouth/AT&T, and Comcast Business (1997-2018). He earned President's Council, Rookie of the Year, and other awards. In addition, Steve taught Dale Carnegie Sales Training from 1988-1999.

Steve is married to Jeanne. They live in Miami Springs, Florida, and have one son, Eric.

Steve can be reached at CBMC South Florida—ssolomon@cbmc.com, or 954-805-0351.

A Nice Jewish Kid from Yonkers

By Steve Solomon

Whenever I get to know somebody and tell them my story, I always start by saying, "God has a great sense of humor…He took a nice Jewish kid from Yonkers, NY, and made him the Area Director of the Christian Business Men's Connection (CBMC) marketplace ministry in South Florida…and I don't speak a lick of Spanish!!!" It's all true! Thankfully, neither my past failings nor language barriers have prohibited CBMC from impacting hundreds of men for God's glory.

This is God's incredible story of where I came from, how I got where I am, and where He continues to take me!

Let's begin with my mom and dad, who met late in 1943. My dad was stationed in the Upper Peninsula of Michigan, training on airplanes at Michigan Tech in Houghton for the US Army Air Corps (predecessor to the US Air Force). My dad, Sidney Solomon, was an Orthodox Jew from The Bronx. My mom was a local girl, Rita Neault, a French American Roman Catholic. In those days, this was a marriage that was never supposed to happen—Orthodox Jews did not marry out of their faith, especially during World War II when the genocide of Jews was happening throughout Europe. Still, my parents married against all resistance from their families, which came especially from my dad's side, who pretty much wanted to disown him.

My parents' wedding was in March of 1944. Regarding their faith, they reached a compromise, deciding that as each of their children became old enough, the child could pick the religion (Catholic or Jewish) they wanted to be trained for, practice, and go through all the ceremonies. In addition, as a family unit, they would celebrate all the holidays related to the two religions, including Christmas, Easter, Rosh Hashanah, and Chanukkah.

In mid-1944, Sid got shipped out to the South Pacific in the war against Japan, not knowing if he would ever return. In June 1945, Rita gave birth to their first child, a boy named Jack. When Sid did return, he picked up Rita and baby Jack in Michigan, and the young Solomon family relocated to The Bronx. All were accepted by the Solomon clan, and the faith compromise continued to be honored for baby Linda, born in 1949, and Steve, born in 1955. As the years went by, my older brother Jack and older sister Linda hung out with friends with Irish and Italian backgrounds. Wanting to be like their friends, Jack and Linda decided to train in the Catholic religion.

By the time my decision was at hand, we were ready to set sail for Yonkers. My friends in Yonkers were all Jewish. They had their Bar Mitzvahs and all the gifts that went with it. I wanted a Bar Mitzvah. So, I picked Jewish. That's what I figured I would practice and celebrate according to everything I learned in Hebrew school for the rest of my life! However, as He often does, God had another plan!

GOD'S ROADWORK BEGINS

As I grew up, my family always celebrated Easter and Christmas together among our extended Jewish family—so there wasn't much spirituality to the holiday. When I spent summers in the Upper Peninsula of Michigan with my mom's family, I would go to church with my grandma, aunts, uncles, and cousins. It was just something we did with the family without much spiritual alignment.

Fit 2 Fight: Are You Armored Up?

On the Jewish side, we commemorated all the major holidays. We conducted the Passover Sedar at our house, with Mom cooking for the entire Solomon clan. I went to synagogue with Dad on Rosh Hashanah and Yom Kippur. Of course, we all celebrated Hanukah with all the gifts.

So, as I grew older, the pattern and habits were in place, but I was still a Jewish kid from Yonkers, no matter what!

My first real job after college was working as a manager trainee in the general office at Korvette's Department Store on 45th Street and Lexington Avenue in New York City. I was all grown up, a college graduate, a manager trainee, engaged to a beautiful gal, and ready to handle the world.

One of my co-workers, Chris, a former Hindu who had converted to Christianity, pastored a home Bible church. We spent a lot of time together; he always asked me questions about my beliefs in God and the Jewish faith. At first, I did pretty well answering. All I had to do was repeat the answers I had memorized in Hebrew school.

Then he started to dig a little. He asked me questions about Jesus Christ. They were superficial questions at first; I was able to handle those pretty well because of my grandma and my Catholic background.

Then, one day, he asked me if I had ever read Isaiah 53. I told him I probably had, as it was in the Old Testament. That opened more dialogue about its meaning and how it related to Jesus. Chris planted a seed that I wasn't ready to receive. It wouldn't matter what he said; at that point, I knew for sure I was Jewish and always would be Jewish. In fact, I told Chris that I would always be Jewish, and he could take that Isaiah 53 stuff and shove it! After all, my fiancé was Jewish, and we were going to raise a Jewish family together.

MY PATH TO NOWHERE

In 1979, I was on the path of success that the world said would lead to wealth and happiness! I was married to a great gal. We both came from good families and made pretty good money. We lived in the Fleetwood section of Mt. Vernon, next door to my beloved Yonkers. It was 30 minutes by train to Manhattan. We had two cars, went on vacations, and hung out with friends. It was all that we had dreamed of.

However, our fantasy life started to unravel in 1985. Since high school, I always enjoyed having more than one drink with the guys. In college, I ended up cracking up a car while I had a buzz but was able to walk away. I also tended to get a little frisky with inviting ladies if the opportunity availed itself.

Now that I was married, I started staying out late to have a good time with the guys. I left my wife at home alone a couple of times a month. It got bad enough for us to enter counseling, but that proved to be quite ineffective. It was alright, though; we had a better solution. We bought a house and moved to a Long Island beach community. Atlantic Beach, here we come! As you may have guessed, it was a temporary fix.

Things were good for a while. I scored a sales job and started making really good money, and my wife was happy to live near her parents. But then old habits crept back in, and I started to stay out all night again. It was almost acceptable to us both. She accepted it because she was getting the material things she wanted. I accepted it because I was having my fun playing the big shot—drinking, laughing it up, and eventually being unfaithful.

So, in the spring of 1989, I made the executive decision that I could do better and asked her for a divorce. She couldn't agree fast enough. It was an easy, uncontested, one-attorney divorce. She got the house; I got the good car and some money. It was a great plan because we were both ready to move on.

I quickly started dating a gal who had previously worked for me. My next success plan was in the making. We moved in together, and when the company transferred me to South Florida in May 1990, we planned to get married in August. I figured that control was mine and this wife would depend on me. Little did I know, I was wrong on both counts. But hey, It was all good since I could still hang out and drink with the guys a couple of nights a month and have a blast.

GOD'S PLAN

God's plan was in motion. In November 1991, my marriage was nearly a total disaster. She was seven months pregnant, and we constantly fought. I coped by drinking more "socially," ya' know? No problem there. I lost $85,000.00 in expected commission when Southeast Bank declared Chapter 7 bankruptcy. That was the equivalent of $195,000.00 today. To compensate, I worked my sales job while clerking at an overnight convenience store on Fridays. I also taught the Dale Carnegie Sales Courses part-time in Miami, Ft. Lauderdale, and West Palm Beach. Because my wife was pregnant, she helped out by babysitting.

The pressure was on. My great plans were tanking. The challenges of my first marriage were my fault; my first wife was a great gal. My second marriage was not working out primarily because we should never have gotten married. There had to be a better way. Although I admittedly had not prayed, I know now others were, namely my sister, who was now a born-again Christian, and Chris, the Isaiah 53 guy. Just after Thanksgiving 1991, God's plan for this South Floridian Jewish kid from Yonkers started to move into the next gear!

I met with a fellow Dale Carnegie Sales Course Instructor, Dave Roberts, at his Nationwide Insurance Agency office in Boca Raton. We met to review the new sales course curriculum that would be rolled out in January 1992. As He often does, God had other plans for our meeting.

Dave made coffee in the little kitchen in the back, and then he turned to me and said, "Steve, you are the most unhappy person I know. What is going on?"

That question struck home. For the next two hours, I growled, moped, and cried. I let it all out.

Then Dave replied," Are you done?"

I nodded.

The next thing he said changed my life forever. Dave said, "You need Jesus in your life."

At first, I pushed back since I was going to be Jewish forever, ya' know? Also, I knew all about Jesus since Grandma took me to church when I was a kid and we celebrated the Jesus holidays, like Christmas and Easter.

Dave's next words still stand out to me to this very day. He said, "Yes, but do you have a personal relationship with Jesus?"

I was stopped in my tracks. I said, "Is that what you have? Explain!"

Dave shared Romans 3:23-24, *For all have sinned and fall short of the glory of God, and all are justified freely by his grace through the redemption that came by Christ Jesus* (NIV).

He also asserted, *So, we are made right with God through faith and not by obeying the law* (Romans 3:28 NLT).

He further shared the Lord's most common truth from John's gospel.

For God so loved the world, that he gave his only begotten Son,
that whosoever believeth in him should not perish,
but have everlasting life.
(John 3:16-17 KJV)

And for the Jew in me, he pulled out THE Isaiah 53:4-5. (Sorry, Chris.) The prophet Isaiah proclaims, *Surely, He hath borne our griefs and carried our sorrows; yet we did esteem him stricken, smitten of God, and afflicted. But he was wounded for our transgressions, he was bruised for our iniquities; the chastisement for our peace was upon him, and by his stripes we are healed* (ASV).

Dave explained that Jesus died for me on that cross and that all my sins would be forgiven if I accepted Jesus Christ in faith.

I knew Dave's wife was leaving him after 25+ years of marriage, and although he wasn't happy, he was at peace. I also knew another Christian named Guillermo—a twenty-two-year-old who fixed the equipment I sold. Guillermo was born in Cuba, had survived coming to Miami in 1980 on the Mariel boatlift, and currently lived with five other guys—but he was peacefully happy. I wanted the peace through the storms that these guys had. I told Dave I wanted that kind of peace. Twenty minutes later, I was on my knees, accepting Jesus as my Savior. His plan for my life was on its way. I felt five hundred pounds lifted from my shoulders. That weight has never come back!

It was just as the Apostle Paul declared, *And the peace of God, which transcends all understanding, will guard your hearts and minds in Christ Jesus* (Philippians 4:7 NIV).

NEXT STEPS ALONG THE ROAD

Dave encouraged me to plug into a church as soon as possible. Wouldn't you know it, God found me one. One week later, I was listening to Moody Radio South Florida when I heard a Messianic Rabbi in Boca Raton discussing the significance of Hanukkah and Jesus. I called Rabbi Ira, and his church became mine for the next three years.

Two weeks later, our son Eric was born prematurely. He only weighed two pounds, four ounces and was fourteen inches long. That was December 1991, when babies like Eric had a thirty to forty percent survival rate. The only one in our entire family who was not freaking out was me. I knew that God had it! Today, Eric is a thirty-two-year-old Christian making his way as a voice actor.

My wife was indifferent to my new Christianity. She tried it for a while, but we slowly drifted apart between 1998 and 2001, when our marriage ended. However, even then, God had a better plan that led me to my impactful calling for many others.

In 1994, I was still in sales but was moving on to telecommunications. I attended chamber of commerce meetings, networking events, and other social events to develop business relationships. Someone told me about a monthly luncheon in Ft. Lauderdale that was sponsored by Christian businessmen. It sounded like a winner to me. I attended my first meeting in the Spring of 1994; I loved it so much that I kept attending. During my third time there, I started talking with a member of the sponsoring group, Steve Estler. We made the connection and met for lunch another time. Steve explained that the group was the Christian Business Mens Committee (CBMC). Their mission was to disciple and evangelize to men in the marketplace. He asked if I'd like his mentorship through the discipleship program, Operation Timothy. I accepted, and 30 years later, Steve is still my mentor. I continued my sales career working for BellSouth, AT&T, and finally, Comcast while serving on the board with CBMC.

Having Steve Estler as my mentor/discipler helped me grow in my great faith walk with Jesus! My life wasn't perfect. For example, my marriage wasn't working even as we tried. I was challenged with the "good time" syndrome's excessive partying and pornography. However, with Steve's support, I have been able to overcome these temporary battles.

GOD HAD MORE

In 2003, I met the most wonderful woman I know, my future wife, Jeanne! Aiming for ensured clarity, we dated for thirteen years. Ours is a long story but a good one for another time. We married in 2016 and have been happy together since. I lead with her because without God putting her in my life, the next part of my life would never have happened.

In 2010, I met another mentor, Seann Maxwell. Seann's teachings emphasized that regardless of my career, as long as I did it with and for God as my Director, the venture would always be worthy. Paul affirms the same when he writes, *Whatever you do, do you work heartily, as for the Lord and not for people* (Colossians 3:23 NASB). That is when I knew that working with men in the marketplace was where I should be.

I returned to the board of CBMC South Florida in 2016 after a ten-year hiatus. We all knew we needed to do something new. So, we started a Boca Raton Luncheon and a Cooper City Luncheon. Yet it wasn't enough. I felt a sense that God's calling was stronger for more. Our marketplace men needed more! So, I retired from thirty years in telecom in July of 2018 and became the Area Director for CBMC South Florida. God called our team of leaders to connect more with God and each other in the marketplace.

In 2018, we had three lunch outreaches, reaching about fifty to seventy-five men monthly. Now, we have three lunch outreaches, four cigar fellowship nights, thirty weekly or bi-weekly connect groups, two monthly business owner peer advisory groups, and two monthly young professional groups. Altogether, 400+ men connect each month.

Additionally, over 300 men have completed Operation Timothy and attended our four men's retreats and two marriage retreats. CBMC spans 150 miles from Miami-Dade County to Port St. Lucie, with remote groups in South Africa and on Florida's west coast in Naples. Thanks to the work of CBMC, over 300 men have accepted Jesus Christ as their Savior, and another 300+ have recommitted their lives to Jesus Christ.

All this might never have happened if the Jewish kid from Yonkers hadn't made his long and troubled way to South Florida—God can and will use everything for His good when we love Him.

> And we know that God causes all things to work together
> for good to those who love God, to those who are
> called according to His purpose.
> (Romans 8:28 NASB)

I have learned a lot through my journey from being that nice Jewish kid from Yonkers—the greatest lesson is that God's plan is the best plan!

You can believe and trust Him. My life verse says it all:

> Trust in the LORD with all your heart and lean not on your
> own understanding; in all your ways acknowledge him,
> and he will make your paths straight.
> (Proverbs 3:5-6 NASB)

Eddie Gonzalez

Eddie Gonzalez, his loving wife Sandra of 23 years, and his two amazing children, Gabe and Alyssa, live between Westchester County, New York, and West Palm Beach, Florida. He enjoys a successful career of almost 29 years in the financial industry. He sits on four different investment boards and committees, is a co-author, and has ownership of 15 offices with Primerica Financial Services across several states with currently over 5,000 clients.

Born and raised in the heart of the southeast Bronx, New York, Eddie is a proud 2nd generation nuyorican, stemming from his loving parents, Angel and Nelida, who migrated to the US from San Juan, Puerto Rico. He is the proud sibling of his great brother Angel and heartfelt sister Maria.

Eddie strives to empower and equip others, always breathing hope, self-love, belief, and potential into others. His hobbies include photography, horseback riding, helicopter touring, boating, traveling, self-development, and spending quality time with his wife, family, and friends.

Lessons Learned, Changes Made

By Eddie Gonzalez

Having grown up in an extremely dangerous environment, I always wondered what those who are dimensionally successful did in their life to succeed. I refer to those who have a great walk with the Lord, are physically fit, emotionally fit, relationally successful, and likely, financially successful. What did these individuals do differently? Did they have innate advantages, talents, or better genetics?

I learned certain desires, habits, gratitude, and attitudes are present in those who experience great adversity or tragedy and still come out on top. How can we learn from the examples of these individuals?

As men, many of us were raised not to show emotion or hurt but to be tough no matter what. We were taught not to trust, asking for help is to appear weak, and if you want something done right, you must do it yourself. How do we deal with these issues and, for some, the scars and deep wounds we may be scared to face that come with this way of thinking?

For the record, I, too, was a victim of this early indoctrination and inaccurate teachings. Growing up as a 2nd generation young Hispanic male who was born and raised in the Southeast Bronx during the 60s and 70s, there were so many answers I searched for. Trust did not come easy, being raised in city housing, but tragedy and tribulations did. In fact, trust became quite impossible. So, my quest to develop trust took decades and was filled with many doubts until the Lord gifted me with some answers.

Thriving is difficult when your daily objective is to survive—when getting home safely each day without being robbed, beaten, or killed is your number one goal. Our neighborhood was riddled with street gangs, violent crime, drug and alcohol addiction, and occasional prostitution. The fact that I made it out alive without incarceration or addiction was clearly the work of the Lord. As we all know, it is easy to become a product of our environment. Somewhere within me, I always felt that the Lord had much bigger plans for me to carry out His work, though I wondered what God was trying to tell me. My quest for these answers didn't begin in earnest until my parents were able to remove us from that toxic environment in 1977.

I had wonderful parents who were happily married for 64 years. I am the youngest of three. My amazing brother Angel and amazing sister Maria were always role models to me and still are today. Mom and Dad were an outstanding couple who were loved by everyone. They were filled with love and joy and appreciated life every day. They were grateful, simple, and humble immigrants from Puerto Rico. But they were tough, and they were determined.

Mom and Dad never finished high school since they had to work as teenagers to support the family. However, they taught us great morals, values, self-love, respect, and old traditional disciplines. Angel Sr. and Nelly fought every day to keep us close, safe, clothed, fed, and educated—putting the three of us through Catholic schools on Dad's modest salary from working as a printer. Mom stayed home and raised the kids. We weren't a perfect family, but we were a happy family.

As most siblings, we fought over trivial things but were always alert and looked out for one another. Growing up in the South Bronx for many years under these conditions posed a great challenge. Housing was scarce. Because of crime and tenants who did not pay rent habitually, many landlords burned their own properties to collect the insurance. It was a sad and scary time, but there was an advantage—either you got tough or you didn't survive. We learned to fight mentally as well as physically. We grew a thick skin to avoid becoming a victim. Our scars became trophies, and our reputation became our defense. These lessons transformed into assets. In fact, this disadvantage became what is called the "advantage of the disadvantaged."

In 1977, when I was 16, we moved to the Northeast Bronx, which initiated a new chapter for all of us. My sister married soon after and moved to a new place close to my parents, and my brother did the same. Their apartments were in the same building one city block away. Although we all lived separately, we were still united. The foundation Mom and Dad set for us was strong. My brother and sister pursued successful careers as my quest for answers began.

I did very well during my school years, considering my environment. In fact, I was in the top of my classes. I received scholarships to two private schools and was accepted to some of the best high schools that required entrance exams. The curriculum in our Catholic school was very advanced, which helped me excel. However, high school soon began to bore me. Somehow, somewhere, I knew there was more.

I picked up a couple of retail jobs after school and started to feel the independence of having my own income. The experience was addictive. I began to study how the owners and managers ran the companies I worked for and quickly lost interest in high school. I soon walked away from high school with less than two years completed. I handed in my resignation, passed my GED exam in less than 30 days, and decided to go into business for myself.

To gain experience, I took on a position with an auto electrical installation company designing security systems and high-end audio equipment. That then branched into many other things in that same field involving low-voltage wiring. I was 19 at the time. Within six months, I took on my first independent contract with an auto dealership, spearheading their installation department. By 20, I had contracts with seven car dealerships, which required hiring five employees. My registered company was soon servicing 15-20 cars a day. I was still living with my parents, operating out of my small bedroom. The business obviously outgrew my bedroom. I soon rented an apartment with a two-car garage to take on private clients. By 23, my business was pulling in six figures.

I learned a lot about relationships and negotiations and began to understand profit margins, tax write-offs, balance sheets, and how to work with distributors. However, by the mid-80s, technology had progressed quickly, and much of the equipment we specialized in became factory-installed. I saw an end coming to this boom quickly.

So, I shifted gears and decided to pursue real estate.

I studied for my real estate licenses part-time while still working my auto business. I got the knack of it pretty quickly and, with some good mentorship, eventually walked away from the auto business. Within two years, I had enough experience and sales history to become my own broker, so I opened two offices—engaging in sales and rentals from one office and property management from the other. I had a crew of 14 associates working with me, managing over 170 units for landlords and property owners. We did very well.

At 27, I purchased my first home with no initial down payment. Again, I learned many great lessons from this experience.

After 13 years, I started to see the flaws in the real estate model. Often, after I trained leaders in my organization, they left to open their own offices and compete against me with what I had taught them. Again, my journey began to find better answers.

I was introduced to the financial services industry in 1995 and decided to walk away from my strong six-figure real estate income. After obtaining all my necessary financial licenses, I closed my real estate offices to work in finance full-time. Although many colleagues and people I thought were my friends criticized, mocked, and laughed at me for this bold move, it was one of the best decisions I've ever made. Again, I learned many lessons through that great experience.

One of the best things that came from that decision to change careers was meeting Sandra, who is now my loving wife, best friend, and soulmate. Sandra had also walked away from a successful career, and we decided to join forces, start a family, and pursue our dreams together. Today, we have two wonderful kids, Gabe and Alyssa, who are the light of our lives. They are both amazing adults. Today, Sandra and I are celebrating 23 years together. We own and operate 15 offices, and the Lord continues to bless us. Our business is still growing, giving us the opportunity to educate and empower thousands of people. We love our life, and we love what we do.

Along the way to success, I've learned some important dynamics I'd like to share with you.

First, I learned to harness the power of relationships. One of the most significant dynamics of life is the power of learning through mentorship. People with great experience can become your best cheat sheet to being dimensionally successful. Starting from childhood, the most prominent mentors in my life were my parents, my brother, and my sister. As I got closer to the Lord, He, too, became a prominent mentor in my life. I learned His principles through Scripture via the Holy Spirit. My best friend of 44 years, Alvin Ortiz, and other leaders from my industry—starting with Lou Vitale, Bill Whittle, and Frank Dillon—also guided me. My great friend and brother in Christ, Ken Hobbs II, completely reshaped my life and helped me move closer to the Lord. I have many others to thank who reached me through the hundreds of books I've read and seminars I've attended. Reading every day was vital to finding the answers I was searching for.

My wife Sandra is one of the most prominent mentors in my life. Sharing this quest with her has been an exhilarating experience. Since the day we met, she has taught me countless lessons. Even my kids, Gabe and Alyssa, have mentored me directly and indirectly with the valuable lessons they've taught me.

To be successful, begin with getting rich in relationships, which is far more important than getting rich financially. I truly believe you cannot have one without the other.

Besides relationships, gratitude is at the center of a successful individual. Each morning you can get out of bed is a gift from God. What you do with that day and the lives you touch is your gift back to God. Most people try to get through the day instead of giving to the day. Our gratitude for waking up, breathing, and functioning must be paid forward by impacting others. It is our responsibility to pass on the lessons we have learned.

We must seek gratitude before knowledge and happiness—it is the primary key to peace and fulfillment. There is a great power in humility. If you learn to teach others what you've discovered and have been taught, your impact will be monumental, as will your personal fulfillment. Remember, when you serve others, you are serving the Lord.

Another invaluable lesson was one I learned from my parents: persistence. We all know life will hit you hard and keep you down if you let it. However, life will also give you whatever you are willing to fight for. Persistently moving toward all God has called you to is a choice. Along the way, there will be pain, but know that pain is temporary! Eventually, it will subside, and something else will take its place, but if you quit, that pain will last forever! Ironically, the right pain is actually good. It can be an indication that something is wrong, which requires adjustments, or it can be a sign that something is growing. You will never grow muscle unless you tear it the night before. You can either retreat, moving away from pain, or you can move towards pain and grow.

Over the years, I've learned and taught many how to use pain as a motivator. Sometimes, the things you don't want to happen will motivate you more than the things you are after. What is at stake if I do not pursue change and make these adjustments? Where would I be today? Would I be able to live with myself knowing I did not pursue my full potential? What's at stake if I don't adjust? These are questions I challenge you to ask yourself every day.

The pain of change is temporary, but the pain of regret can last forever. What would I not be able to give to my family if I threw in the towel? How much better can I serve the Lord if I have the resources and time to do so? Success is not about acquiring abilities; it is about the awareness that you already have it and are moving persistently.

Finally, there is the power of persistence that is unmatched. You must push through with passion. You either hate losing so much that you're willing to change, or you hate change so much that you're willing to lose. This choice is within your control.

While you persist, remember to process. Question the rules so you can find the potential that already exists. Here is some food for thought: business success is not everything. Business success alone does nothing for your soul. We must learn to question the rules of how we were raised and the things we were indoctrinated with by our teachers, spiritual influencers, family, and closest friends. Our parents did the best they could with what they had. They meant well, but their resources were limited. I never questioned my own parents' values and morals, for they were impeccable. But, when it came to money and business, that was a very different dynamic. Most never question the rules they learned in their youth because they view that as being disrespectful. Not true. All of our parents wanted us to live a better life than they did. "At the age of 18, you look like your parents. When we die, we look like our decisions." My soul sister Ida Brian taught me that.

Obviously, where we come from does not dictate our potential; it only dictates what we were previously taught. It has no bearing on what the future holds if you allow yourself to become a student of life, push yourself, and allow yourself to be guided. To resist is weak. It takes a strong man to surrender to growth and mentorship. Because He was meek, Jesus Christ may have been viewed as a weak man. Not so. Although His gentle love for us is unlimited, Jesus was a warrior. Many times, His humility and His lessons were His shield and His sword.

Last, but certainly not least, stay close to Christ. Only Christ can expertly guide us through hardships and spiritual warfare. Remember this: the Lord creates, and the devil imitates. The enemy wants us weak, but the *joy of the Lord is your strength!* (Nehemiah 8:10b NIV). James expounds on this point when he asserts, *Submit yourselves, then, to God. Resist the devil, and he will flee from you. Come near to God and he will come near to you* (James 4:7-8 NIV).

Getting close to the Lord is your responsibility. Don't resist, specifically when the right people come along. I thank my great wife for getting me closer to God. She has and continues to make a massive impact in my life. Although I grew up with much religion, with all my business ventures, deadlines, and compelling goals, it was easy to stray. The enemy loves to keep all men and women in isolation. We are at risk when we stray. I once heard someone say, "I am no longer close to the Lord." My question was, "Who moved?"

Life constantly changes. It's what we learn and how we meet life that creates our path. If we're willing to appreciate and harness our relationships, be grateful through the ups and downs, persist when the going gets tough, process all we see and learn, and stay close to God in the process, the path we travel will be better than we can imagine.

Just as the Lord spoke life over His exiled people through Jeremiah, so are we His people here in the twenty-first century. Hence, His Word stands true today just as It did then. The prophet speaks, *"For I know that plans that I have for you,"* declares the Lord, *"plans to prosper you and not to harm you, plans for a hope and a future"* (Jeremiah 29:11 NIV).

Although many experiences will be extremely difficult, our attitude must be "We never lose, we learn." This is how you prepare to overcome any circumstance. The humility to prepare will give you the ability to execute. Learning is preparation, and preparation teaches you these principles. Remember, there is never a shortage of opportunities, but when those opportunities come along, make sure you are prepared.

Develop strong relationships with those you respect. I would not be where I am without my family and mentors.

Set yourself up by always submitting in gratitude. The disadvantages in my upbringing positioned me to be grateful so I could take advantage of these gifts the Lord eventually blessed me with.

And hold close to God, who will give you the strength to persist and the wisdom to process your situations, opportunities, and even failures.

> *If God is for us, who can be against us?*
> (Romans 8:31 NIV)

When it's all said and done, we must accept what we can change and what we cannot. Focus on answers and not problems. Focus on what you can change, and do not worry about what you can't. The Serenity Prayer says it all and has always been my go-to for behavioral guidance. "God, grant me the serenity to accept the things I cannot change, the courage to change the things I can, and the wisdom to know the difference."

The changes we need to make come from the lessons we chose to learn. Lessons were designed to be learned, and changes were designed so we can serve.

Lessons Learned, Changes Made. Only then can we truly be *Fit 2 Fight* and serve the way the Lord designed us.

Fit 2 Fight Fear

By Ken A. Hobbs II

Two types of fear are mentioned in the Bible—one is beneficial and encouraged, but the second type of fear is detrimental and must be overcome.

The first fear spoken of in the Bible is the fear (respect) of the Lord, which brings about blessings and benefits and is also the beginning of all wisdom. *The fear of the Lord is the beginning of wisdom, and knowledge of the Holy One is understanding* (Proverbs 9:10 NIV).

The other biblical fear, the "spirit of fear," can come upon us at any moment and is something we must be prepared to fight against. Trusting and loving God completely helps us rise above this type of fear.

> *Be watchful, stand firm in faith, act like men, be strong.*
> *Let all you do be done in love.*
> (1 Corinthians 16:13-14 ESV)

The fear of man is a trap, a snare that can lure, entangle, and overpower us. When we make people big and give in to their power, we inadvertently make God small. Peer pressure, codependency, and other things can lead us to succumb to men and threaten to immobilize us.

> *Fear of man will prove to be a snare, but whoever trusts*
> *in the Lord is kept safe.*
> (Proverbs 29:25 NIV)

The fear of man can be one of the most significant roadblocks in life and in serving the Lord. It causes us to allow people to control how we think, feel, and act. We are negatively affected when we consider other people to be more significant than God. How can we possibly be obedient to God's Word when we are more concerned with what others think of us?

When you look to God, He will give you the power to do what you are not capable of doing yourself. Despite feeling fearful, if you go to Him, He will enable you to be obedient to Him. Looking to God allows you to move in faith as you trust that He will get you through any situation that may attempt to hold you back. Take a step through the fear even when you do not feel like it, ask God to help you, and watch His miraculous movement as He gives you the power to get beyond the fear.

Once you have learned to put your trust in God and bravely walk forward by faith into the unknown, you will find it easier to stand against the things that come against you. God takes our hand when we take the first step of faith forward. You serve the God of heaven's armies.

To overcome fear, we must be aware of its traps and prepared to face them down. Without God, fear has the power to paralyze. But we can go right to God's Word to see His life instructions for us; in the Bible, He tells us to "Fear not" 365 times—once for every day of the year.

Be a man of strength and valor. Be brave and of good merit in your home, work, church, and community. Fear has no dominion over you when you armor up and stay *Fit 2 Fight!* Serve others and teach them to be the worthy man of God who fears God in all they do but does not fear man.

> *"Be strong and of good courage, do not fear nor be afraid of them; for the Lord your God, He is the One who goes with you. He will not leave you nor forsake you."*
> (Deuteronomy 31:6 NKJV)

Even when your path takes me through the valley of deepest darkness, fear will never conquer me, for you already have! Your authority is my strength and my peace. The comfort of your love takes away my fear. I will never be lonely, for you are near.
(Psalm 23:4 TPT)

Fit 2 Fight: Are You Armored Up?

Brett Dabe

Brett Dabe is an accomplished entrepreneur, author, and visionary founder of Godfident. com, a platform that guides men toward biblical success in an unbiblical world. Alongside his wife, Maria, he also co-founded the Ready Set Go Experience, a ministry that prepares Christians for covenant marriages.

Brett's journey to success was paved with decades of adversity and numerous trials. He uncovered the essential elements for living an abundant life through perseverance and faith. Empowered by God's grace, Brett has developed transformative tools and resources that have not only changed his life but also inspired and uplifted many others.

As a dynamic speaker, mentor, and leader, Brett's work continues to have a profound impact. He excels as both a business professional in the payments processing industry and a dedicated ministry leader. His and Maria's story reflects their commitment to spreading hope and encouragement, a mission they continue to pursue with unwavering dedication.

WAKE-UP CALL

By Brett Dabe

It was a normal cold night in December when I heard an abnormal knock on my door after dark. One minute later, I found myself face-to-face with two police officers from the county sheriff's office. They were there to serve me with a notice—I had been indicted on multiple felony charges earlier that day, and a warrant had been issued for my arrest. As the reality of the situation sunk in, I realized I had hit rock bottom. Over the years, I had struggled with procrastination and poor decision-making, leading to failures and setbacks. Despite my efforts to turn things around, I was always one step behind.

The next few months were a blur of legal battles, strained relationships, and personal struggles. I found myself grappling with the consequences of my actions, facing the prospect of prison time and the loss of everything I held dear. But amidst the chaos, I also began to find clarity. Locked away in a jail cell, I knew I had to confront my demons head-on if I ever wanted to move forward. At 42 years old, I was forced to contend with my deepest fears and insecurities. It was a wake-up call—a reminder that I couldn't keep running from my problems forever. But it was also an opportunity—a chance to chart a new course for the future. Fortunately, I learned early on that divine intervention and revelation would be the foundation for positive change.

The legal issue was my failure to pay child support. Although I'd always had huge dreams and aspirations, they were more like visions of delusional grandeur. In fact, for the previous few years, I had lived practically as a vagabond at times with no home, car, or driver's license. My entire identity was in question. I did not know who I was or what I was doing, and it showed up in my behavior and decision-making, including but not limited to:

- I failed to secure a steady income and meet the financial obligations to my four children.

- I looked for love in all the wrong places and remarried when I had no business being in any relationship.

- I embarked on risky business endeavors, hurting those who financially supported the initiatives.

- I lived in approximately ten residences in less than three years and was evicted from most of them.

Challenges and obstacles were not a new experience in my life. I had floundered in utter survival mode for nearly two decades since entering adulthood, as I always tried to hit the ball out of the park personally and professionally. But instead of winning, I was losing in practically every possible area of my life. I had attempted to fake it till I made it, but now I was behind real bars in an actual jail cell, asking myself, "Is this really happening?" There was no more hiding from the truth of my dismal existence.

For the first week after my arrest, I was a resident of the county jail and had ample time to consider how I had ended up there. Between the jailhouse attire, 5 am wake-up call head counts, less-than-appetizing meals, being locked up in a small cell for about 19 hours a day, and shuffling around in shackles for transport to court hearings, I became determined to figure out what had gone so very wrong.

During the next few months, I was on the receiving end of vengeance from my first marriage, watched my second marriage permanently implode, pleaded guilty to the felony charges against me, and was sentenced to 33 months in state prison. Fortunately, since I was a first-time offender of the law, I was placed on probation instead of being sent to prison.

Unfortunately, my woes continued as the relationships with my children deteriorated further; I faced yet another failed business effort and then humbly was forced to move in with my parents as I licked my wounds. Now, at the age of 43, I considered myself an idiot and a loser. I had lost practically everything as I sought to break free from my very confused place in life. Fear made me lazy, and being lazy made what I feared come true. My deepest fears were now my reality, and things needed to change.

During the next few years, I began to slowly recapture my psychological mojo and move toward transforming my life. Although I wish it could have happened quickly, the process was slow and, at times, very difficult. The process was more like a procMESS. It was more difficult than it had to be, but despite that, it ushered me into a state of being for which I am now extremely thankful.

I've learned that after a life crisis, there is no magic wand you can wave to instantly become an amazing dad, restore every broken relationship, solve every challenge, and pay back every debt. However, when you surrender your past to God, He overcomes it. The truth is that anything can happen in your present and everything is possible for your future.

Although there may be consequences from the past, you do not have to remain a slave to those consequences. You can be free from the fear that created them and establish a new existence despite them. If you can envision a different and improved condition in any area of your life, God will guide your brain to coordinate with your body to make it happen. I discovered from the age of 43 to 53 that there is a difference between knowing who God is and personally knowing God. I also found that the key to transformation is to become what I call GODFIDENT, which is: Being in a state of physical, emotional, and spiritual surrender to God's grace, mercy, and love that delivers God's peace, provision, and power on earth as it is in heaven.

While living at my parent's house for nearly a year and a half, God began to reveal a series of truths through His Word.

The Apostle Paul wrote in 2 Corinthians 13:5-7: *Test yourselves to see if you are in the faith; examine yourselves! Or do you not recognize this about yourselves, that Jesus Christ is in you—unless indeed you fail the test? But I expect that you will realize that we ourselves do not fail the test. Now we pray to God that you do nothing wrong; not so that we ourselves may appear approved, but that you may do what is right, though we may appear unapproved* (NASB).

After growing up in church and attending it all of my life, it occurred to me that I had been blind to the truth contained in the Bible. I was living in the world and for the world—full of fear, pride, and lust. The idea that Jesus Christ could be in me, lead me, and set me "free from me" was not something I had ever really grasped. I read Bible scriptures but consistently did not apply them in my life. Rather, my existence was full of B.S.—Bad Strategies. More specifically, there were ten bad strategies that I was suffering from. In no particular order, they include complaining, worrying, blaming, lying, faking, judging, wasting, lusting, boasting and isolating. I want to take a brief look at each of these. I hope you can learn from my mistakes.

COMPLAINING

From an early age, I found that even though I would try to turn negative circumstances into positive outcomes, I was consistently not content with the blessings God gave me.

> *Do all things without complaining or arguments; so that*
> *you will prove yourselves to be blameless and innocent,*
> *children of God above reproach in the midst of a crooked*
> *and perverse generation.*
> (Philippians 2:14-15 NASB)

My pattern of never being satisfied perpetually put me in survival mode, firmly establishing poor character. This poor character was the foundation from which I began my adult life. Looking back now, it is clear that the house of cards would ultimately fall apart.

WORRYING

I was married right out of college, and two years later, my wife gave birth to our daughter Faith, who has special needs. During the pregnancy, we knew there was a significant problem. Faith was not expected to breathe on her own after delivery, so we planned that we would be burying her the following week. I had already made arrangements for the funeral and grave site. To our surprise, Faith survived; however, her health needs and the responsibilities associated with her care brought a substantial amount of pressure to our life and marriage.

> *"So do not worry about tomorrow; for tomorrow will worry*
> *about itself. Each day has enough trouble of its own."*
> (Matthew 6:34 NASB)

Throughout my entire adult life, I was behind on bills. I mostly ran my own business initiatives as an independent contractor, and concerns over keeping the lights on and paying rent were consistent issues. My reality was a life of constant worry, but I masked this from most people. I thought I was operating in faith, but I was really rotting away inside.

BLAMING

It was always easier to come up with excuses as to why I was not doing what I was capable of instead of looking in the mirror and saying, "Mirror, Mirror, on the wall, who is the cause of all my problems?" I became good at placing blame on conjured-up circumstances or people.

After my wife gave birth to another two daughters and there seemed to be light at the end of my financial tunnel, I rented a very large, brand new custom home on a gated street. It was a foolish decision; as it became clear that we could not afford to live there, I became desperate and made additional poor decisions.

> *One who conceals his wrongdoings will not prosper, But one who confesses and abandons them will find compassion.*
> (Proverbs 28:13 NASB)

My marriage had never been healthy, but for some reason, we believed that having more children would help. My wife became pregnant with our son, and when she was eight months pregnant, there was a knock on the door from the landlord demanding that we leave. I needed to catch up on the rent, which had been late many times. I had committed to purchasing the home after leasing it for two years; however, at that point, it was evident that I could not do that. I created this mess but attempted to blame the landlord for not being "reasonable."

LYING

Over many years, I became a master manipulator. Although I did not consciously seek to lie, cheat, and steal, that is what I did. I subconsciously justified it because I needed to care for my family and keep up the image that I was doing better than I was. It became a very unhealthy and vicious cycle. Unmanaged chaos was my day-in and day-out experience.

> *Lying lips are an abomination to the LORD,*
> *But those who deal faithfully are His delight.*
> (Proverbs 12:22 NASB)

I deluded myself into thinking I would "hit it big" at some point, allowing me to make things right in every area where I was wrong. The hole I continued to dig for myself and my family would eventually come crashing in.

FAKING

Because I did not have a real relationship with my Lord and Savior, Jesus Christ, one of the most significant areas where I faked it was in church. I became an "elder" in my late twenties, led a teenage group each Sunday, and became an example of the hypocrite that so many people outside the church despise.

> *Therefore if anyone is in Christ, this person is a new creation;*
> *the old things passed away; behold, new things have come.*
> (2 Corinthians 5:17 NASB)

I did not see myself as a new creation. I saw myself as a "poor, miserable sinner" who was unable to do what he was truly called to do. Although I was not aware of this consciously, my behavior proved otherwise.

JUDGING

I thought I was better than others. In my twisted mind, I justified my irresponsibility because I believed I was special. I thought I was talented enough to pull a rabbit out of a hat and, through a series of magic tricks, solve my problems and help others solve theirs.

> *"Do not judge so that you will not be judged. For in the way you judge, you will be judged; and by your standard of measure, it will be measured to you."*
> (Matthew 7:1-2 NASB)

I did not respect or honor my parents, who had bailed me out of many financial challenges. I was getting back what I was sowing in the world. Year after year, poor life management led to an epic downfall.

WASTING

I was a pro at procrastination. Fear of failing and a lack of self-respect made the lack of necessary action a lifestyle.

So then, be careful how you walk, not as unwise people but as wise, making the most of your time, because the days are evil. Therefore do not be foolish, but understand what the will of the Lord is (Ephesians 5:15-17 NASB).

I would read books and study how to be successful far more than taking steps toward accomplishing things. Ignoring and avoiding challenges was a pattern that would lead to troubling times.

LUSTING

From my early teenage years, I had seen nude pictures of women, and that established an appetite for what ultimately became an addiction to pornography in my late twenties. The desire to have passionate sex would ultimately take me down a path of destruction.

But each one is tempted when he is carried away and enticed by his own lust. Then when lust has conceived, it gives birth to sin; and when sin is accomplished, it brings forth death (James 1:14-15 NASB).

I would have never conceived of having an affair, getting divorced, spending limited time with my children, becoming a felon for not paying child support, or living with my parents in my early forties. If I had to pick one Bad Strategy that caused most of it, lust is at the top of the list. I never understood sex, the desire for it, why God created it, and how to properly channel the need. This undoubtedly is one of the greatest challenges for men, and I was no exception. Memorizing the scriptures in Proverbs warning against lust and what happens when you tolerate the "Jezebel spirit" (Revelation 2:18-29) are something that should be required for all young men.

BOASTING

When someone is ignorant, that is one thing. When someone is arrogant, that is another. When someone is both, it is painfully obvious and very annoying. I was both. I am humbled looking back on how I operated and how I was seen by many people in my circles, especially those close to me.

> *For by grace you have been saved through faith;*
> *and this is not of yourselves, it is the gift of God;*
> *not a result of works, so that no one may boast.*
> (Ephesians 2: 8-9 NASB)

It is impossible to know what you do not know. I did not know how bad my boasting was. I could not see how poorly I was missing the mark in so many areas. Ignorance is not bliss. It leads to heartache for you and those you care about.

ISOLATING

Men are especially good at this. I certainly was. I desperately could have used a strong inner circle of men who would call me out and give me wisdom. However, I isolated myself into my shell of stupidity early on in my twenties, and it became a way of life.

> One who separates himself seeks his own desire;
> He quarrels against all sound wisdom.
> (Proverbs 18:1 NASB)

It was not until well into my forties that I began to get serious about setting myself up for success and surrounding myself with men who could help me out of my own way. As I did, however, I became a man who can honestly say he has a "peace that transcends understanding."

If you are seeking to produce results in any area of your life, I advise you to meditate on the scriptures in this Chapter and be aware of the following principles:

- Practicing unconditional surrender to God and abiding in His presence is freedom.

- Your brain will often tell you to quit. God calls you to follow His timeline and guidance.

- How you view yourself will typically determine what you do.

- Your past is done. This moment is a miracle.

- Whatever isn't measured remains confined. Measurement unleashes boundless potential.

- Action free from fear produces fulfillment. Action rooted in fear produces regret.

- Deliberating deeply on who and what is worthy of your attention and resources is powerful; therein lies your path.

- Freedom pays emotional dividends but requires delayed gratification. Slavery pays instant gratification but leads to emotional bankruptcy.

- Criticizing yourself or others, whether in silence or speech, is destructive to yourself and those God has called you to serve.

- "Will my present actions have eternal significance?" is a question worth asking daily.

I pray you have learned from my wake-up call. Lean into the Lord; He will give you all you need to serve Him as He has called.

> *The LORD bless you, and keep you;*
> *The LORD cause His face to shine on you,*
> *And be gracious to you;*
> *The LORD lift up His face to you.*
> *And give you peace.*
> (Numbers 6:24-26 NASB)

JASON PERRY

Jason Perry is a distinguished voice in the Christian community and the realm of security and emergency preparedness. As the founder and pastor of Christian Warrior Mission, a home church, community, ministry, farm, and podcast, Jason disciples men and women to embrace their role as good shepherds and become warriors for Jesus Christ.

Additionally, as the founder of Trident Shield, an emergency preparedness, security training, and consulting firm in Johnson City, Tennessee, Jason masterfully integrates biblical principles with practical safety training. Jason's approach to active shooter and workplace violence prevention, as well as emergency preparedness and personal safety, is deeply rooted in real-world experience and guided by his faith. His extensive background (32+ years) encompasses his role as a Navy SEAL, Independent Duty Corpsman, Paramedic, SWAT Officer, Executive Protection Specialist, and Corporate Security Expert. Jason's expertise in crisis management is enriched by his spiritual leadership, offering a perspective that encompasses both physical readiness and spiritual insight. His methodology extends beyond conventional security tactics, fostering a spirit of vigilance and resilience deeply anchored in biblical wisdom.

A Battle for Generations

By Jason Perry

> *And I looked and arose and said to the nobles and to the officials and to the rest of the people, "Do not be afraid of them. Remember the Lord, who is great and awesome, and fight for your brothers, your sons, your daughters, your wives, and your homes."*
> (Nehemiah 4:14 ESV)

BORN INTO DARKNESS

I was a rabid atheist and enemy of God for thirty-seven years of my life. I grew up in Quincy and South Boston, Massachusetts, in a secular home that was loving and caring in a worldly way. My family did the best they knew how, raising me in a godless, broken, and lost environment. Buried in alcohol and drug addictions, broken despair and tragedy seemed constant.

My story from darkness to light begins with my maternal grandfather. He was an orphan in a notorious orphanage in Newfoundland, Canada, where sexual abuse, beatings, and other cruelties from the Catholic priests were routine. His severe abuse soured him on a faithful church life. I believe we are born empty vessels to be filled by either the Holy Spirit in obedience and love or the world in rebellion and wrath. Because of his wicked priest wounds, we scorned faith and defaulted to the world's wrathful rebellion.

My family loved as best they could. Sadly, without God and solid discipling, worldly love is tragically broken. Godlessness led to immense family despair. My grandfather's alcoholism was inevitable. He was kind and loving through life but consumed by bitter resentment in his final years as his health failed. Sorrowfully, several close relatives were molested by a Canadian uncle in childhood. Such abuse was their catalyst for wounded despair that led them all down very dark paths.

At fifteen, my mother got pregnant by my seventeen-year-old father. They married just after my birth and divorced soon thereafter. Heinous addiction ran rampant on my father's side. He was already well on his way to becoming a third-generation addict and alcoholic with a spotted jail career. I was surrounded by godlessness and the hopelessly broken. Not that I was interested at the time, but the Lord had a plan for this walking wounded warrior.

THE WOUNDING

My father remarried, started a new family, and continued his downward spiral for decades. I was sent to live with my maternal grandparents, which marked the beginning of my abandonment wounds that caused a profound emptiness in me. We all have a deep need to know that we are loved and worth fighting for. When trusted parents and guardians refuse the fight, abandonment wounds ensue.

Believers of our Lord and Savior, Jesus Christ, understand that God loves us enough that He fought for us by sending His only Son to die for our sins and reconcile us to Him. However, like many others, I projected my father's failures onto the heavenly Father. As such, I was bitterly angry toward God.

Several years later, my mother remarried and had two more children, one with Down Syndrome. When I moved back with her, it marked my second abandonment wound—because my grandparents didn't fight for me. This caused what felt like a growing void in my chest. My mother's marriage ended shortly after her husband was caught cheating, and we became a welfare family. She was a single mother of three now, and it was hard. I remember sleeping in front of the electric stove during a cold Massachusetts winter because my mom couldn't afford the oil bill. She wasn't prepared for this burdensome time. Eventually, she kept my youngest brother, released my special needs brother for adoption, and sent me back to my grandparents. Watching my brother being given to strangers destroyed my trust in my family. Abandonment's wound exploded when my brother and I were sent away. Over time, I was passed around between my grandparents and my mother until I was sixteen.

INDOCTRINATION AND ANGER

Unfortunately, Massachusetts' public school education meant that I was indoctrinated deeper into God-opposing atheism. Early repetitive abandonment wounds left me extremely vulnerable to God's enemies. So, the world offered all the godlessness that I could handle.

I discovered anger as a fuel source and used it daily. I started working out and doing boxing/martial arts as an outlet for my anger. I believe music is a potent weapon that can be used for good or evil. Music can bypass our conscious mind and start manipulating us into various emotional and spiritual states that can take us to good or evil places. I use music as a mood accelerant, a catalyst for mood change, or a foundation to set the mood I want to be in. Unfortunately, when I was younger, I used music as a weapon to fuel my anger. I started listening to the angriest and most vile music I could find, like heavy metal and gangster rap. Music was the fuel to make me burn angrier, which is precisely what I wanted. Evil music dragged me willingly to hell's gates, where I was banging on the gate, screaming to let me in. Today, it disgusts me that my favorite song on Gym Blast was Slayer's *God Hates Us All*. In hindsight, I know we must be extremely cautious when listening to music and about what we let into our and our family's minds. External stimulation influences us far more than we realize and can be treasonous to God, leading us into deeper darkness.

Like many men challenged with abandonment wounds, I tried to fill the void with unbiblical sex with women. I dropped out of school at sixteen and started hanging out with older guys at the gym. I got a job bouncing at seventeen in a popular nightclub by lying about my age and spent nearly all my energy chasing older women. The club spawned my first ungodly love relationship, and I poured my worldly heart into it. When she broke up with me, my betrayal and abandonment trigger elevated to a critical state. In such woundedness, my sole perspective was through the abandonment void inside me. Anger was my superpower, and I vowed defensively never to be hurt again. I became a monster—the wounded had become the serial wounder.

Those with untreated wounds bear a dismally dark worldview. The deep-seated wounds taint and twist all that we see and experience. Through the wound, I believed I couldn't trust anyone. I had been abandoned and rejected by all that I loved. I knew I couldn't live with this painful void deep inside me; I tried filling it with everything but what I needed. Womanizing's false idol failed to fill the void first. I lived in dishonest conquests built on deceptive lies as I dated as many women as I could at one time. If one left me, hey, that was fine; I laughed it off and moved on to whoever was left. The drinking and drug-filled parties failed to fill the void as well and only ushered me deeper into misery's dark depths.

BECOMING A WARRIOR

When I was twenty, I stared at my ceiling fan while lying in bed at 10 AM. I couldn't sleep; my nose hurt from drugs, and I felt awful. I remember thinking, *I paid a lot to feel this way, and I feel like garbage.*

I thought about my last three years and how far I had fallen. I was a thug, a liar, and a cheat. I looked into the mirror and hated myself. I considered my friends; they were either on their way to jail, in jail, or on their way to an early grave. I had to redeem myself. I wanted to be a "good guy." I wanted to be a hero! But I wasn't. I was a villain. As an atheist, I could not turn to God for redemption. So, I turned to my second false idol: my country.

I loved my country and was patriotic despite being a thug. Being raised in and around Boston, the birthplace of the American Revolution, was inspiring. American history was so real to me and was all around me: the USS Constitution, the Mayflower, Plymouth Rock, Fort Independence, the Freedom Trail, John Quincy Adams' House, Paul Revere's House, Bunker Hill, and more. I believed if I could serve my country honorably, I could redeem myself from this thug life. I enlisted in the Navy to face the greatest challenge available. I chose to become a Navy SEAL. I believed the brotherhood and camaraderie in a SEAL Platoon would provide safety. Surely those guys wouldn't ever let me down. Off to Bootcamp I went and left my thug life behind. I was, however, still a womanizer, a liar, and a cheat. I tried to rack up as many "serious" girlfriends as I could before I went into the military because I feared they would all cheat on me and leave me. So, I did it to them first.

In Bootcamp, I started to run into Christians. I would notice them praying at mealtimes. I had never encountered this in my twenty-one years of life. I challenged, mocked, and made fun of their faith. One day during Basic Underwater Demolition School, known to most as BUDS, we were in the infamous week of training called "Hell Week." I sat down at a table with my new boat crew for a rushed three-minute meal at the chow hall (as people quit, you are constantly reassigned new boat crews by height) when I noticed a couple of them giving thanks to the Lord for getting them through that day of training and asking for His help to get through that night. I became enraged and shouted at them, "No one is going to help you get through training! YOU HAVE TO DO IT!" Every chance I got to try to shake the faith of Christians, I would go after them. I would ask them hard questions about creation, the age of the universe, Noah's Ark, Jonah and the whale, and make them defend their beliefs. Sadly, none of them could, and I have repented many times for the harm I did to poorly discipled Christians during this time of my life. Finding a Christian who could defend their faith took me decades, but more on that later.

I got through SEAL training by relying on my superpower—anger. No matter how scared, overwhelmed, in pain, cold, or miserable, I would burn hotter and hotter, screaming the vilest music and language inside my head and, at times, out loud. I would hate and burn with anger and fury to overcome all my obstacles, challenges, and opponents. I had no peace, only anger, conquest, and camaraderie. Regardless of how much womanizing, friendships, parties, and adrenaline I poured in, the void was bottomless. The anger raged on, and it wasn't a clean fuel. Anger doesn't discriminate. It burns everything! It burns down family, friends, and self just as swiftly as it incinerates challenging enemies.

The problem with always looking for a fight is, far too often, you find one. Even if there is no fight to begin with, anger finds an enemy to burn. When we believe that everyone will eventually betray us, we do our best to keep everyone at arm's length before they can hurt us. I've learned through the challenges that this lonely existence is NOT God's will for us. He created us to be in communion with Him and with others of His body, the church. The enemy wants us isolated because it is always easier to pull down a lone warrior than a shield wall of warriors working as a team. The enemy knows he cannot have us once we turn to our heavenly Father and become His children. The Holy Spirit becomes part of us—His life is in us! Jesus declares, *"I give them eternal life, and they will never perish, and no one will snatch them out of my hand"* (John 10:28 ESV). Knowing this, the enemy works overtime to keep us from knowing our heavenly Father. Because of my wound and betrayal's fear, I caused a lot of emotional pain and left all previous relationships, including my first marriage, in ruins.

I continued to serve as a Navy SEAL for about sixteen years. I found out that betrayal existed even in the SEAL Teams. I witnessed countless double standards and politics being played by senior leadership that would eventually cost my teammate and friend his life. Their trust breach broke my heart again. I deployed to Iraq, Kosovo, Southeast Asia, Colombia, and other places. The men I served with were amazing. Sadly, most were as broken and lost as I was. While I and many of the godless SEALs were womanizing and partying to cope with the stress and tragic loss that come with a warrior's duty, I saw godly SEALs who were more resilient than others. They had what Paul described as God's peace, which surpasses all understanding. His peace guarded their hearts and minds in Christ Jesus (Philippians 4:7 ESV). While we were thrashing in life's storms, they remained calm in the storm's eye.

Nevertheless, I was still God's enemy, trying to shake believers' faith wherever I could. However, I looked at the lives and relationships of these Christian Team Guys, and they were rock solid and full of love and peace. These godly men couldn't be shaken by logical debate skills, and they just laughed at my challenges. Somewhat jealously, I came to admire their peaceful confidence.

THE TURNING POINT

During my last deployment to Iraq, I had a cancer scare. The doctors thought I was in real trouble, but I refused to go home. I assured them that

I would handle it when I got home. When I returned, my command sent me to shore duty to take care of the possible cancer. People said to pray, but I was too wounded and bitter about losing to cancer after several near-death SEAL experiences. I foolishly said that I was not coming to God on my knees with cancer. Instead, I revisited living like a rock star at high velocity! I didn't want to die a shriveled-up cancer patient. After a year of living like I was dying, the doctors removed one of my adrenal glands, and the cancer was gone! Now what?

My marriage was thriving, so I decided to get out of the Navy and become a Boston cop to help fight the drug epidemic that took so many lives, including my younger brother's. God came for me in Boston. It started with Norman Geisler and Frank Turek's amazing book, *I Don't Have Enough Faith to Be an Atheist.* Their book CHANGED EVERYTHING! In thirty-seven years, I had never had the scientific case for creationism and intelligent design presented to me in any logical manner. Norman and Frank effortlessly countered all my argumentative points, and after about 377 pages, they destroyed my entire belief system. Like a baseball bat smashing a house of cards, it all came down! My deciding factor was looking at DNA after reading the book. DNA is a code, and a code requires a coder.

I felt like a completely betrayed fool. Why had no one ever explained God like this? Why did all my public schooling feed me so much garbage and lies? How could I believe such nonsense? Why didn't my parents know about Jesus? I gave my life to God the next night while lying in bed and joined the battle for eternity. It can be quite shocking how quickly the Holy Spirit moves and begins our sanctification. I remember being in the gym the next day and reflexively starting to play the angry music. GOD immediately convicted me of those songs to the point I was disgusted by them and could no longer listen.

THE BATTLE CONTINUES

> *Be sober-minded; be watchful. Your adversary the devil prowls around like a roaring lion, seeking someone to devour.*
> (1 Peter 5:8 ESV)

So, that's the end? Easy days now, right? Not even close. This was just the beach landing at Normandy on D-Day. I fought several battles in the following years. I won most; I lost some, but those are stories for another day.

Team, it's vital to understand that we are on the largest POW rescue mission ever! What we do with the rest of our lives matters in eternity. Jesus Christ won the war! Now, it's our job to help rescue those behind enemy lines. This includes our families. My family's godless suffering isn't unique. Sadly, it's somewhat normal in our secular society. Without proper discipling, countless more families are doomed to generations of suffering and eternal damnation.

Our families are in enemy territory. We must fight for them with His everything because the enemy is coming for them unless we guide them to the Great News of Jesus Christ as Savior! Recall Jesus' affirmation: *"The thief comes only to steal and kill and destroy. I came that they may have life and have it abundantly"* (John 10:10 ESV).

Our most important job as men is passing our Christian identity onto our families. Nothing else matters! Our current or future wives and children will be under attack 24/7 by this world's dark forces. Don't be distracted by the endless entertainment designed to keep your attention away from what is happening in your family, community, and country.

We have a mission from God! Our holy duty is to disciple our families and prepare and safeguard them in Christ for eternity's war. Then, from His firm foundation, our godly families go with us, in Jesus' name, to save the POWs drowning in an ocean of sin and death. Together, we are here to pull them onto Jesus Christ's eternal life raft.

WE MUST NOT FAIL!

Only fully in Christ's power and authority are we *Fit 2 Fight!*

Embracing a Fit 2 Fight Stance

By Allen L. Thorne

If we are to learn and grow as we advance through life, we must embrace change and a *Fit 2 Fight* stance. But how? As a man who resisted change for the better part of three decades, I attest to the Apostle Paul's truth recorded in Romans 8:6. He recognizes, *For the mind set on the flesh is death, but the mind set on the Spirit is life and peace* (NASB).

In simple terms, operating in the flesh is living by the world's carnal standards, whereas living in the Spirit is only possible inside our relational confession of Jesus Christ as Lord and Savior of our lives.

Flesh desires are hostile toward the Lord's will and way. They require a never-ending pursuit of "more" while, in reality, that "more" diminishes over time and leaves us with minimal (if any) lasting satisfaction. In contrast, new life in Christ welcomes fresh perspectives concerning lives lived with eternal benefits on earth as in heaven.

Jesus asserts in John's Gospel that *when the Spirit of truth comes, He will guide you into all the truth; for He will not speak on His own initiative, but whatever He hears, He will speak; and He will disclose to you what is to come* (John 16:13 NASB).

God has a plan for all of us, friends. However, in order to partake in His higher and greater plan, we must intentionally step away from the world's plan and follow Jesus' will and guidance. For believers, Jesus, the light for all mankind, presents us with God's righteousness, and the Holy Spirit communicates the plan to us when we choose to listen, align, and abide in Him.

So, how do we begin? Jesus' disciples asked the same question. *Jesus answered and said to them, "This is the work of God, that you believe in Him whom He has sent"* (John 6:29 NASB). Our initial move is only to believe that Jesus Christ is who He says He is. Mind you, Jesus didn't tell us we must fully understand; He said we are to believe. Believing requires faith; faith is the *certainty of things hoped for and a proof of things not seen* (Hebrews 11:1 NASB), so it is alright if we don't understand everything; we can begin with simply believing. You won't regret taking the initial move of faith. To add a bit of viable perspective, Augustine differentiates between belief and understanding. He affirms, *Seek not to understand that you may believe, but believe that you may understand*.[1]

As we embrace this vital transformation from having our mind set on the flesh to being set on the Spirit, we observe that the Lord's "full armor" is only attainable through our faith-filled belief transformation.

The Apostle Paul announces that we must gird our loins with truth (Ephesians 6:14a). Our faith confession has received such protection in Jesus as He does not just *present* a truth, He *is* the truth, as well as the way and the life. (John 14:6) Paul also calls us to avail ourselves of the breastplate of righteousness to guard our heart, only accessible through Christ, who reconciles our righteousness before the Father (2 Corinthians 5:21). Likewise, Paul encourages our faith walk be fortified by the shoes of peace (Ephesians 6:15), which are also only accessible via Jesus who informs *"Peace I leave with you; My peace I give to you; not as the world gives do I give to you"* (John 14:27 NASB). Further, we wield off satan's flaming arrow attacks with the shield of faith (Ephesians 6:16), proclaiming as Peter did that Jesus is, indeed, *"the Messiah, the Son of the living God"* (Matthew 16:16 NIV). We must also guard our minds set on the Spirit with the helmet of salvation, which is found in no one else but Jesus Christ the Nazarene (Acts 4:10, 12).

Finally, we brandish the sword of the Spirit, the Word of God (Ephesians 6:17), which has testified over centuries that Jesus Christ is King of kings and Lord of lords (Revelation 19:16).

As you prepare to be *Fit 2 Fight*, embrace the transformation that begins with a faithful belief in the One whom the Father sent, Jesus. A mind set on the Spirit and taking full advantage of the Father's full authoritative armor, solely defined by Jesus Himself, invites new life and peace, fortifying our fitness to fight.

Only Jesus presents a newness of life and can offer us the fitness necessary to fight. His presence, protection, and wisdom are more than we could ever ask or imagine! Praise Him!

. . . .

[1] Word Counter, St. Augustine Quotes, 2024, https://word-counter.com/popular/saint-augustine-quotes/

ERIC FAZZI

Eric Fazzi grew up in a small rural town in Florida and then moved to Miami in his early teens. He became a world-class freediver/spearfisherman and an avid hunter; he enjoys just spending time in nature connecting with God.

In high school, Eric met his wife, Jennifer, the love of his life. After high school, Jennifer went to college and became a registered nurse, and Eric became a firefighter. They have three beautiful children and enjoy spending time together as a family.

Eric began his career as a firefighter/paramedic. Throughout his prestigious and distinguished career, Eric was promoted through the ranks to Battalion Chief. He also served on the Rescue Task Force for Active Shooter and Hostile Events, the Rapid Intervention Team, the Dive Rescue Team, the Hazardous Materials Team, and the High Angle Rope Rescue Team—just to name a few of his specialties.

After leaving the fire department, Eric began work in the private sector. He now serves on the leadership team for the Florida Band of Brothers.

Finding My Father

By Eric Fazzi

I grew up in Belle Glade, Florida—a small city near Lake Okeechobee in South Florida—with my Cuban maternal grandparents and my mother. I spent much of my early childhood outdoors playing, fishing, hunting, and riding my bicycle around our rural Florida town.

My grandparents had fled the murderous communist dictatorship of Fidel Castro, which took over their home and tropical paradise of Cuba. Shortly after the revolution in 1961, they left everything behind and escaped communism with their three children—my mother, my uncle, and my godfather. After arriving in Florida with their children and nothing but the shirts on their backs, they worked any job they could find to make ends meet.

Fast forward about 20 years, my grandparents had established themselves as citizens of the greatest country on earth: the United States of America. My grandmother worked as a local bank administrator, and my grandfather was a local sugar mill welder for thirty-five years, after which he retired. My mother was a young bride, marrying my biological father when she was twenty-one years old. Shortly after they were married, I was born. My mother never shared the details with me, but my biological father left her before my birth. To this day, I have never met or spoken to him.

About ten months after I was born, a female drunk driver killed my godfather in a motor vehicle accident. Our family's devastation from his loss still resides today. So my life began surrounded by all this turmoil. But I was treasured—the family's new baby boy and first US-born member.

My relationship with my mother was more of a sibling relationship, with my grandparents posing as my parental figures for the majority of my life. I received lots of love and attention from both my grandparents, but they fought constantly. My grandfather drank heavily and left the house often. On several occasions, my grandmother locked us in her room with the lock only accessible from the inside, so my grandfather couldn't get in when he returned. Mama did a good job shielding me from the family turbulence, so I always looked up to my grandfather for his hard work and the dedicated support he offered our family.

People always asked me about my unique last name and why it was different from my mom's. I was embarrassed and never knew how to answer. At a young age, I got into a fight with a boy who called my grandfather old. I still have a scar on my hand from that day. I constantly felt like an outcast, as if I was the only boy in the world who didn't know who his dad was. It didn't help that nobody ever talked about him.

I thank my grandmother for my relationship with Jesus Christ. She was a devout Catholic; she ensured I attended Sunday School and mass every week and participated as an altar server. She also took me to her Bible studies and church events, where we made crafts to sell to raise money for our small church. And we prepared food and delivered it to needy families in our community. I believe this is where I received my calling to help others.

My mom met her boyfriend, who later became my stepfather (although they were never officially married). He had also fled Cuba's communism with his son, daughter, and wife at the time. He came to America, like many, in search of freedom. He eventually divorced his wife and met my mom at the sugar mill where they both worked. My mother was a secretary, and my stepfather was the chief engineer. Mom took me on the weekends to his apartment in Miami, and we would go out on his 19' Donzi boat, which he towed with an old Buick with holes in the floorboard. I remember it as an exciting time as a little boy. He was an avid world-class freediver/spearfisherman and competed several times in the US national competition. He treated me very well and introduced me to the world of freediving/spearfishing long before its popularity here in the US.

However, not all of those trips to Miami were fun memories. My stepfather and mom often argued; since he lived in a small one-bedroom apartment, there was nowhere for me to hide from the turmoil. They broke up on many occasions. My mom would pack us into her car, and we'd leave. One particular time, I recall Mom telling me it was my fault that they were breaking up; I wrote my stepfather an apology letter covered in my tears because I really thought it was my fault. Please understand this, though: my mom was not a bad mother. She tried the best that she could, but she'd gone through a lot of trauma early on. I honestly believe that she was doing the best she could. Despite her outward actions, I knew she loved me immensely. My childhood experiences built one resiliently tough little boy.

My grandparents divorced when I was in fourth grade. Since they were most of my world, I was devastated! They immediately sold the house where I had grown up, and my grandfather moved in with my great-grandparents in West Palm Beach. In the upcoming months, I bounced around with my grandmother, from friends to family members' houses, while she and my mother figured out what to do. I also stayed with my grandfather once a week; we would go out to eat and enjoy great times. Our dinners together are some of my treasured memories from this tough time.

The summer before my sixth-grade year, my grandfather moved to South Miami with his girlfriend. My grandmother also moved to Miami—into an efficiency apartment, and my mother moved in with her boyfriend. I wanted to stay with my grandmother, but she thought it would be best for me to live with my mom. So, I moved in with my mom and stepdad in a two-bedroom apartment in Miami Lakes. Going from a house in a small rural town where I spent days roaming the outdoors to a two-bedroom apartment in the city surrounded by cars and people made me feel like a fish out of water. I started sixth grade as one of 3500 sixth to eighth-grade students. My previous school had about 150 students from kindergarten to twelfth grade. My new school was a large concrete building with very few windows. Security guards and police patrolled the hallways. Sex, gangs, and drugs were everywhere in the big city school. It was like overload for me! I was a shy young boy who felt like an outcast with no identity. I was not a bad kid. However, in a system like this, trouble just finds you.

> Be sober, be vigilant; because your adversary the devil walks
> about like a roaring lion, seeking whom he may devour.
> (I Peter 5:8 NKJV)

As a shy boy who was new in town, I was picked on and made fun of a lot. I got into fights and was frequently in detention and suspended from school. Luckily for me, that was when God sent me my first real friend, Tomas. He was also a shy kid; we developed a great friendship and spent a lot of our time together as he lived about two blocks away from me in a house with his parents and two siblings. I attribute this friendship to keeping me out of any serious trouble; I was looking for acceptance and validation and could have easily gone in the wrong direction. Tomas's family was traditional, and his parents were quite strict. This was a good thing because I had free reign and could basically do whatever I wanted. Tomas's parents' rules affected me and helped keep me out of trouble.

By eighth grade, I was acclimated to living in the city with my mom and stepdad. My stepdad was and is a great man who cared for me and provided me with another father figure. It was a little confusing, though, and I didn't know what to call him. So, I called him by his first name for the majority of my life. Honestly, I was confused, embarrassed, and ashamed that I didn't have someone to call Dad. As such, I put up walls and hid behind different masks.

Look out! Here comes high school! After seeing what the middle and high schools were like, my mother and grandmother did not want me to attend public school any longer. So, they registered me at a private Catholic school in Opa-Locka, FL. However, I failed my entrance exam and had to attend summer school. Since my grandfather was retired, I stayed with him and his girlfriend in South Miami for the summer. He drove me and picked me up from summer school. This school had a pretty large campus with lots of windows in the classrooms, trees, and walkways throughout. I felt a lot better there than in the prison-style school I had been attending. My mother could not afford the tuition. I was constantly called to the office to pick up Mom's bounced checks. She tried her best to pay for it, but her job just was not enough to cover the expense. So my grandmother covered the school's cost.

As awkward as the high school transition was, I will forever be grateful for the shift because that is where I met the love of my life—my wife, Jennifer—and several lifelong friends. I also played football, developing a passion for the "team" environment. Unfortunately, I lost one great thing: my friend Tomas. Since we were in different schools, we drifted apart. However, God continued blessing my path with great friends, brothers, and mentors.

Through the challenges of my youth, the Lord showed me that He sees us through our storms when we trust Him. As I am grateful for the growth through challenges, I recall His Word, reminding me to *Make sure that your character is free from the love of money, being content with what you have. For He Himself has said, "I will never desert you nor will I ever abandon you"* (Hebrews 13:5 NASB).

After high school, I entered the workforce. I worked at my friend Jason's uncle's business, repairing medical equipment, loading shipping containers, and doing various other tasks. During my time there, Jason's uncle exposed us to drugs, strippers, and prostitution. Regardless of our underage status, he took us out to party all night at strip clubs and various other locations. Disturbingly enough, the scene was filled with alcohol and drugs. In hindsight, it was only because of God's protective grace that I did not ever partake in any of the drug usage. I did, however, drink quite heavily.

Along with Jason, my friend David—who would later be the godfather to all my children—and I worked at that business together. Eventually, David and I decided to become firefighters, and Jason joined the Army.

Shortly after high school, I married Jennifer. I cannot expound enough about the wonderful woman the Lord has given me. She's remained by my side through life's most difficult battles. Jennifer is the love of my life, and I thank God for our lives together. I could not ask for a more supportive lady through all our life's endeavors.

> *He who finds a wife finds a good thing,*
> *And obtains favor from the Lord.*
> (Proverbs 18:22 NASB)

As a firefighter, I was strong, tough, smart, and motivated. I thought I was invincible. I joined and excelled in every department specialty team. I was an instructor and received promotions several times as a respected leader in the department. Because I never knew my biological father, I had always looked to others to fill that void. This search continued at the fire department. My superiors were my role models who gave me advice and guidance. The challenge was that the latter part of my career introduced toxic leadership that failed to lead as I needed. I felt lost again because I had no one to guide me. I quickly fell out of love with the profession and struggled with anxiety and depression. I reached out for help at the fire department and was told to contact the Employee Assistance Program (EAP). Unfortunately, the EAP was nothing but a contact list of list of doctors. I was lost and spiraling down depression's dark tunnels, and all of my relationships were affected. Then God put another person in my life to help guide me, my friend and brother-from-another-mother, Jay.

> A man who has friends must himself be friendly,
> But there is a friend who sticks closer than a brother.
> (Proverbs 18:24 NKJV)

I remember one of my darkest pits. I was just lying alone in bed at our Central Florida ranch, sobbing uncontrollably and praying as hard as I could for a miracle to get me out of that place. Suddenly, out of nowhere, I felt a warmth come over me; it was a peace I cannot explain. I related to Paul's declaration.

> Be anxious for nothing, but in everything by prayer
> and supplication, with thanksgiving, let your requests
> be made known to God; and the peace of God which
> surpasses all understanding, will guard your hearts
> and minds through Christ Jesus.
> (Philippians 4:6-7 NKJV)

With unthinkable peace, I felt God speaking to me, telling me it was time for something new, time to leave the fire department. I had no idea how I would leave or where I would go. So, I talked to Jay about it, and he said, "Don't worry. If this is really what you want, do it. I got you."

This was such a blessing. By then, my grandparents had passed, my mom and stepdad had separated, and my relationships with my remaining friends were slipping. I felt like I was all alone. BUT GOD had other plans.

As if dealing with this drastic life change wasn't hard enough, imagine me telling my wife and kids this news—that their husband and father was about to abruptly leave the fire department and move away from South Florida.

Fortunately, the Lord blessed me with a supportive wife who could see I was struggling inside and quickly agreed to the plan. She left her comfort zone, family, and friends... for me. I could not ever thank her enough for her sacrificial support.

We sold our house in South Florida, and, along with Jay and his family, we bought houses in Central Florida that were only ten minutes apart. I started a small company; with Jay's help, I worked day and night to build it.

The road forward was not the trouble-free one I was expecting. We had family struggles, along with additional bouts of depression, anxiety, and financial burdens. Jay invited me to attend a Florida Band of Brothers Rally Point; at that event, I heard from God again. He now reminded me, *For I know the thoughts that I think toward you, says the Lord, thoughts of peace and not of evil, to give you a future and a hope* (Jeremiah 29:11 NKJV).

I gave my life to Jesus Christ at the Rally Point and acknowledged that living for Him was all I needed. As I came to Him, I came to know and believe that I had always had my Father in my life. His name is Jesus. Looking to Him for the answers and guidance I longed for my whole life meant I would never be lost again. I also realized I am not perfect and will never be perfect. But If I look to Jesus when I fall off the path, He will always be there to pick me up. And that, like a father, He would correct me and push me toward greatness because He cares for me.

> *Therefore, humble yourselves under the mighty hand of God, that He may exalt you in due time, casting all your cares upon Him, for He cares for you.*
> (1 Peter 5:6-7 NKJV)

I had felt lost, confused, and outcast for my entire life because I didn't know my biological father. BUT GOD knew what He was doing the whole time. He sent me the people I needed when I needed them. Today, I no longer feel ashamed or confused because I had my Father with me the entire time, and now I know exactly who He is. I have realized the importance of living a life for Jesus, not only for me but also for my family and friends.

Now, I wake up every day and put on the whole armor of God, starting my day by reading His Word.

Armor up, my brothers! You are not alone!

> Finally, my brethren, be strong in the Lord and in the power of His might. Put on the whole armor of God, that you may be able to stand against the wiles of the devil. For we do not wrestle against flesh and blood, but against principalities, against powers, against the rulers of the darkness of this age, against spiritual hosts of wickedness in the heavenly places. Therefore, take up the whole armor of God, that you may be able to withstand in the evil day, and having done all, to stand. Stand therefore, having girded your waist with truth, having put on the breastplate of righteousness, and having shod your feet with the preparation of the gospel of peace; above all, taking the shield of faith with which you will be able to quench all the fiery darts of the wicked one. And take the helmet of salvation, and the sword of the Spirit, which is the word of God.
> (Ephesians 6:10-17 NKJV)

John Riggs

John Riggs was born on May 20th, 1964, in Cumberland, Maryland, to George and Margaret Riggs. He has one older brother, George William Riggs. In 1968, the family relocated to South Florida to begin a new chapter in life. After growing up in the Fort Lauderdale area, John accepted Jesus as his savior at the age of 16 and continues to serve the Lord to this day.

John has had an extensive career in law enforcement and security management, which has spanned over 40 years. He now works as a federal security contractor for the Department of Homeland Security.

John married Dawn Michelle Riggs in 2010. They have seven children and ten grandchildren. Throughout the years, John has been involved in youth and men's ministries, as well as setting up and managing security teams for several churches. John's steadfast love for the Lord grows stronger every day. His main ministry is his wife and family, whom he loves deeply.

GOD'S LOVE
THROUGH LOSS
FOR CRYSTAL

By John Riggs

There are many different forms of loss—from the most trivial to the most severe.

You can lose your keys, your wallet, or your place in line at the coffee shop—these are frustrating and can sometimes cause a minor inconvenience. Some losses are a little bit more troubling—the loss of a job or a vehicle that is your only form of transportation. Then, there are the life-altering losses that affect your soul and spirit—perhaps a medical diagnosis or severe injury that causes the loss of your health or even threatens your very life. As Christians, we know God's love for us is vast and enduring; it can carry us through the most difficult and painful times.

However, there is at least one loss that may cut deeper than the rest and usher in emotional pain beyond what we can imagine: the death of a child, no matter their age. This kind of loss may even cause us to question the foundation of our faith.

We all will, at some time, experience loss; we may even experience profound, gut-wrenching loss. How we respond will define our remaining time here on earth.

The pages ahead tell of losing my thirty-three-year-old daughter, Crystal, to a drunk driver in September of 2020 and how her death left our family and dear friends broken on the inside. However, take heart because the victory rings through this story in the form of God's all-consuming love, the power in the blood of Jesus Christ, and the Holy Spirit's restorative rule. Before we get started, let's take a moment to read Psalm 136 and enjoy the psalmist's common theme that God's love endures forever.

> "Give thanks to the Lord, for he is good.
> *His love endures forever.*
> Give thanks to the God of gods.
> *His love endures forever.*
> Give thanks to the Lord of lords:
> *His love endures forever.*
> to him who alone does great wonders,
> *His love endures forever.*
> who by his understanding made the heavens,
> *His love endures forever.*
> who spread out the earth upon the waters,
> *His love endures forever.*
> who made the great lights—
> *His love endures forever.*
> the sun to govern the day,
> *His love endures forever.*
> the moon and stars to govern the night;
> *His love endures forever.*
> to him who struck down the firstborn of Egypt
> *His love endures forever.*
> and brought Israel out from among them
> *His love endures forever.*

with a mighty hand and outstretched arm;
His love endures forever.
to him who divided the Red Sea asunder
His love endures forever.
and brought Israel through the midst of it,
His love endures forever.
but swept Pharaoh and his army into the Red Sea;
His love endures forever.
to him who led his people through the wilderness;
His love endures forever.
to him who struck down great kings,
His love endures forever.
and killed mighty kings—
His love endures forever.
Sihon king of the Amorites
His love endures forever.
and Og king of Bashan—
His love endures forever.
and gave their land as an inheritance,
His love endures forever.
an inheritance to his servant Israel.
His love endures forever.
He remembered us in our low estate
His love endures forever.
and freed us from our enemies.
His love endures forever.
He gives food to every creature.
His love endures forever.
Give thanks to the God of heaven.
His love endures forever. "
(Psalm 136 NIV)

DADDY'S LITTLE GIRL

Crystal was absolutely daddy's little girl. Even though she was my stepdaughter by marriage to her mother, Debra, I loved her deeply, as if she were my own. (Just so there's no confusion, Debra and I were divorced in 2007, but we remain good friends to this day.)

Crystal was always a happy baby. As a blonde-haired and blue-eyed toddler, she captured my heart and exuded a devout love and connection for her family. My girl became quite independent early on. For example, as soon as she learned to talk, Crystal would push your hand away and say "myself" whenever you tried to help her. As she grew through her preschool and elementary school years, she boldly declared her evident independence via her ever-present "I can do it myself!" Crystal grew up with four brothers: Jon, John, Devon, and Joshua. (Yes, there are two boys with the same name, and my name is also John. Trust me, it got quite confusing in our home at times). You can bet that she was always with her brothers, and as the only girl, she viewed herself as their second mother, especially to the younger ones.

As a South Florida church-going family, we tried to keep a love for Christ at the forefront of the children's lives. However, we were not perfect. We did our best and admittedly made some mistakes along the way. Just as the psalmist notes, *Hear my prayer, Lord; let my cry for help come to you* (Psalm 102:1 NIV), we believe praying over our children is key to helping them navigate life. Life can be scary for kids, but for parents raising right-minded children, it can be utterly terrifying. So, we learned from Paul's statement: *Do not be anxious about anything, but in every situation, by prayer and petition, with thanksgiving, present your requests to God. And the peace of God, which transcends all understanding, will guard your hearts and your minds in Christ Jesus* (Philippians 4:6-7 NIV).

The fact that Crystal was very smart became apparent in middle and high school. Because of her independent spirit, she excelled at academics and sports and was even a very gifted cheerleader. For a time, I thought she might go into law because she loved to argue her point of view. However, she also had a wonderful business and administrative mind that she put to effective use when entering the workforce after high school. I married my wife Michelle in 2010, and Crystal gained a stepmom, a sister, Maegan, and another brother, Sean. She was so happy that our family kept growing and was so loving and accepting towards one another. Crystal had grown into a young woman who constantly approached the world with drive and determination and later became a wonderful mother of two boys.

Crystal always had a love for Jesus. She knew of His sacrifice on the cross and of his resurrection. Despite giving her life to Him as her Savior, she had trouble giving Him full control due to her independent spirit. The Apostle Paul recognizes the reality of giving up control of our lives when he writes, *Now the Lord is the Spirit, and where the Spirit of the Lord is, there is freedom* (2 Corinthians 3:17 NIV). We must give control of our lives to God. It is the only way to live and truly be free.

THE CALL

It was Labor Day—Monday, September 7, 2020, at about 10:15 PM. My wife Michelle and I were getting ready for bed after a long day, and that's when the call came. It was Debra; I could hear the fear in her voice. She told me that Crystal had been in a bad accident in front of her house; she did not have any more information.

I got dressed and left my house right away. Being a former law enforcement officer, I knew how to get information quickly. As I was driving the ten minutes to Crystal's house, I spoke to an officer on the scene who told me that Crystal's two children were not involved in the accident and were safe. However, Crystal was hit as a pedestrian in front of her house by a suspected drunk driver. He said that two neighbors walking their dog found her.

I later realized that God sent the neighbors to find and minister to Crystal so that she did not have to die alone in the street. Finally, the officer told me she was being transported to the trauma unit at Broward General Medical Center instead of the closest hospital. A wave of fear and panic swept over me because I knew what that meant. They were bypassing the nearest hospital and opting for a trauma center because my little girl was in bad shape.

Knowing what I knew, I drove directly to the hospital, crying out to God as a psalmist beckoning, *"Hear my prayer, Lord; listen to my cry for mercy. When I am in distress, I call to you, and you answer me"* (Psalm 86:6-7 NIV). In anguish, I pleaded with the Lord not to take my baby girl! Remember, God always hears you. He always walks through life's pain with you, and He will strengthen you beyond what you can imagine.

THE HOSPITAL

When I arrived at the hospital, the trauma center staff advised Debra and me that Crystal was in critical condition, and they were working to stabilize her. It was the height of the COVID-19 pandemic, so the hospital was very restrictive about entry, especially in the trauma center. I began a group text to family, friends, and our pastor to update them and ask for prayer. We remained in the critical care waiting area for what seemed like an eternity.

Finally, one of the trauma doctors came in to give us an update. The devastating news was that Crystal had sustained massive crush injuries, damage to her lungs, and was still in critical condition.

After a little more time passed, Debra and I were able to go back and see her. When we first saw Crystal, we were in shock. She was covered in blood, as were her sheets and pillow. You could tell the doctors went to great lengths to get her stabilized. She was intubated, had splints everywhere, and was wrapped from head to toe to try to stop the bleeding. Because my baby girl was so severely hurt, a deep, unrelenting, painful sadness set in. I felt anger towards the drunk driver and even towards God. I wanted nothing more than to scream, "God, why?!?"

While we were there, Crystal regained consciousness for a moment. Her selfless first thought was of her children. She made a cradling motion as best she could, as if to ask, "Are they ok?"

We told her they were safe, and that we loved her. I told her that Jesus loves her, and that Daddy was here. Then, after a few moments, she lost consciousness again.

The visit was short. We had to return to the waiting room so the staff could work on her. Crystal's brothers had arrived; I made sure that her brother John, who was in the US Army stationed in Germany, was told what was happening. I told her sister, Maegan, and her brother, Sean, and asked them to pray. Maegan was about eight months pregnant with Crystal's soon-to-be niece. Crystal was so excited about her sister's little girl coming that she set up a COVID-19 drive-thru baby shower just one week before the accident.

The entire family was in shock. Everyone had been notified by then, including her biological father (also named Jon), who lived in Tampa, Florida. We were all afraid of what the future would bring. Then, God brought me this Scripture: *So do not fear, for I am with you; do not be dismayed, for I am your God. I will strengthen you and help you; I will uphold you with my righteous right hand* (Isaiah 41:10 NIV).

There were many broken hearts and much despair; we needed hope and strength. We needed to *be strong, take heart...[and] hope in the Lord* (Psalm 31:24 NIV). We recalled that *The Lord is close to the brokenhearted and saves those who are crushed in spirit* (Psalm 34:18 NIV).

As hours turned into days and days turned into weeks, we could see that Crystal was weakening. With each surgery and medical procedure, we felt her slipping away. The doctors continued to fight for Crystal, but they were simply running out of options. I was still praying for a miracle, hoping beyond hope, and struggling with the thought of what life would be like without my little girl. I was trying to be strong for my family, but I could feel a part of me dying on the inside, along with my daughter. The one thing you must never do, no matter how you feel, is break communication with God. He hears your cry, and He saves you. The psalmist knowingly writes, *Lord, you are the God who saves me; day and night I cry out to you. May my prayers come before you; turn your ear to my cry* (Psalm 88:1-2 NIV). God hears and loves us. He always answers us. However, His answer isn't always what we think it should be.

On Friday, September 25, 2020, 18 days after the accident, the doctors told us to call the family to the hospital. They had done all they could do for Crystal; she did not have much time left. We needed to say goodbye. They allowed the entire immediate family into the critical care unit, even though there were so many of us. The staff was wonderful. We told them how much we appreciated the care they had given Crystal.

The doctor explained the situation to me and gently asked if we were ready to let her go. I asked him if she would go quietly and without pain, and he said yes. I told him to let my baby go to be with her Savior Jesus. We all waited by her side, speaking words of love and comfort until she passed away a short time later. My little angel, my little love, my little girl was gone. I was heartbroken, but through it, I believed, *The Lord is my rock, my fortress and my deliverer; my God is my rock, in whom I take refuge, my shield and the horn of my salvation, my stronghold* (Psalm 18:2 NIV). God was always my rock through the heartbreak, but it was challenging to remember it at that painful time.

The family supported one another and held each other for what seemed like hours until we slowly started to move out of the critical care unit and head for our cars. I told Debra and my children to call me or come and see me—day or night—if they needed to pray, talk, or cry.

As my wife Michelle and I were walking to our car, and we got out of sight, she stopped me and, with wisdom, said, "It's ok to cry."

I thought I had to be strong for everybody, but the sorrow was so deep and so painful that I had to let go and cry.

The only words I could say were, "That's my baby," and, "Why, God?"

I did not see it right away, but I later realized this was the starting point of my long journey to God's merciful healing.

> *Be merciful to me, Lord, for I am in distress; my eyes grow weak with sorrow, my soul and body with grief.*
> (Psalm 31:9 NIV)

> *He heals the brokenhearted and binds up their wounds.*
> (Psalm 147:3 NIV)

When we experience loss, we must allow ourselves to grieve so God's healing can begin.

THE LONG JOURNEY AHEAD

We spent the next few weeks in a bit of a daze, planning the funeral and trying to come to terms with Crystal's death and how she died. The police identified the vehicle and the drunk driver, and, as suspected, it was someone we knew. I can't discuss it because it's an active case, but suffice it to say that

I could feel anger welling up in me. Over time, God reminded me that it is for Him to avenge, which is a gift because holding on to bitterness can destroy us.

> Do not take revenge, my dear friends, but leave room for
> God's wrath, for it is written: "It is mine to avenge;
> I will repay," says the Lord.
> (Romans 12:19 NIV)

> Get rid of all bitterness, rage and anger, brawling and slander,
> along with every form of malice.
> (Ephesians 4:31 NIV)

You can be sure that Satan is looking for a way to destroy you in your pain and loss. Whether your loved one's death is caused by illness, accident, or crime, the devil wants nothing less than despair, loneliness, and pain for you. Such is affirmed by Peter when he writes, *Be alert and of sober mind. Your enemy the devil prowls around like a roaring lion looking for someone to devour* (1 Peter 5:8 NIV).

We live in a sinful and fallen world, and bad things happen. You must not let it destroy you. It is so vital to "armor up!" Paul asserts, *Finally, be strong in the Lord and in his mighty power. Put on the full armor of God, so that you can take your stand against the devil's schemes* (Ephesians 6:10-11 NIV). When you are going through times of loss, put on the belt of truth, the breastplate of righteousness, and fit your feet with the gospel of peace. Don the shield of faith, the helmet of salvation, and the sword of the Spirit—the Word of God. Our armor is God's gift. Learn and apply it to your life. It saves you.

The funeral was difficult. The whole family helped with the planning, and all of Crystal's family and friends came to show their love for her. One of the hardest things that I've ever had to do was give the eulogy for my little girl. I spoke about what a wonderful mother, daughter, sister, and aunt she was. I let everyone know that our Crystal would always be in our hearts and minds and that she was safe in the arms of her Savior.

As we started, I asked you to read Psalm 136 because its theme is uplifting¬— *His love endures forever.* I also told you that you will experience loss—of that, you can be sure. Loss is simply a part of this broken world.

Not a day goes by that I don't think about my Crystal. Sometimes, the tears still come. I would never tell you that the pain of losing a loved one will just be gone one day, but you can still find joy in your life.

God loves each one of us. Jesus died on the cross and rose again for each one of us, and the Holy Spirit uplifts all of us.

Embrace Paul's written truth: *But the fruit of the Spirit is love, joy, peace, forbearance, kindness, goodness, faithfulness, gentleness, and self-control* (Galatians 5:22-23 NIV).

> *Choose light and Shout for joy to the Lord, all the earth.*
> (Psalms 100:1 NIV)

You will have good days and bad days after the loss of a loved one, but we are overcomers. Choose joy over pain daily. Put on the full armor of God and remain a warrior for Christ. Don't give up, and don't give in.

God's got you!

FIT 2 FIGHT FROM VICTORY

By Allen L. Thorne

We can most likely agree that our life challenges have, over time, tainted our worldview. Have distractions pulled you away from what matters most? Do you feel that it's time to reset your zeros, catch your breath, and return to faith's basics? You are not alone. We are all challenged occasionally. Remember, Jesus never promised us a rose garden. However, He did warn us that distracting challenges would be imminent.

> "These things I have spoken to you, so that in Me you may have peace. In the world you will have tribulation, but take courage; I have overcome the world."
> (John 16:33 NASB)

While John's familiar passage contains Jesus' authoritative statement, we can ask if the passage is just ancient text or is appropriate for current life application. Is God's peace just something we talk about or is it a truth we *believe?* Friends, having faith in Christ is the core of understanding *how* He equips our fighting fitness. Consider this: Are you relying on Jesus to help you fight *for* victory, or do you *believe* that His work on the cross equips you to fight *from* victory? Let's dig in!

John's Gospel recalls that just before Jesus gave up His spirit, He affirmed, *"It is finished"* (John 19:30 NIV). What was finished? Understanding what was finished empowers our ability to stand in adversity's face when we decide to believe His truth. After all, Jesus doesn't merely present some truth; He *is* the Truth.

Jesus said...*"I am the way, and the truth, and the life; no one comes to the Father except through Me"* (John 14:6 NASB).

Jesus also declares in John's Gospel that He came to fulfill God the Father's plan for humanity as He announces, *"For I have come down from heaven, not to do My own will, but the will of Him who sent Me"* (John 6:38 NASB).

To answer the *"What was finished"* question, it's helpful to know why Jesus was sent by the Father. As His public ministry began, Jesus excited the religious leaders when He affirmed that He was the fulfillment of Isaiah's prophecy by reading, *"The Spirit of the Lord is upon Me, Because He has anointed Me to bring good news to the poor. He has sent Me to proclaim release to captives, And recovery of sight to the blind, To set free those who are oppressed, To proclaim the favorable year of the Lord"* (Luke 4:18-19 NASB).

Throughout His ministry, Jesus cleansed lepers, cast out demons, healed the sick, and raised the dead while sending His disciples out to do the same. Luke scribes, *Now He called the twelve together and gave them power and authority over all demons and the power to heal diseases. And He sent them out to proclaim the kingdom of God and to perform healing* (Luke 9:1-2 NASB).

Part of the Father's plan was to foil satan's plan. Jesus asserts that the *thief comes only to steal and kill and destroy; I came so that they would have life, and have it abundantly* (John 10:10 NASB).

Also, when interrogated by Pilate, Jesus affirmed that He came into the world to testify to the *truth* (John 18:37 NIV).

But wait! There's more!

That's the cool thing about Jesus; when we're ready to believe and receive, He always has more of His goodness and lovingkindness for us.

The prophet Isaiah foretold Jesus' ministry seven to eight hundred years before He arrived. The prophet declares, *Surely, he has borne our infirmities and carried our diseases; yet we accounted him stricken, struck down by God and afflicted. But he was wounded for our transgressions, crushed for our iniquities; upon him was the punishment that made us whole, and by his bruises we are healed* (Isaiah 53:4-5 NRSV).

Isaiah 53 recognizes that Jesus died for our sinful disobedience and selfish tendencies as well as our physical and emotional pain—so that we could be made whole!

WOW! What a plan! So, what was finished? His ministry of reconciling believers to the Father is *finished!*

Indeed, Jesus' death, and more so, His resurrection, paid it *all* for us. When we *believe* this truth, everything changes! Accepting His finished work is more than receiving sin forgiveness and a *get-out-of-hell-free* ticket. It's about more than Jesus meeting our needs and *maybe* helping us through challenges.

Jesus doesn't do *"maybe!"*

Jesus does *"absolutely!"* He died (John 19:30), defeated death (Revelation 1:18), and rose again (John 20) for us to believe *for* a few victories? NO! He paid it all for us to believe IT IS FINISHED!

Of course, our battles are real, but God has already won the war! Believing and receiving His Truth empowers us to be *Fit 2 Fight* from the victory He gained forever over satan.

. . . .

Jan Scher

Jan Scher and his wife Melanie have been married for 43 years and reside in Sunrise, Florida. They have three daughters—Samantha, Melissa, and Heather; three grandkids—Camden, Riley, and Wyatt; and two sons-in-law—Charles and Jake.

Jan grew up in Queens, New York, and relocated to South Florida after graduating high school. He received an AA from Miami Dade Community College and his Bachelor of Science in Criminal Justice from Florida International University.

Jan worked 18 years in law enforcement before retiring to run and operate his own Primerica Financial Services Company with his wife. As Regional Vice Presidents, they have served the South Florida community for over 39 years, helping families become properly protected, debt-free, and financially independent. He loves spending time with his family and friends, especially cooking Sunday breakfast for his grandkids.

Jan is a #1 best-selling author in United Men of Honor: Overcoming Adversity Through Faith. He serves on the Florida Band of Brothers, is on the Bootcamp Ministry Leadership Team, and is a Forgiving Forward coach.

Contact Jan at 954-520-4592.

www.Bandofbrothersfl.com

www.forgivingforward.com

Stroke of Faith

By Jan Scher

It all started with an invitation to something new. My business mentor and friend Guy Shashaty invited me to the inaugural Band of Brothers Florida Bootcamp in 2013. I didn't know what to expect, but I discovered the event would be based on John Eldredge's book *Wild at Heart*.

That Bootcamp changed my life as God worked on my heart and soul during the quiet meditation sessions. Admittedly, His transformation wasn't instant. However, the Lord's seeds were planted in 2013, and His harvest was set in motion. Unbeknownst to me, He was preparing me spiritually for what I would endure medically, mentally, and emotionally in November 2023, when I experienced my *Stroke of Faith*.

The prophet Jeremiah reminds us that the Lord knows the plans that He has for us. His plans aim to prosper and not harm us (Jeremiah 29:11).

As I share my story, my prayerful hope is that someone going through difficult challenges will discover God's comfort and peace and the strength to embrace their difficult times through faith and the power of prayer. I have learned that through our difficulties, God can offer us a greater calling. With the strength He develops in us, He empowers us to sow seeds of His goodness and the gospel truth into the lives of others.

That is why, for Christ's sake, I delight in weaknesses, in insults, in hardships, in persecutions, in difficulties. For when I am weak then I am strong (2

Corinthians 12:10 NIV).

Let's get started!

I was preparing for the upcoming Band of Brothers Bootcamp around 10 PM on Friday, November 3, 2023. As I reviewed the camp checklist, I started getting chills and a severe headache on the right side of my head. I initially ignored the symptoms for a few minutes. But when the vision in my right eye was challenged, I rose to find my wife, Melanie. Feeling dizzy and having trouble walking, I called out, "Mel, call fire rescue! I think I'm having a stroke!"

She immediately called 911. While waiting, a mirror revealed my face and eye's drooping distortion—like a bad abstract painting. My reflection confirmed our possible stroke suspicions.

The fire rescue unit arrived and initiated their stroke protocols as they transported me to the Cleveland Clinic Hospital near our home. Upon arrival, my condition had worsened. My speech was slurred, walking was difficult, and I was very disoriented. The neurological emergency team met us at the doors and rushed me into radiology for head and neck CAT scans.

After discovering no artery blockages in my head or neck, they swarmed around me and Melanie, strongly recommending we give them permission to administer the TNK or "clot buster" injection. After a few reasonable questions, we agreed to the head emergency room neurologist's recommendation.

Before the injection, per protocol, they had to insert a Foley catheter. When I questioned, hoping for sedation, they responded by implanting the catheter. Thus, my hopes were answered with a resounding "No!"

After a few more tests, they admitted me to the intensive care unit for observation. I subsequently learned that the "clot buster" shot can only be administered within the first four hours after a stroke and that it is a very powerful injection designed to dissolve most blood clots but could cause intracranial hemorrhages and fatal bleeding. So, that's exciting!

The Cleveland Clinic is a teaching hospital, so the next morning, the head neurologist and several neurological medical interns greeted me with the normal post-stroke bedside exam. We played follow-the-light, how-many-fingers-am-I-holding-up, what-day-is-it, and my favorite, can-you-move-your-arms-and-legs. I asked the doctor if I had a stroke, and to my surprise, he said no. He advised that the TNK injection precluded me from having the stroke and that I was one of the 30%-plus patients for which the injection worked. He said that I'd have to remain another night for observation to make sure there were no bleeding challenges from the TNK injection and that I could possibly be discharged on Sunday if everything was good.

All my stroke symptoms were gone, and I was as normal as I could be—depending on who you asked. I had no slurred speech. My right eye was normal. The disorienting dizziness had ceased. And I was eating and drinking with no challenges. I felt 100% better and was making ride arrangements to attend the Band of Brothers Bootcamp the following week.

Melanie stayed with me despite her own medical challenges and finally went home to rest and freshen up at 4:30 PM on Saturday when our daughter Heather relieved her. Approximately an hour later, the seventeenth or eighteenth hour from the time I received the shot, I had an Ischemic Stroke caused by a blockage or damaged artery. I went from great to horrible in a New York minute!

The blockage of a small artery on the rear right side of the base of my neck caused the stroke. I couldn't see from my right eye. My voice was broken to a whisper, and I couldn't walk. Also, my esophagus and epiglottis were out of alignment, causing any food or drink I tried to swallow to go into my lungs. I'd aspirate on my own fluids, which resulted in projectile vomit whenever I tried to eat or drink anything.

Again, I was rushed to radiology for CAT scans with contrast. I had to be still for fifteen to twenty-five minutes, which seemed like an eternity inside that tube. I was getting dizzy, nauseous, and disoriented. I started having a panic attack when they wheeled me to radiology, and I vomited consistently.

When I was in the tube, I prayed to my Lord and Savior Jesus Christ to help me not panic. I cried out to Him to give me His peace, comfort, and love through the Holy Spirit's presence. "Lord, please get me through the test without throwing up or having a panic attack in the tube," I requested. HE DID BOTH!

I often quote memorized Scripture verses to get me through difficult times like this. For example, I affirm Moses' words, *"The Lord will fight for you; you need only to be still"* (Exodus 14:14 NIV), or *The righteous person may have many troubles, but the Lord delivers him from them all* (Psalm 34:19 NIV).

Despite my challenging panic attacks, unknown future, and diminished physical condition, I had the Lord's inner peace and knew two certainties. First, I was exactly where God wanted me to be. Second, my faith in Him would get me through this difficult time. Through His Word and prayer's power, I was armored up, empowered, and enabled to be spiritually *Fit 2 Fight*. Like the Apostle Paul, we must *Rejoice always, pray continually, give thanks in all circumstances; for this is God's will for you in Christ Jesus* (1 Thessalonians 5:16-18 NIV).

Let's take a pause for the cause right here, friends. Before we go too much deeper, I'd like to share a little bit about my personal journey of how God used various people and events to lead me to my current spiritually faithful life.

My parents raised my older siblings and me in our lower/middle-income liberal Jewish household in New York City. At thirteen, per tradition, I had my bar mitzvah. Honestly, though, if I were any less religious, I'd have been a borderline atheist.

My parents divorced after twenty-six years of marriage. I know they loved us, but they could only do what they knew—and hurt people hurt people. My father isolated, refused emotion, and never told us he loved us; my mother only loved us conditionally. In hindsight, they were complete opposites.

I was in law enforcement for eighteen years before retiring to start a financial services business. I joined a Bible study group via the business because I was looking for direction. I wasn't where I wanted to be in my life, and I couldn't get out of my own way. I was merely existing and was frustrated and stressed, which affected my life negatively. That Bible study taught me that I could have a personal relationship with God instead of adhering to *religion;* I also learned that Jesus Christ was a Rabbi. Who knew?

I accepted Jesus Christ as my personal Lord and Savior on January 27, 1999. I also made several subsequent altar calls, but nothing really changed in my life because I was stuck in my head instead of my heart.

Fire tests the purity of silver and gold, but the Lord tests the heart.
(Proverbs 17:3 NLT)

As previously mentioned, I attended my first Band of Brothers Bootcamp in 2013, and through the years, God has taught me so much through this organization. I have attended Bootcamp every year since except for 2023, when I was dealing with my severe health issues.

In 2013, I learned that we live on a battleship, not a cruise ship. God and Satan are in a battle for our hearts. The experience at Bootcamp that year inspired me to become active in the Leadership team and guided me to rely on these Bible passages to help me recall God's truth through challenges.

For our struggle is not against flesh and blood, but against the authorities, against the powers of the dark world and against the spiritual forces of evil in the heavenly realms (Ephesians 6:12 NIV).

In 2014, I learned about prayer's power when my mom passed from cancer. Our entire Band of Brothers Team prayed over my family's loss. I felt the Spirit's presence when they prayed for our family. It's crucial that we exercise bold faith as prayer warriors who know that there's no wrong way to pray when it's coming from the heart. That's why it's important to, *Above all else guard your heart, for everything you do flows from it* (Proverbs 4:23 NIV).

In 2015, I met the author of F*orgiving Forward,* Dr/Pastor Bruce Hebel. He isn't a normal part of the program, but I believe he was there for me that weekend. We spent two hours together as he walked me through the protocols in *Forgiving Forward* and shared the gospel's message of forgiveness. Until then, I had been challenged by the value of self-forgiveness. I was my own worst critic. Spurred on by all I was learning, I forgave all who had wounded me, asked for forgiveness from those I had wounded, and *forgave myself.* Praise the Lord! I eventually became a Forgiving Forward Coach; now I love sharing that message with others.

In 2017, certain challenges made my personal and business lives implode. I finally *surrendered my heart* to God, asked for His forgiveness, and lost egotistical pride. Dealing with my life required all of Him and none of me.

He must become greater; I must become less (John 3:30 NIV).

This brings us back to 2023. I was in the hospital from a stroke. But because of my FAITH journey, I *KNEW* God had me where He wanted me. He had my back, and I knew I would be okay.

I spent a total of 27 days in various hospitals. We celebrated my 70th birthday, my wife's birthday, and Thanksgiving recovering in the hospital.

I couldn't eat or drink without choking, so I was fed intravenously through a feeding tube. I had that wonderful tube for nine days before one of the night staff dislodged it accidentally. To remedy the situation, the medical staff could either remove or reinsert the tube. Due to its drastic initial pain, I politely declined their offer to reinsert it.

On the Thursday or Friday of Bootcamp 2023, all four hundred Band of Brothers prayed for me and the family. That prayer cleared my vocal cords and gave me back my voice! That's the Holy Spirit's Prayer Power!

I couldn't get out of bed and had to learn to walk again. The Foley catheter had been in for five days and caused a urinary tract infection. After a week in the intensive care unit, I was moved to the intermediate care floor, room 413. I appreciated the Holy Spirit's confirming reminder here. Paul declares in Philippians 4:13, *I can do all this through Him who gives me strength* (Philippians 4:13 NIV).

The fun continued. I had limited speech, physical and occupational therapy, blood drawn several times daily, injections and pills, continuous stroke-preventing medications, and no food or shower for nineteen days. After stabilizing my medications and condition, they were to transfer me to the Acute Rehab (AR) facility for intensive therapy. However, AR doesn't receive patients with dislodged feeding tube challenges. So, they surgically placed the tube in my stomach so that I could be transferred to AR. We waited twenty-four hours to ensure all was well and the tube was working properly.

In the late afternoon of November 19, a private ambulance transported me to the AR hospital. The ride was about as pleasant as early-on law enforcement high-speed chases. Oi Vey!

Upon arrival, I was taken to room 623, where the charge nurse assessed my condition to determine the treatment therapy plan. This room number was another comforting Spirit assurance. He reminded me of God's words for Gideon before facing the Midianites. Our sovereign Lord declared, *"Peace! Do not be afraid. You are not going to die"* (Judges 6:23 NIV). So, I had that going for me!

The Lord also reminded me how Daniel's trust saw him through. *The king was overjoyed and gave orders to let Daniel out of the den. And when Daniel was lifted from the den, no wound was found on him, because he had trusted in his God* (Daniel 6:23 NIV).

God's favor was turning my way. Only two days after receiving the feeding tube, I could eat on my own again and didn't need it. However, I had to keep it for a minimum of six to eight weeks for scar tissue formation—its premature removal could be harmful.

I was coachable and worked hard as I learned to walk and regain my balance again. I felt like a mess. I wanted this just to be done! I wanted to drive. I wanted to be off the blood-thinner meds but understood that they were a necessary evil to complete physical and occupational therapy by February's end. I prayed for God's blessing and praised Him in advance for all He had done, was doing, and would do in my future.

> Give praise to the Lord, proclaim his name: make known
> among the nations what HE has done.
> (Psalm 105:1 NIV, emphasis added)

I passed all cognitive tests in the acute rehab and was scheduled for discharge on November 27. However, the adventure continued as an infection developed around the feeding tube, which was treated with large antibiotic doses before I was finally discharged on Thursday, November 30. *The Wizard of Oz's* Dorothy and I agreed. Indeed, there is no place like home!

Through all of these challenges, my family portrayed amazing love and support. The amount of prayer warriors, family, and friends who prayed and visited me was incredible! I'm highly blessed, humbled, and grateful to have them all in our lives.

From the stroke and through the recovery, I did what I believe GOD wants and calls us to do: I allowed His light to shine through me onto others. As Christ followers, we're called to carry His gospel truth high! So, in my own challenges, I prayed with several hospital staff members and shared my one-minute gospel message with as many people as I could. His Word instructs us, *Each of you should use whatever gift you have received to serve others, as faithful stewards of God's grace in its various forms* (1 Peter 4:10 NIV).

Whatever challenges you may face, remember God's instructions: *"Go into all the world and preach the gospel to all creation"* (Mark 16:15 NIV).

God encourages us that our actions and calling matter. *This is to my Father's glory. That you bear much fruit, showing yourselves to be my disciples* (John 15:8 NIV).

As you step into God's evangelistic calling on your life, here are some shared one-minute gospel message acronyms that helped me embrace all God had for me:

1) *EGO—Easing God Out.* We must lose our pride/ego and fully surrender.

2) *BIBLE—Basic Instructions Before Leaving Earth.* Once we surrender,

we must embrace God's Word to develop our personal relationship with Him instead of exercising religious knowledge about Him.

3) *GRACE—God's Riches At Christ's Expense.* God calls us to develop a personal relationship with our Lord and Savior. He longs for us to walk in faith covered by His grace as we spread His good news. In faith, fear falls.

4) *GOSPEL—God's Only Son Providing Eternal Life.* This is the centerpiece of the message we are to share with others: through His death and resurrection, Jesus made a way for us to live eternally with our Father in heaven.

I don't recall how many people I prayed and shared the gospel message with during my hospitalization. I, most likely, won't see them again in my lifetime. I cannot be certain what spiritual impact our meeting had on them. However, the reality is that the result is not up to me. I can only control my obedience to God's Word. Through His power, I've obediently planted the seed. The rest is between God and them.

God saw me through it all. The feeding tube was removed successfully, the blood thinner meds were stopped, and I successfully completed physical and occupational therapy. By February 2024, I also passed a comprehensive driver evaluation test with flying colors. Praise JESUS!

Although the battle was difficult, my *Stroke of Faith* reflection depicts how God prepared me to be *Fit 2 Fight* through several medical challenges. I grew in and exhibited the discerning wisdom that our Savior Christ imparted to me.

Friends, life is short. Nothing is promised. And the only things that truly matter are our faith in God, family, and friends.

We must learn from the past and not live in it. Regardless of our circumstances, we must enjoy the present as His gift and treat each day as our last because it could be.

Don't live in fear. Faithfully trust in Christ as you plan for your future.

ANDRE HARRIS

Andre Harris is a seasoned professional with a strong background in business development, real estate, and financial advising.

Andre's personal life is deeply rooted in faith and family. Married to Krista Beth Harris, he navigates the joys and challenges of their blended family, which includes three children from her prior marriage and one child together, emphasizing love and resilience. His spiritual journey, shaped by his upbringing in an African American Baptist Church and currently Christ Fellowship Church, inspires his writing, particularly his current work, "The Strength of Surrender: What It Means to Surrender to God."

Passionate about empowering others mentally, financially, and spiritually, Andre seeks to partner with other Christians to offer hope and direction to Jesus. His innovative spirit and commitment to excellence define his professional and personal pursuits. Andre Harris embodies leadership, integrity, and a dedication to meaningful connections and community.

Jeremiah 29:11 is his favorite verse.

You can follow him @andre.levan.harris on Instagram and Facebook.

SURRENDERING PRIDE

By Andre Harris

When was the last time you asked yourself, "Have I totally surrendered to God?"

What does it mean to surrender to God? For many Christians, surrendering to God has different interpretations. While many may have a conceptual grasp of surrender, truly internalizing and practicing it can be more challenging. The first step to surrendering is sanctification. Surrendering voluntarily places you under Jesus' direction in your life. Surrender must be an everyday practice for Christians.

If you had asked me five years ago, I would have confidently said I was totally surrendered to God. However, looking back, that was not the case. I tried to be in control and create the outcomes I wanted. I set high expectations for myself and others. I was a poser, trying to look self-assured and put-together. This meant having control over my face, emotions, body, food, as well as my words, house, schedule, yard, money, reputation, and future.

I grew up in a traditional African American Baptist Church. My dad was the youth pastor and deacon; my mom was the church secretary and led her own women's ministry. My life was the church. Something was going on every day—sometimes all day or night. One day, while setting up chairs and music equipment for an outreach street service in a challenging section of the city, I made my decision to follow Christ. I was eight years old and afraid to go to hell, so Jesus became my Savior. In hindsight, I realized that I didn't make Him Lord. The first commandment, *You shall have no other gods before me* (Exodus 20:3 ESV), is about Lordship. We must humbly admit that we cannot save or change ourselves into the person Jesus desires. We must surrender our identity to Christ.

My upbringing was strict. I went to a Christian school until I was 16, wasn't allowed to date, and couldn't go to friend's homes or have company without adult supervision. My parents shielded me from the secular world: no bad movies, music, books, magazines, dating, or hanging out with the wrong crowd.

My life was on the right track. I was learning how to be a man of God, a great athlete, a friend, a son, and a community leader. My brothers were amazing football players and made it to the highest level. I graduated from Penn State, traveled the world modeling, worked hard, and was involved in churches. I had a great reputation as a Christian and a community man. Dad always reminded me that *A good name is more desired than great wealth, Favor is better than silver and gold.* (Proverbs 22:1 NASB) Likewise, I recalled, *The reward for humility and fear of the Lord is riches and honor and life* (Proverbs 22:4 NRSV).

My life was amazing. I was well-traveled, served in different ministries, coached people, and was sought after for advice and guidance. As I ponder all this, my thoughts go to Galatians 5:19-21a, which says, *Now the works of the flesh are manifest, which are these: Adultery, fornication, uncleanness, lasciviousness, Idolatry, witchcraft, hatred, variance, emulations, wrath, strife, seditions, heresies, envyings, murders, drunkenness, revellings* (KJV). I did not struggle with many of the sins of the flesh. I thought I was better than everyone else because my reputation and good works seemed better than others my age or in my situation with status or financial means. I was the guy females would call for help with some of the men they were dating or had challenges with. I was the guy men called to help them become better.

What does the Bible say about the fruit of the Spirit? *But the fruit of the Spirit is love, joy, peace, forbearance, kindness, goodness, faithfulness, gentleness, and self-control. Against such things there is no law* (Galatians 5:22-23 NIV). I was legalistically just trying to keep the law. I was *posing* as a Christian doing good works but not producing spiritual fruit. Keeping the law is an exercise of self-improvement of the flesh, but Jesus calls us to crucify the flesh (Galatians 5:24).

Believers must focus on walking in the Spirit rather than following rules. Rule-following justifies fleshly behavior. However Spirit-following unleashes the resurrection power of Jesus. When we choose to walk in the Spirit, we manifest completely different behaviors. Rather than me-centered behaviors, we manifest behavior that yields a harvest for others, which is what Jesus calls us to.

> Jesus replied: "'Love the Lord your God with all your heart and with all your soul and with all your mind.' This is the first and greatest commandment. And the second is like it: 'Love your neighbor as yourself'."
> (Matthew 22:37–39 NIV)

Let's go a little deeper into my life: 2021 is a year I won't forget. God exposed my struggle with pride.

Pride is having a high opinion of our own identity, importance, merit, or superiority, whether held in our minds or exhibited in our conduct (John Piper, Founder & Teacher, desiringGod.org). Pride is thinking highly of ourselves or being overtly critical of ourselves. Pride is a false sense of identity. Our identity should be found in Christ.

"For God knows that when you eat from it your eyes will be opened, and you will be like God, knowing good and evil" (Genesis 3:5 NIV).

The devil encourages us to be prideful and judgmental of others. Pride stops us from loving others, it causes us to forget that God created us equally and only God can judge. When we take the credit for our accomplishments, it is helpful to recall 1 Corinthians 4:7's statement, *For who makes you different from anyone else? What do you have that you did not receive? And if you did receive it, why do you boast as though you did not?* (NIV).

Pride causes us to disobey God's command to love Him above all else and love our neighbors as ourselves. God loves us enough to discipline our pride.

> *I will punish the world for its evil, the wicked for their sins.*
> *I will put an end to the arrogance of the haughty and will*
> *humble the pride of the ruthless.*
> (Isaiah 13:11 NIV)

Early in 2021, I got my girlfriend pregnant. I had just moved into a new high-rise Orlando apartment with a rooftop pool, gyms, and every accommodation available. I was thriving in business and life. She told me she was pregnant, and my life just crashed. *What was I going to do?* The devil encouraged me to commit suicide.

You see, the Andre Harris I just told you about, who was amazing and living a great life, was just humbled.

> *Pride goes before destruction, a haughty spirit before a fall.*
> (Proverbs 16:18 NIV)

That night, I thought about suicide. I heard sirens and looked over my balcony and saw a young man lying there in blood after being struck by a car. I watched as they blocked the road off and covered his body with a sheet. I also witnessed his family screaming and crying over his lifeless body.

I couldn't possibly hurt my parents. I also couldn't tell them of my current situation after all they had sacrificed to raise me. I couldn't tell my youth pastor or the other Board of Directors members for Global Youth Ministry. No, not Andre Harris! I thought everyone would judge me like I had judged others.

My pride got in the way; I was held accountable but was given grace. I received the very things I did not give out. I appeared to have all these things, but as you can see, judgment's fire burns away impurities. The devil wanted me to kill myself, BUT GOD told me to man up and take responsibility for my actions.

People embraced me even more because of my humility. I had tried so hard to be perfect and was playing god in other lives while I was sitting on the throne of my life. I was met with even more love than I had before because people saw the real me. The poser was gone.

My girlfriend and I got married a month after getting the news of our child. It was twenty-nine days after my birthday. I had a very good reputation at forty-seven. God was not interested in my reputation; He wanted me to surrender.

> *But we are all as an unclean thing, and all our righteousnesses are as filthy rags; and we all do fade as a leaf; and our iniquities, like the wind, have taken us away.*
> (Isaiah 64:6 KJV)

God had had enough of me and my pride. We got married, and I assumed I was back on track. I assumed everything would be smooth and almost perfect again like they were before, right? Wrong again! God was not finished humbling and correcting me. I still had pride.

Once married, all hell broke loose. Our marital relationship was tested. My new family relations were under fire. You see, my wife had two sons and a daughter. The three-year relationship with her ex-husband became intense after we married. We had to move while dealing with COVID and the lack of school openings. We were also financially challenged. We got COVID from the same hospital where we would be delivering our baby. My car was totaled the same month. My mom and dad came to visit and got COVID and became very ill. What else could possibly go wrong!?! Thirteen days after my daughter's birth and three days after Facetiming, my grandmother unexpectedly passed away.

Life was challenging; I became angry, bitter, resentful, and isolated because I lost the life I had planned. I had thought I was in control. It's one thing to control myself and my life; it's another to have no control of a wife, four children, my wife's ex-husband, and additional family members. It was also challenging giving up my comfort zone with Christians I had known all my life and my strong family. Unfortunately, I wasn't planted in a church, squad, or men's ministry.

I attended Band of Brothers Bootcamp event in 2021. I prayed that I would make it to the event. Once I arrived, God immediately started to work on me. I was broken and lost. The men prayed and interceded for me. God never gave up on me.

You see, as I grew up, I was equipped with the Word of God. However, when it came to fighting for good and against evil, I had no power. I was not *Fit 2 Fight*. I didn't know how to use the armor of God in this new season. I depended on *my* relationships, *my* power, *my* strength, and *my* pride. God had to strip everything from me and let me get to the end of myself. It wasn't until I surrendered and realized that I was on the throne that He became my Lord and not just my Savior.

I did not surrender to Him. So, I was losing the real fight with marriage, family, and my new life. The devil was trying to take me down. I was reliving old victories. However, God sought to create a new thing in my life. He was teaching me to be the man I needed to be to gain victory in my marriage, family, and legacy.

> *"Forget the former things; do not dwell on the past.*
> *See, I am doing a new thing! Now it springs up; do you*
> *not perceive it? I am making a way in the wilderness."*
> (Isaiah 43:18-19 NIV)

The devil constantly reminded me of how good I thought my life was before and how hard my life was now. When the Bible says forget the former things, it doesn't just mean negative things; it means everything! God wants to do a new thing. Leave it all behind so we don't put God in a box and limit who He is and who we can become.

This means: Do not allow your past experience—those "former things"— whether good or bad, to color your perception of the present or your expectations for the future. When consumed with the "former things," we view our future through a distorted past lens. We cannot take full advantage of our current trials or appreciate the joy God has provided us.

This is the way of sight (treating our circumstances as bigger than God) and not of faith (treating God as bigger than our circumstances). God does not want His children to live delusionally. Therefore, we must plead for Him to free us from being mastered by "former things" because that mindset is rooted in a small, disbelieving view of God.

The power to forget the former things can only be accomplished through focusing on God's will for you. The Bible tells us to forget the former things; that means everything. We need to move on from the negative things that have happened as well as the positive things God has blessed us with. This process is possible when we trust Him with our future.

My takeaways regarding surrendering to God,

Surrender to God Is Essential:

- Surrender is letting go of everything to be in God's presence.

- Allow Christ to take His place as Lord, Savior, and King of your life.

God Wants Us To Reflect and Grow:

- I struggled, only surrendering what was comfortable, which halted my growth.

- I would take some things back I tried to surrender, causing me to become more distant from God.

- Surrendering did not make me weak. Surrending made me strong because it allowed God to be in control.

God Knows We Struggle with Pride and Legalism:

- I struggled with pride and legalism, which fed my self-righteousness.

- Legalistic behavior is a product of focusing on good works. The Holy Spirit allows us to grow. According to Jesus, the Holy Spirit guides, speaks, hears, discloses, and glorifies (John 16:13-14 NASB). The Holy Spirit also teaches and reminds us (John 14:26). He dwells in us (John 14:17), He testifies (John 15:24, John 15:26) and He convicts (John 16:8)

God Allows Challenges, and He Allows Us to Fall:

- My challenges led me to a deeper understanding of surrender and humility.

- God used these challenges and experiences as correction and protection.

Sometimes, God whispers to get our attention.

Other Times, He Disciplines Us in Public:

- Significant life events, such as unexpected pregnancy or marriage and family struggles, serve as opportunities for deeper surrender and transformation.

God Calls Us to Surrender:

- *Submit yourselves, then, to God. Resist the devil, and he will flee from you. Come near to God and he will come near to you. Wash your hands, you sinners, and purify your hearts, you double-minded. Grieve, mourn and wail. Change your laughter to mourning and your joy to gloom. Humble yourselves before the Lord, and he will lift you up* (James 4:7-10 NIV).

When you fight pride, I encourage you to intentionally surrender to God daily. One way to do that is to process your inner thoughts through journaling. Along with allowing God to speak to you regarding your daily struggles and victories in your journaling time, I'd like to challenge you to answer these questions at least once every six months. You will be amazed how your answers change as you grow in the Lord.

What does it truly mean to surrender to God?

How can I fully trust God when surrendering control?

What areas of my life am I holding back from God?

How do I know if I've truly surrendered to God?

Why is surrendering to God so difficult?

What happens after I surrender to God?

How can I surrender to God in times of trials and suffering?

What role does prayer play in surrendering to God?

How do I surrender my fears and anxieties to God?

When I take back control of my life, what are the consequences?

I hope my testimony makes an impact on your life and encourages you to totally surrender to God.

Remember, even when we fall or make mistakes, if we totally surrender to God, we already have the victory.

Being Fit 2 Fight Requires Surrender

By Allen L. Thorne

What if I told you that being *Fit 2 Fight* requires total surrender? That doesn't sound right, does it? Even as illogical as it sounds, it's true! This paradigm shift is worth considering, friends.

Are you caught up in a seemingly never-ending pursuit of more? We often get caught up in what I refer to as shiny lies. One shiny lie is that we can find our identity anywhere besides in Jesus Christ.

The Apostle Paul recognizes our beneficial perspective shift in his letter to the Romans when he asserts, *For the mind set on the flesh is death, but the mind set on the Spirit is life and peace* (Romans 8:6 NASB).

Perhaps we find our worth in our chosen profession, financial gains or losses, social status, possessions, knowledge, or even relationships. Please don't misunderstand me; none of these pursuits, in and of themselves, are bad. However, if they consume our identity, we operate in the *"flesh"* as we insist on sitting upon our own life's *throne*.

Unfortunately, based on our experience, when we choose to sit on our own thrones and live life by the world's standards, we get what the world has to offer in the way of stress-ridden anxiety, fear, depression, and the like. Such is not the Lord's intention for any of His children.

Through life, it's invaluable to recognize that even as we may be successful parents, business people, spouses, friends, or leaders, any one of us proves to be a fairly insufficient god. Thus, would it not stand to reason that we ought to surrender our throne to the One whose thoughts and ways are higher and greater than our own?

The Lord declares, *"For as the heavens are higher than the earth, so are My ways higher than your ways, and My thoughts than your thoughts"* (Isaiah 55:9 NASB).

Perhaps you are tangled up on a "throne" of fear and addiction, just hoping life will be okay if you can numb the pain away just a little longer. Perhaps you are high atop the corporate working "throne," believing the lie that all will be well if you can just get to that next level. Maybe you are lost on the "he-who-dies-with-the-most-toys-wins" throne, where your possessions own you instead of the other way around. Regardless of what your throne looks like, the worldly *flesh* context never provides lasting satisfaction, only the need for more. God is calling each of us to recognize that we are insufficient gods; when we surrender our "thrones" to His insight above ours, we will experience more fulfilling encounters.

The psalmist recognizes, *Your throne, God, is forever and ever* (Psalm 45:6a NASB).

Jesus, as our high priest, is noted to have *taken His seat at the right hand of the throne of the Majesty in the heavens* (Hebrews 8:1 NASB).

Likewise, the Apostle Paul scribes, *Therefore, if you have been raised up with Christ, keep seeking the things that are above, where Christ is, seated at the right hand of God* (Colossians 3:1 NASB).

All through the Old and New Testaments, two of three persons of our Triune Godhead are noted as seated on their heavenly thrones. So, where is the Holy Spirit seated? Would you believe that He is here with us? Yes indeedy-doody-daddy! He is here with us!

Jesus declares in John's Gospel, *"But the Helper, the Holy Spirit whom the Father will send in My name, He will teach you all things, and remind you of all that I said to you*" (John 14:25 NASB).

The Holy Spirit is here to counsel us in the way we were created to live. He is here to sit on our "thrones" and guide our hearts and minds to the Lord's intended life and peace. He is the Spirit of truth who guides us into all truth (John 16:13a NASB). His truth overcomes the enemy's lies every time, as long as we surrender and believe it!

Friends, we encourage you to dethrone yourself and humbly surrender your throne to the Holy Spirit, allowing His instruction to permeate the eyes of your heart with His vision for your life. Surrendering our life's throne and following His vision is the most responsible and life-altering decision you will ever make.

Fit 2 Fight = Surrender!

Believe. Receive. Align. Abide. Follow... Freedom.

BERNIE MENA

Bernie Mena was born in Paterson, New Jersey. When he was ten years old, he and his family relocated to the Dominican Republic for five years, and then they moved to Miami in 1985. Florida has been his home state since.

Bernie graduated from Hialeah High School in 1988 and received his business degree from Trinity International University in 2015. At fifteen, he made a decision to follow Christ and immediately felt an unbelievable amount of peace that remains as part of his life. When Bernie was 22, he prayed for a wife, requesting many very detailed and specific physical and intellectual characteristics. Four days later, he met his wife, Lissette. They have raised three awesome kids: Bernie Jr, Michael, and Alyssa.

Today, Bernie is a financial coach who helps people overcome money concerns. He leads a connect team at Elevate Church and also serves at the Florida Band of Brothers, a Christian ministry that helps men align with their purpose in life.

Peace in the Storm

By Bernie Mena

Friends, life's storms are inevitable! At some point, we will all get jerked right out of our comfort zone. The Lord's truth verifies this when our Savior King encourages His followers to find peace in Him. He further affirms, *In this world you will have trouble. But take heart! I have overcome the world* (John 16:33 NIV). When we are in a tough spot, the choice is always ours to fight from victory or fall to the world's victim mentality. What we decide in the challenges defines our character. Choosing to rely on God provides us with His peace.

It began as a typical day for me. Then, I started feeling an uncomfortable pain in my stomach; at first, I didn't think much of it, figuring maybe I had eaten something that upset my stomach. I went to bed that evening, expecting to wake up fine. In the morning, sharp pains jarred me from my sleep. It was nearly the time we would normally get up to go to church, but instead of waking my wife, I felt a strong urge to go to the ER. Once there, they ran all kinds of tests: bloodwork, x-rays, a CT scan—you name it. When it was all said and done, they didn't have an answer for what was going on with me. They said all the tests came back normal, gave me some medication for the symptoms, and advised me to follow up with a specialist first thing in the morning.

At that point, everything seemed like any other ailment. Shortly after, I met up with a gastroenterologist who ran further tests; he couldn't find what was causing my abdominal pains. He prescribed some medication to ease the pain and said to keep monitoring it and follow up with him in a few weeks. He also asked me if I had ever had a colonoscopy. My reply was that I never felt like I needed it. He told me I was overdue (since I was 51 years old) and wrote me a prescription for both an endoscopy and a colonoscopy just as a precautionary measure because of my complaints.

I went home unsatisfied with the doctor's answers. I shared the information with my wife, who told me to move forward with the additional tests. But instead of listening to her, stubborn me just took the meds and put off the colonoscopy. After a few short weeks, my pains subsided, and I stopped taking the meds. My wife kept telling me to have the tests the doctor had ordered; I continued to ignore her suggestions.

I've felt God's presence throughout my life, but I often forget He is *always* there guiding me. Many people say that when they start trusting God, something noticeable changes in them—for me, it was an inconceivable peace. Philippians 4:7 says that God grants a peace beyond our understanding, and in some very troubling circumstances, I can say I have felt an indescribable amount of peace.

My wife and I had just celebrated our 29th anniversary and have three amazing children. Although we've had our ups and downs, we have a pretty good marriage. God has blessed us greatly. After thinking about all I had experienced and everything my wife has done for me over the years, I finally set up appointments for the tests to surprise her (happy wife, happy life). The colonoscopy was scheduled right before my 52nd birthday. The day finally came when I went to the medical facility to do what I thought would be a routine checkup. I was incredibly oblivious to the journey God was about to send me on.

On the morning of June 25, 2022, my wife drove me to my procedures. We were casually chatting in the waiting room like any regular day. I was a little uneasy about the procedures, but I wasn't nervous since I knew I would be sleeping right through them. After prepping me, they rolled my bed into the room, where the doctor, anesthesiologist, and several other hospital personnel were waiting. The anesthesiologist started to administer the medication to put me to sleep, and I stared at the clock on the wall to see if I could remember the moment I would be out. I looked at the clock, and then I don't remember anything after that. I was out cold.

The next thing I knew, the doctor was waking me up. She had a serious and urgent tone as she told me that they removed numerous polyps and found a malignant mass in my rectum she believed was cancer. She said I needed to get a CT scan immediately and set up an appointment with a colorectal surgeon right away. It was so surprising to me that I thought this had to be some kind of joke or a mistake. Then, reality set in, and God got my attention.

I shared the news with my wife and family; they were all very distressed. I, on the other hand, felt very calm. I felt I was in God's hands. Many people commended me for my attitude, but I simply felt God's peace. Sure, I had some thoughts about leaving my loved ones behind to be with Jesus, but I figured that was going to be up to Him. By this time, I knew I needed to reassure my wife, trust God, and be thankful. That was easier said than done, but I did my best to stand firm and be a source of confidence for her. Romans 8:28 kept coming to my mind: *And we know that in all things God works for the good of those who love Him* (NIV). Even though we did not know how, I knew God would bring about His purpose in what was happening to us.

I kept praying for God to provide the answer, a solution, a way out. I prayed for strength, healing, and God's will to be done in my circumstances. My years of hearing preachers, reading the Bible, and listening to the audio Bible as I drove helped me prepare for difficult times. I felt the Holy Spirit point things out to me from all I had learned.

Something I immediately recognized was Philippians 4:6, *Do not be anxious about anything, but in every situation, by prayer and petition, with thanksgiving, present your requests to God* (NIV). God's Word says to not be anxious about ANYTHING. What I was going through definitely didn't feel like just "anything," but I put my trust in God and was not anxious. The verse says to offer prayer and petitions. I was praying and asking like never before. The verse also says to do this "with thanksgiving." At first glance, it seems the opposite to thank God for the same thing you are asking Him to remove from your life. But He is above us and can see things we don't. So, I trusted Him and gave thanks for EVERYTHING in my life, including my diagnosis and health concerns.

I don't really like sharing my personal business with many people, but this was different. I needed a very special kind of help. So, I sought those in my life from whom I could ask for prayers. I know that God gives His ear to our requests and petitions. First John 5:14 says, *If we ask anything according to his will, he hears us* (NIV). So, I knew that my best chance would be to trust in God and in His Word. I called on my family, my Band of Brothers, and my friends, and then I started brainstorming about which acquaintances I could reach out to for even more prayer requests. I don't know the exact number, but there was an army of people in the thousands who were praying for me. God heard them all!

All those around me seemed very upset, especially my wife and kids, but they tried to hide their worrisome feelings for me. I knew I had to be a pillar of strength for them, and I continually spoke words of encouragement to them. There is a joke between my wife and me—she says that I have a direct line of communication with Jesus. Whenever we run into serious trouble, she tells me to take out my walkie-talkie. She believes God listens to me more than He does her, although I continually remind her that He also listens to her.

In the weeks that followed, many people reached out to me. They offered me their prayers; some suggested books, while others gave me advice and shared testimonies of friends who had gone through cancer treatment. A close friend even gave me the name of a surgeon, Dr. Gustavo Plasencia, who had operated on his cancer 23 years ago. I started researching online, watched many videos, and read a few books on the subject. I saw a common theme that I personally wanted to avoid. I dreaded the side effects that many people reported about chemo and radiation treatments. Still, I went through a list of doctors covered by my insurance plan.

The words from the first surgeon I met with were far less than encouraging. He read my diagnosis: adenocarcinoma located in the lower part of my rectum, very near the sphincter muscles. He said that he could likely operate but cited a fifty percent chance of me needing a permanent colostomy bag after the surgery. He scheduled a sigmoidoscopy exam so he could personally see the tumor and referred me to an oncologist for possible chemotherapy.

Days before the exam, I met with the oncologist, who immediately wanted to schedule chemo and radiation that same day. I was taken by surprise at the immediate availability and urgency of these procedures. I decided to wait until after the surgeon's exam before committing to any treatment. And when that day came, the surgeon advised that the tumor was too close to the anal verge and recommended I attempt the chemo and radiation first in the hopes the tumor would shrink and thereby minimize chances of living with a permanent bag attached to my abdomen to collect my bowel movements. I was not happy with his assessment.

I started praying for an alternative, pleading with God to give me a better solution. My Band of Brothers prayed over me, and the next day at church, Dan, one of my pastors, recommended that I meet with a doctor who attended the church. I met with this doctor, who spoke hopefully to me. After several meetings, he offered me a non-conventional treatment that was not covered by insurance. Thanks to his suggestions for diet and exercise, I got much healthier as my immune system greatly improved.

The change in my diet was radical. I eliminated many foods I was used to eating and added new foods. Meal prepping was a new daily activity. The ingredients, condiments, and cooking instructions posed a welcomed challenge. I started eating healthier than ever before, and I started feeling great. It was a commitment I made, and my family helped me along the way. In addition to diet, I started taking numerous supplements to promote healing: liquid solutions, pills, and other natural supplements. I had heard and read about people beating cancer with these methods.

After about four months of intense dieting and rigorous adherence to doctors' orders, I lost 40 pounds and felt better than ever. I had transformed my body to a much healthier state. I had another test to monitor my progress; unfortunately, the non-conventional treatment did not bring about all the results I wanted. The tumor had not decreased in size, so it was time to seek another treatment solution. I was still at peace, but my family was frustrated by the lack of progress and was desperate for a solution. God was working, just not the way we were expecting. Instead, He was putting people in my path to bring about the right outcome.

The non-conventional doctor referred me to a colleague friend, who, in turn, referred me to a well-known colorectal surgeon. After months of searching, I was eventually connected with none other than the doctor who had operated on my friend decades before, the one and only Dr. Plasencia.

After reviewing my records and examining me, my new doctor told me the last one hundred similar surgeries he had performed had been successful, and some were even worse cases than mine. He spoke in a very reassuring manner, telling me I would need an ileostomy temporarily while the rectal surgery healed, and the subsequent reversal could take place as early as 6-8 weeks after the operation. Finally, we got a glimpse of hope; we saw light at the end of the tunnel. My wife felt some relief after a long period of uncertainty. God had sent the right person to help me and had provided a way for me to prepare for the outcome He wanted.

I had my initial surgery on April 5, 2023. All went well, and after a biopsy of the removed tissue, the doctor confirmed the cancer had not spread. Although I needed an ileostomy, I knew it would be temporary. It was still a bit of a shock to have a bag stuck to my stomach with adhesive to collect my waste. The manual emptying of the bag was a challenging new process, but eventually, I got the hang of it. I kept thinking, *God has given me a new opportunity. He provided an outcome that could have been much worse.*

At times, the bag's adhesive would get loose, and the surrounding skin would get painfully irritated and even bleed. My wife was so amazing and truly lived up to her vows of "for better or worse." The Lord God said, *"It is not good for the man to be alone. I will make a helper suitable for him"* (Genesis 2:18 NIV). She was my beautiful helper and stood by me every step of the way. I am so thankful for her and praise God that she is in my life.

After about two months, I was healing well and my doctor said I could have the ileostomy reversed. I was happy to get the bag removed, but I knew the next phase would be challenging. The reversal was completed. After, a painful process of my body expelling air that was put in me for expansion during the operation began. The pain was excruciating, and I couldn't leave the hospital until I had a satisfactory bowel movement. They told me to walk up and down the hallway to help my body restart. That seemed like the last thing I wanted to do because of the pain I was in.

They gave me meds to supposedly alleviate pain. The relief was minimal and helped me get a few hours of sleep. I remember getting out of bed and trying to find relief. I would stand, then sit, stretch, and lie on the hospital couch. I was desperately seeking what might make me feel better. I walked the halls numerous times, but the pain in my abdomen just seemed unbearably constant. The song "Praise You in This Storm" by Casting Crowns came to mind, and I started singing worship to God at all hours of the night. It was as though my soul wanted to praise despite the pain. I was in pain for several months, though it slowly faded.

After about a week, I was able to go to the bathroom and was eventually discharged. Prayers had been answered; my health continued to improve while I recovered at home. The gas pains persisted for several weeks and would keep me up some nights, but even those pains eventually subsided. Life was getting back to normal.

Today, I am so thankful for what God has done. It has been a roller coaster of emotions and events, and I am still recovering, but I know that God's got me no matter what happens.

What started as something uneventful and inconsequential slowly developed into an unforgettable life event. A friend once told me God made us frail in one way or another so we can remember He is the source of our life and recognize our need for Him. Although we are independent and self-sufficient, we depend on Him for our very lives. The sooner we acknowledge this truth, the sooner we can rest in His protection and embrace.

God had been training me in the years leading up to this time by putting the right people in my path and teaching me His scripture. God was building my trust in Him and helping me become fit for this fight. I am humbled by all those who supported me and prayed for me. And I am so thankful to them and to our almighty God.

> *Lord my God, I called to you for help, and you healed me.*
> (Psalm 30:2 NIV)

God is our great healer; He healed me in so many ways.

I pray this story will also help you become better *Fit 2 Fight* as you trust and praise Him through your inevitable storms.

ANTOINE THURSTON

Antoine Thurston is a prolific author, community engagement specialist, licensed minister, and ordained elder who has been preaching the gospel since January 2013. His passion for the youth and the despondent led him to do multiple evangelistic outreach events in his community and continue his education by pursuing a bachelor's degree at South Florida Bible College (sfbc.edu) in pastoral leadership.

Antoine's two books, *My Bondage and My Freedom: From the Mental Institution to the Pulpit,* the memoir and Volume 2, the Workbook, have been instrumental in the revitalization of the health and healing of people facing hardships both mentally and physically. As a result of inspiring many with his captivating life story of how God restored him from battles of suicidal tendencies, bouts of depression, exposure to witchcraft, and many other addictions, his testimony has increased social awareness of the mental health industry to a new level. Antoine can be experienced on social media platforms everywhere.

Becoming a Sober Soldier

By Antoine Thurston

I stalked her on social media and had dreams and visions about her with angels who were trying to make her notice me. She told me she wasn't interested, but my desire for her became my crutch, a crutch I couldn't see or notice. For the love of me, I thought God told me in these dreams and visions that she was my wife, but there was no reciprocity AT ALL. When I wouldn't let up, she blocked me on social media.

Things became even more intense as I prayed that God would bring us together, that He would open her eyes to see that I was right for her and she was suitable for me. Unfortunately, that never happened, and I realized I had been hoodwinked again by Satan because of my desire for her and, ultimately, a wife.

This was a torment to me until I started to learn to become sober. However, my road to sobriety wasn't easy.

In my obsession, I had reached a place where I confided in and consulted several friends about the object of my infatuation. One older leader had previously told me to let her go, that she wasn't suitable for me then. Consequently, I thought he was wrong; therefore, I pursued her with passion.

I had another friend praying on my behalf, and after speaking with him, he sent me a quote saying, "The person you want may not be worthy of you."

After a year and four months of this torment, I decided to consider *letting this go*. I started to feel as though this attraction really may not be from God at all and may be an obsessive desire, a compulsive target. I decided to delete all my dreams of her, and boy, was it hard. I was afraid because I did not want to lose the chance of possibly being in a relationship with her. I eventually deleted every dream and document and finally gave it to God.

I could not see Satan nor his schemes until I let go.

Through this process, I learned that we must often pause and ask ourselves: What am I holding on to that hinders and distorts my perception? What lies am I believing that may be bringing torment to my soul?

> *Therefore, humble yourselves under the mighty hand of God,*
> *so that He may exalt you at the proper time, having cast all your*
> *anxiety on Him, because He cares about you. Be of sober spirit,*
> *be on the alert. Your adversary, the devil, prowls around*
> *like a roaring lion, seeking someone to devour.*
> (1 Peter 5:6-8 NASB)

Merriam-Webster defines drunk as having the faculties impaired by alcohol, dominated by an intense feeling, or controlled by some feeling as if under the influence of alcohol. I realized I was drunk, under the influence of an outside force that was affecting my views and actions. I worked to no longer hold on; I finally let her go. As I began to mature and become sober, I had several dreams about this situation.

On December 1, 2023, I had a dream about past women. In this dream, God spoke to me about women from my past and women I was interested in. I saw how my dreams and visions of women being my wives were distractions sent from the enemy. Satan was manipulating my *desire* for a woman/wife, intoxicating me.

Talk about a slap in my face. For almost two years, my yearning for this woman had NOT been from God but a culmination of my desire and Satan's manipulation. I could not see the enemy using my longing for companionship until I released my desire back to God, giving it to Him to manage, control, and handle.

In early 2024, my close friend and I had a discussion about this ordeal I had endured the previous year. They further confirmed what had been happening, affirming, "Antoine, when you told me those dreams at first, I thought it was God, but after a while, I thought to myself, *Maybe this isn't God; maybe Satan is using his desires to torment him.*"

My past traumas and insecurities created cracks in my spirit that the enemy used to slide in and control and torment me. For one, I became angry, and I allowed my anger to fester. Although anger in and of itself is not a sin, anger can lead us to sin when we allow it to be unresolved. Apostle Paul warns us in his letter to born-again believers in Ephesus, saying, *Be angry, and yet do not sin; do not let the sun go down on your anger, and do not give the devil an opportunity* (Ephesians 4:26-27 NASB). This is a protection for us. God knows harboring anger gives Satan the opportunity to place his arsenal of unforgiveness, resentment, hate, and malice in our hearts. I had anger in me prior to having the desire for that young lady; I had years of unconscious anger toward other women because of rejections.

Do you have suppressed anger? Do you have anger you're not aware of? Be aware that Satan can use your unresolved anger against you. With it, he can influence, control, and torment you.

As a result of my anger, I had no peace, joy, or rest until I released it. Now, I have the discernment to know where my anger originates—whether that be from within me as a by-product of life, from God as a means of pruning me or stirring me to action, or from Satan as a way to destroy me. Understanding my anger allows me to harness it, using it positively—even when it DOES come from Satan.

> *As for you, you meant evil against me,*
> *but God meant it for good.*
> (Genesis 50:20 NASB)

Resentment against women from my past who had rejected me had built up in me, unchecked, for years; I internalized it and took it personally. I harbored unforgiveness against women, especially African American women, with whom I had most of my relationship failures. Therefore, I concluded that African American women were the problem—*NOT ANTOINE*. I was in full-blown denial and stuck in a victim mentality.

When you think of someone intoxicated, you often think of them holding a beer can, wine, or liquor in their hands as they stumble, fall, and act irrationally. But there is another kind of intoxication; it does not come from wine, liquor, or alcohol. It is the intoxication of desire and mind.

> *He looks on everything that is high;*
> *He is king over all the sons of pride.*
> (Job 41:34 NASB)

In the above scripture, God describes Satan to Job as a large dragon that is drawn to and attracted to pride. Pride empowers Satan and gives him access to our lives. In contrast, humility is a fortress that produces a sober perspective concerning God, self, sin, and Satan. Humility gives us a balanced God-view and worldview, but pride and ego distort it. Those who are not sober are impaired by their emotions instead of being Spirit-led.

I was caught up in this worldly living. Being led by our feelings is a form of carnality. We should not disregard our feelings but instead submit them to the Holy Spirit. According to the Apostle Peter, sobriety of spirit and mind results from submission to God rooted in humility. Humility submits everything to God and releases what we want to hold on to. Humility is a constant dependence on God and a casting away of pride. Pride loves to HOLD ON because pride is controlling. When we operate in pride, we want to control our cares, our lives, and our situations. However, when we humble ourselves, we give that responsibility to God alone, and He TAKES CARE OF IT FOR US.

Without sobriety, losing is one's birthright. Neither can we be alert, nor can we be practical or successful without humility. We must clothe ourselves in humility to win the war. Pride hinders us from becoming self-aware and conscious of our blind spots, errors, and self-deception. Pride makes us emotionally and mentally impaired. It takes away our ability to think critically, rationally, and appropriately while aligning with the Spirit of God.

Our battles cannot be won as long as we are in denial. When we allow Satan and his forces to influence our minds, we enter a state that is the opposite of mental and emotional sobriety, and our struggles intensify. Spiritual maturity is rooted in tempered thinking and emotional sobriety. False and distorted narratives that live in our minds make us easy targets for Satan. Emotional and thoughtful sobriety are foundational to spiritual warfare. As long as you concern yourself with only yourself, Satan, our enemy, will use your self-absorption to worsen the trap you are caught in. He will use your ego and pride to devour you. He will use your lack of trust and submission to God to gain a foothold and torment you.

Have you ever met someone drunk or under the influence of alcohol? It changes their demeanor, speech, and language. The same thing happens when we are under the devil's influence. How do we know if we have become emotionally or spiritually impaired?

First, we can become compulsive, obsessive, and hypervigilant.

Second, we can become so black and white in our thinking that there is no room for a healthy alternative. Healthy perspectives aren't welcome by Satan. Correction is despised, and constructive criticism is offensive.

> *Do not be wise in your own eyes; Fear the LORD*
> *and turn away from evil.*
> (Proverbs 3:7 NASB)

Third, we refuse to RELEASE our affected emotions to God, allowing them to become our idols, a god we bow to, yield to, and submit to. When we submit to anything that fights for the supremacy of Jesus Christ in our hearts and minds, we risk losing our connection with the Lord.

Fourth, we may become controlling, manipulative, and angry as we stalk or bully individuals or use intimidation or even tactics of seduction.

Lastly, we can tell that we are emotionally or spiritually impaired when we harbor bitterness, unforgiveness, and hate. We may even devise ways to retaliate and become vengeful.

So, what is the solution to this challenge of overcoming emotional or spiritual impairment?

First, when we become aware that we have taken our eyes off Jesus and allowed the devil to sway us to follow him, we must confess our sin.

> *Therefore, confess your sins to one another, and pray for*
> *one another so that you may be healed.*
> (James 5:16 NASB)

Secrecy, privacy, and a closed mouth give the enemy so much power over our lives. The above scripture encourages us to confess our sins to each other, not just to God. When I acknowledged and accepted that seeking a relationship with that young lady wasn't God's will, it was then that healing, liberation, and sobriety took place.

> If we confess our sins, He is faithful and righteous, so that He will forgive us our sins and cleanse us from all unrighteousness.
> (1 John 1:9 NASB)

Whatever we don't confess will keep us broken and in bondage, and Satan will use it to manipulate and torment us. Confession is the prescription for healing and restoration; secrecy will keep us in our current state. If we want to be healed, we must heed John's valuable advice.

The second part of the solution is to stop drinking the poison. When I was admitted into the mental institution over a decade ago, there was a man there who was accepted for alcohol detox. The purpose of detox is to allow your body to clear itself of the alcohol and its effects, but detox can't happen if the person continues to drink. They have to put themselves in an institution or an environment where alcohol is no longer available. Similarly, we can never become sober by continuously drinking the lie that impaired us in the first place. After acknowledging the lie that has infiltrated our lives, we have to separate ourselves from that lie and trust in the truth that Jesus will impart to us.

> [Jesus said] "And you will know the truth, and the truth will set you free." They answered Him, "We are Abraham's descendants and have never been enslaved to anyone; how is it that You say, 'You will become free'?"
> (John 8:32-33 NASB)

For truth to be effective, we must acknowledge the lies we believe. The Israelites could not be set free because they were still in denial that they needed freedom. Sometimes, not thinking that we are in bondage is a sign that we are.

Thirdly, we must surround ourselves with godly community. Apostle Peter said Satan prowls around like a roaring lion seeking whom he can devour. Satan has a nature like that of a predator.

As a child, I loved the Discovery Channel; it often shows animals in their environment and how they lived. I was always fascinated by it. One of the things I noticed about lions, wolves, and many other predators is that they always look for an animal in the pack or family that is young, weak, sick, or elderly. Launching their attack, they scatter the prey to isolate and devour it. The enemy uses this same tactic; he's looking for those who are arrogant, not submitted to God, depend only on themselves, and are isolated. Isolation makes it easier for Satan to devour us. I once saw a pride of lions hunting a herd of cape buffalo; instead of running, the cape buffalo surrounded the young and stood their ground. That day, the lions went home hungry. Why? Not only did the cape buffalo stick together, but they also protected each other. Satan cannot pierce through a community that stands together and holds each other accountable. We all need a community that will stand with us when Satan attacks, not flee and scatter like prey. If we act like prey around a predator, it will treat us like it. Find people who will stand hand in hand, toe to toe, arm to arm with you in this life. If we isolate ourselves, we become an open target. Community brings strength, courage, transformation, and accountability (Proverbs 27:17).

Lastly, stand strong in God's power by asking for His wisdom and resisting the devil.

God tells us to ask for His wisdom, and He will give it generously, empowering us to persevere under any trial. *But if any of you lacks wisdom, let him ask of God, who gives to all generously and without reproach, and it will be given to him. But he must ask in faith without any doubting, for the one who doubts is like the surf of the sea, driven and tossed by the wind* (James 1:5-6 NASB).

Additionally, Scripture reminds us that we can stand strong by aligning ourselves with the authority of God and resisting the devil. *Submit therefore to God. But resist the devil, and he will flee from you* (James 4:7 NASB). You can't resist Satan with an egotistical, arrogant, unforgiving, driven mindset that won't let go of anything. There is a divine order to defeat Satan: Submit to God. Then, resist the devil. And he WILL flee.

In closing, I couldn't see the enemy manipulating me because he masquerades as an angel of light (2 Corinthians 11:14), and I lacked wisdom. But when I matured and rebuked demonic strongholds in my thought process, the enemy could no longer use my desires against me.

When desires of the heart are not properly vetted, tested, purified, refined, and tempered by cognizant, matured, and skilled individuals AND by the Holy Spirit, it causes emotional drunkenness.

Are you a sober soldier or an emotional wreck? When we can't control and vet our thoughts, we have no chance against the voices of the world and Satan.

A SOBER MIND cannot be manipulated; a sober soldier controls their desires and doesn't allow the enemy, their flesh, or the world to dictate what they think, but instead yields to what God says. A sober soldier is humble and submissive to God and the godly people He puts in our lives; a sober mind doesn't depend on human strength but the strength of the Holy Spirit. A sober soldier submits their emotions, thoughts, and cares and lives at the foot of the cross of Calvary, dying to themselves so that the Holy Spirit can resurrect them to a new life and enable them to live as God desires in the present world. Paul recognized that a sober soldier does not live to please their flesh or this corrupt world, but the One who enlisted Him in His army (2 Timothy 2:4 NASB).

Our authoritative King and Savior affirmed, *"I will not speak much more with you, for the ruler of the world is coming, and he has nothing in regard to Me"* (John 14:30 NASB). Jesus notes that Satan can't find anything in Him that can be used against Him. Although we are not sinless, we should strive to remove those things in us that Satan could use against us. When I got drunk in college, I said things I never would have said in my rational mind; I was staggering and falling on the floor. My college brothers and I were impaired and behaved irrationally. Pride, like alcohol, desensitizes our connection with God. Pride causes our faith walk to stagger irrationally and gives us a loss of control spiritually.

Friends, we would do well to recall King Solomon's warning: *Before destruction, the heart of a man is prideful, but humility goes before honor* (Proverbs 18:12 NASB).

Peter encourages us, *Prepare your minds for action, keep sober in spirit, set your hope completely on the grace to be brought to you at the revelation of Jesus Christ!* (1 Peter 1:13 NASB).

Let's commit to becoming sober soldiers, no longer influenced by Satan and the world! Let's get after it together with sober minds because sober minds are fit to win the fight every time!

Fit 2 Fight in Unity

By Allen L. Thorne

Genesis 2:18 recognizes that we were not created to be alone. The author announces, *Then the Lord God said, "It is not good for the man to be alone; I will make him a helper suitable for him"* (NASB).

From the beginning, we were created for relationships with the Lord and others. Just as our Triune Godhead operates in unity, so are we, as created Christ followers, called into unity with God and each other. Since the last five letters of opportunity are *unity,* let's take an opportunity to unpack our call to unity with God and others.

Jesus affirms the unity amid the Trinity in John 16:13-15. He announces, *"But when He, the Spirit of truth, comes, He will guide you into all the truth; for He will not speak on His own, but whatever He hears, He will speak, and He will disclose to you what is to come. He will glorify Me, for He will take from Mine and will disclose it to you. All things that the Father has are Mine; this is why I said that He takes from Mine and will disclose it to you"* (NASB).

In short, our Savior tells us that the Father's plan for us, in Christ, is through His Son, Jesus, taken from Him by the Holy Spirit and given to us.

Alright, so what does this have to do with our unity? Jesus expounds further concerning the Spirit's role with us. He explains, *"But the Helper, the Holy Spirit, whom the Father will send in My name, He will teach you all things, and remind you of all that I said to you"* (John 14:26 NASB).

So, the Spirit reminds us of what Jesus taught. YES! We believe that nothing is more unifying than love. Hence, we are not reminded of His great "suggestion" but of His Great Commandment. Jesus decrees, *"You shall love the Lord your God with all your heart, and with all your soul, and with all your mind. This is the great and foremost commandment. The second is like it, 'You shall love your neighbor as yourself'"* (Matthew 22:37-39 NASB).

But how can we fulfill such a calling when others aren't as lovable as we'd like? What about the ones who sin against us and treat us poorly? Friends, we are reminded by our Lord, Jesus, that just as the Father has forgiven our debts, so are we to forgive our debtors (Matthew 6:12 NIV).

Because the Word's entirety emphasizes unified relations between Creator and creation as well as between one another, forgiveness is also presented as a command. Jesus affirms, *"But if you do not forgive other people, then your Father will not forgive your offenses"* (Matthew 6:15 NASB).

So, why does the Lord run such a hard line on love and forgiveness? Because we were created for relationships with our Creator and each other, and love and forgiveness are absolutes for strong, wholehearted relationships. Love and forgiveness bring us closer together. Love and forgiveness are commanding parts of His plan and purpose for our lives, and it's crucial to recall Isaiah's prophetic reminder that God's thoughts and ways are always higher and greater than our own.

His plan and purpose keep us moving forward together. We encourage you to embrace love and forgiveness, especially when you don't want to. Friends, our soul's adversary consistently aims to divide us, and he'll use hate, hurt, and resentment to attempt to accomplish his goal. Remember that *all* authority has been given to Jesus in heaven and on earth (Matthew 28:18 NASB). When Jesus has *all* the authority, our disruptive enemy is left with none. Likewise, Christ has given His believing followers authority to tread on serpents and scorpions (demonic symbols) and over *all* the power of the enemy, and nothing will injure us (Luke 10:19).

So, as Christ followers, we have authority over *all* of the adversary's power!

Thus, he has no right to steal our love and forgiveness and damage our relationships!

Let's stand on our God-given authority and expand on Jesus' command to love and forgive as we advance our Band of Brothers to the earth's ends.

Unified in Christ, we are *Fit 2 Fight!*

· ·

MICHAEL C. HOPKINS

Michael C. Hopkins is gentle and genteel. He is able to look at and examine interactions and see many points of view and chooses to believe something good rather than something bad about every person when he has the possibility of doing either.

Michael is a "creative." Early in his childhood, he was fascinated with all aspects of cars. He would spend time drawing his own renderings, paying attention to detail while blending concepts. Speaking of blending, Michael is an excellent cook and enjoys gardening—especially growing herbs.

In high school, Michael was a member of the photo club and yearbook staff. While attending college, he was the Associate Editor of the Adafi Newspaper. In this season, Michael's photography gift has blossomed along with ministry opportunities. He also writes in this season to encourage others.

Michael and his wife are in business together and consider themselves financial freedom fighters.

therealhowmoneyworks.com/us/askjohnson-hopkins

You may connect directly with him at michael.hopkins1@outlook.com

RELUCTANT CAREGIVER

By Michael C. Hopkins

It's not enough to be armored and prepared for your personal battles. God wants you to be ready for trials that affect those around you; when you are, you can help empower and equip others through your gifting and calling. You can actively decide to be an agent for change in the lives of others. It's vital to recall that the Lord knows us as His own and empowers us from victory!

> "For I know the plans I have for you," declares the Lord, "plans to prosper you and not to harm you, plans to give you hope and a future."
> (Jeremiah 29:11 NIV)

> For though we live in the world, we do not wage war as the world does. The weapons we fight with are not the weapons of the world. On the contrary, they have divine power to demolish strongholds. We demolish arguments and every pretension that sets itself up against the knowledge of God, and we take captive every thought to make it obedient to Christ.
> (2 Corinthians 10:3-5 NIV)

My story traces a journey from being thrust into the role of a reluctant caregiver to becoming prepared to boldly meet adversity and uncomfortable challenges through the Holy Spirit's empowerment. Walking this path required me to learn how to use God's provisions to come alongside and empower others. Ultimately, the adventure involved accepting my limitations, embracing responsibilities, expanding my vision of what was possible, and learning to be thankful in all situations. I don't share my story to tell of my parents' shortcomings; I share it to display God's love, faithfulness, abundant provision, uncommon favor, and unanticipated waves of blessings.

My concept of the type of person who fits the description of a caregiver was far removed from my perception of myself. I could not fathom that I had the capacity, gifted desire, or inclination to become that individual. The topic sounded foreign to me. It was something 'those' particularly unusual others-minded people did with their compassion's depth. I, however, considered it as imperceivable. However, as I sought the Lord in this time of uncertainty, He made supernatural provisions all along the way.

> I sought the LORD, and he answered me;
> he delivered me from all my fears.
> (Psalm 34:4 NIV)

The former First Lady, Rosalynn Carter, recognizes that there are only four kinds of people in this world: those who have been caregivers, those who are currently caregivers, those who will be caregivers, and those who will need caregivers. Caregiving is universal *(Rosalynn Carter Institute for Caregiving)*.

On this particular day, so much of my life was forever altered and redirected. It was the starting point of a metamorphosis. Dad had been experiencing multiple health challenges. However, very little information about his condition was shared. He had been hospitalized for an extended period. Word suddenly came to me that he was being released, but the timing and logistics were shrouded in secrecy. In time, I learned that he was in another facility, again with limited information shared. When the fear of the unknown raises its ugly head, God's Word helps me recall whose I am.

> *Do not be anxious about anything, but in every situation, by prayer and petition, with thanksgiving, present your requests to God. And the peace of God, which transcends all understanding, will guard your hearts and your minds in Christ Jesus.*
> (Philippians 4:6-7 NIV)

> *"Fear not, for I am with you; be not dismayed, for I am your God; I will strengthen you, Yes, I will help you, I will uphold you with My righteous right hand."*
> (Isaiah 41:10 NKJV)

I left work and endured the three-hour trip to the hospital because I needed to know what was going on. It was important to know what the situation was, how extensive the physical struggles were, and what help was needed.

When I arrived at the hospital, the person I saw was so far removed from the former vision I had of my father. His face was drawn in, and his body was gaunt and emaciated. His voice was weak, and his speech was difficult to understand. Clearly, his health was rapidly declining.

Mom had been by Dad's side as his health declined, but they were prideful, which caused them to become disconnected from their community. This not-uncommon life situation had become their secret; they were not willing to call on anyone for assistance. Although they had previously been members of a community of believers, they did not want anyone to see them in this condition. As their son, I needed to embrace the responsibility to facilitate this situation amid God's strength and not my own.

> "Have I not commanded you? Be strong and courageous.
> Do not be afraid; do not be discouraged, for the Lord your
> God will be with you wherever you go."
> (Joshua 1:9 NIV)

Even in his diminishing physical condition, my father was still hesitant to accept care. Available senior services had been summarily refused when my parents were still home. Now, close to death, my father remained determined to maintain his pride. Soon after this encounter, he passed into eternity, and Mom came to live with us. Our future challenges were entirely in the Lord's hands.

> Consider it pure joy, my brothers and sisters, whenever you face
> trials of many kinds, because you know that the testing of your
> faith produces perseverance. Let perseverance finish its work so
> that you may be mature and complete, not lacking anything.
> (James 1:2-4 NIV)

> But he said to me, "My grace is sufficient for you, for my power
> is made perfect in weakness." Therefore, I will boast all the more
> gladly of my weaknesses, so that the power of Christ may rest
> upon me. That is why, for Christ's sake, I delight in weaknesses,
> in insults, in hardships, in persecutions, in difficulties.
> For when I am weak, then I am strong.
> (2 Corinthians 12:9-10 NIV)

The time of caregiving for mom in our home commenced. So much of how I now interact with others was formed and cultivated during the six years she lived with us. Mom was unable to care for herself fully, and she was somewhat reluctant to move in with me. The issues with which I contended concerning her care included audio and visual hallucinations, constant disruptive behaviors, demonic associations, blatant deceptive manipulation, unwarranted demands, disparaging commentary concerning family members, overall combative tendencies, mobility challenges, diminishing lung capacity, and cognitive decline. The spiritual warfare levels that ensued showed that although she professed Christ as Lord and Savior, the spiritual forces of evil were still at work.

> *For our struggle is not against flesh and blood, but against the rulers, against the authorities, against the powers of this dark world and against the spiritual forces of evil in the heavenly realms.*
> (Ephesians 6:12 NIV)

The peace in our home was taken, and accepting the responsibility of round-the-clock caregiving during the worldwide pandemic took its toll on confidence, stability, and stress levels. Despite these challenges, I must state without reservation that as I look back on that time, I was honored to have been able to step into this role and offer the level of care my mother deserved. Certainly, at times I was challenged to separate who she was from her condition. Through it all, I learned compassion for others on a level I never could have imagined.

Above all, love each other deeply, because love covers over a multitude of sins. Offer hospitality to one another without grumbling. Each of you should use whatever gift you have received to serve others, as faithful stewards of God's grace in its various forms. If anyone speaks, they should do so as one who speaks the very words of God. If anyone serves, they should do so with the strength God provides, so that in all things God may be praised through Jesus Christ. To him be the glory and the power for ever and ever. Amen (1 Peter 4:8-11 NIV).

When mom was still ambulatory, her care was not particularly consuming for me. A typical day included preparing meals, taking her for a drive, spending time seated outdoors with her, and housekeeping activities. Because of her extremely healthy appetite, extra meals were always available and necessary. She ate four full meals daily with snacks. My food service experience was helpful as I prepared and stored two weeks of meals at a time to stay ahead of demand. As the dementia symptoms progressed, she was no longer in a position to prepare or even heat food for herself. Her mobility declined from using a cane to a walker to a wheelchair to eventually being bedridden and unable to even turn in the bed. At that point, she needed assistance with all her Instrumental Activities of Daily Living (IADLs) and her Activities of Daily Living (ADLs). Since the world was on lockdown, no external care was present.

So, it was Mom and me. I took on her IADLs. These included cognitive organization concerning financial and transportation management, necessity shopping, and consistent housekeeping and living space maintenance. Likewise, communication and medication management rounded out my responsibilities.

As time went on, I also helped her with her ADLs, which were basic self-care tasks that we learned as we grew up. For example, walking, getting dressed, eating meals, bathing, and toilet use were some of the basic tasks with which she needed daily assistance. Likewise, there came a time when she needed help transferring from place to place. I assisted her in standing and even repositioning from one lying or seated position to the next.

I would finish the day just in time to start over again. However, as challenging as it was, it was time well spent honoring her as my mom. I was grateful for the opportunity to serve in such a capacity as the caregiving tasks increased through our time together,

In addition to my extensive caregiving and compassion lessons, I also served with a ministry to help the "houseless" community. Since these houseless individuals are often treated harshly due to social misconceptions, I honestly did not know how I would react in that environment or how the environment would respond to me. However, as I spent valuable time serving others and getting to know them, they empowered and encouraged me. The Lord showed me that everyone has value and purpose. I learned to listen because each person has a narrative worthy of hearing. With experience caring for my mother, I was able to connect with others on another level. I became willing and available to see others as they are, not how our cruel society dictates. God was certainly doing a work in my heart, through my mind, and into our conversations. He showed me His heart and how I should interact with His people. He was tilling up fresh, fertile ground in me, and I was being exposed to a side of myself that had not previously been cultivated. Through my caregiving assignment trials, I was exposed to the Lord's higher calling.

As one assignment led into another, I embraced new opportunities to encourage and empower others on their journey. One of the most rewarding ministries with which I currently serve is our Band of Brothers South Florida leadership team. Since I have been on board with the Band of Brothers, when I need a fraternal support boost, my brothers have had my back! As we are all called to love and support as we have received, God has gifted and empowered me mightily to reciprocate His love.

Many of us may feel stuck in unforgiveness or a despairing lack of hope or direction. Often, we just need to know that someone values us. When someone else recognizes our worth and speaks life into our seemingly hopeless situation, it provides God's light of love and life that people desire at their core. When someone has walked through our challenges and decides to come beside us, we discover that victory through His and their guiding hand is attainable. Hope is made real right in front of them and us. I love that part! Shining His hope onto others who haven't felt it yet is just plain exhilarating! So many are struggling with something, and an experiential conversation makes a world of difference to someone looking for what we have found. His Word literally calls us to such tasks. The Apostle Paul writes, *Therefore, encourage one another and build each other up, just as in fact you are doing* (1 Thessalonians 5:11 NIV).

More so, though, Paul recognizes that this work isn't resourced from ourselves but from God. Friends, we must go to the Source of all love, compassion, and encouragement.

> *Blessed be the God and Father of our Lord Jesus Christ, the Father of mercies and God of all comfort, who comforts us in all our affliction, so that we may be able to comfort those who are in any affliction, with the comfort with which we ourselves are comforted by God.*
> (2 Corinthians 1:3-4 ESV)

What an adventure! When we watch someone's life diminish day by day, it incites an appreciation for the possible quality found only in Christ. Each day, as Mom was nearing the end of life, I would check on her repeatedly, taking comfort in seeing she was at least still breathing. There were decisions she made during her life that affected and contributed to her state at that time. Life-changing decisions affect more than just ourselves. Our decisions have a ripple effect. Watching and internalizing her progress in the final days amplified this truth, causing me to reflect on so much that led up to the final chapter. Somewhere along the path, Mom had given up. Her zeal for life was replaced by an attitude of resignation. She felt she was too old and that it was too late for her to make a change. Watching the daily slow fade was difficult. Eventually, her comfort became my primary goal.

I truly appreciate all that I endured through our caregiving trial. My compassion for others has been heightened beyond my scope of thought. Where a level of apathy once existed, I now find myself going to lengths to impact others.

Further, the importance of clear and open communication cannot be overstated—this is especially true in this post-pandemic era when isolation is said to be at an all-time high. In an era when virtual reality has taken a front seat in how we connect with one another, face-to-face physical connections are greatly reduced but are so vitally necessary. According to the US Surgeon General, social isolation and loneliness are at an epidemic level, perhaps because many groups are either no longer meeting or are operating with greatly reduced attendance.

I have become an advocate for in-person gatherings. Gathering for intended support, encouragement, and networking is crucially important. There is power in physical affiliations. We are stronger together and better equipped to fight our well-being oppositions. Scripture directly warns us about the danger and detrimental effects of not gathering together. Extensive data associates loneliness with heightened health risks such as cardiovascular disease, dementia, stroke, depression, anxiety, and premature death. ("Addressing the Epidemic of Loneliness and Social Isolation," *Psychology Today*, 2024.)

My dear brothers and sisters, be encouraged to take the Lord's Word under advisement and be there for whom He places near you.

> *Let us hold unswervingly to the hope we profess, for he who promised is faithful. And let us consider how we may spur one another on toward love and good deeds, not giving up meeting together, as some are in the habit of doing, but encouraging one another—and all the more as you see the Day approaching.*
> (Hebrews 10:23-25 NIV)

Through our challenging social culture, it's vital to know that the Lord's intended gifts must be shared to elevate and empower others. Friends, we have an obligation to let our light shine brightly before others. We are all endowed with particular skills, mindsets, and resources that must be employed as part of the greater body to achieve His holy purposes. Let us commit to gathering the strength and confident determination to inspire others. We are in a battle! When communities collaborate towards a common goal, according to our higher calling, God is faithful to honor His promises.

I pray you are encouraged by the following scriptures that have emphatically inspired me to be *Fit 2 Fight*. Armor up!

> *Finally, be strong in the Lord and in his mighty power. Put on the full armor of God, so that you can take your stand against the devil's schemes. For our struggle is not against flesh and blood, but against the rulers, against the authorities, against the powers of this dark world and against the spiritual forces of evil in the heavenly realms. Therefore, put on the full armor of God, so that when the day of evil comes, you may be able to stand your ground, and after you have done everything, to stand.*
> (Ephesians 6:10-13 NIV)

The Lord refines us through our trials!

> *Not only so, but we also glory in our sufferings, because we know that suffering produces perseverance, perseverance character, and character, hope. And hope does not put us to shame, because God's love has been poured into our hearts through the Holy Spirit who has been given to us.*
> (Romans 5:3-5 NIV)

Our trials are only temporary!

> *And the God of all grace, who called you to his eternal glory in Christ, after you have suffered a little while, will himself restore you and make you strong, firm and steadfast.*
> (1 Peter 5:10 NIV)

You are NOT alone!

ROB MCLAUGHLIN

Rob McLaughlin and his wife Susan are empty nesters with three strong-willed, grown children—Nicholas, Elisabeth, and David. Rob and Susan have been married for 37 years and live on a small horse farm outside of Durango, Colorado, where Susan rides and breeds Connemara Ponies. She is a Physical Therapist at a local surgery hospital. Rob is a Senior Advisor with McAlvany Precious Metals, a job he has held for 38 years. He has thousands of wonderful clients and manages hundreds of millions of dollars.

Rob is also a Post Certified Reserve Deputy with the La Plata County Sheriff's Office. He works on patrol every other Friday night. He has been a Christian for 48 years and sober for 28. Rob is very involved in the men's ministry at his local Four Square Church and also teaches the fourth and fifth graders.

When asked about his primary focus, Rob will say, "To find where the Lord is moving and get behind Him." When asked about his primary motivation, Rob answers, "To not be the guy looking at his shoes when I stand face to face with my Lord."

You Don't Sharpen a Knife on a Stick of Butter

By Rob McLaughlin

We begin becoming *Fit 2 Fight* the moment we accept Christ, but it is a progressive journey.

I was 19 years old when I first heard the Lord speak. It was a Sunday morning at a small Catholic Church in Independence, Missouri, and I was standing in line to receive the Eucharist. I was incredibly anxious because, the next morning, I would start my summer job—selling books door to door for eighty hours a week and making straight commission. While not the same as a young Marine in full "battle rattle" running towards the sound of gunfire, it was where I was: just me and my sample case on someone's doorstep for 13 hours a day, trying to earn the right to be heard.

Just a year earlier, I had been a cocky, self-absorbed high school athlete. However, as a college freshman, minus football's discipline, I circled the drain of drugs, sex, and alcohol. My grades were in the gutter, and my self-image was even worse. Then, I met two upperclassmen who had sold books for the Southwestern Company. They were poised, outgoing, and self-confident; I wanted what they had. But that Sunday morning in June, the fear of failure loomed like a black hole before me. I doubted I had what it took to do this grueling job for the next three months. As a man all wrapped up in himself, I was a pretty small package. However, that was about to change.

As I waited to receive the Host from the priest and drink from the chalice the altar boy held, it occurred to me that I was taking Christ inside of me, just like the Christians back on campus had been encouraging me to do. I had deliberately rejected Him just six months earlier. I didn't want to give up control of my life. But what a mess I had made of it. Standing there in that church, I thought to myself, Wow, I really need this right now!

Then I heard a quiet voice behind me say, "Come and be satisfied."

A strange feeling swept through me, and I looked around. All that I saw was a tiny, elderly nun standing there. Nope, not her, I thought. Then it hit me Who had spoken. As I took communion, I knew He was coming into me. I felt a peace like I'd never known before. But He wasn't done yet. He was waiting for me down the street at the First Baptist Church.

I located my three fellow first-year-dealers sitting in the fifth row from the front. We were going to go to headquarters together that summer. They all quit within two weeks, but on that Sunday, we were a "Band of Brothers." When the singing ended, the preacher stepped forward in a three-piece suit with his huge Bible. He held up a stack of papers and said, "I have a message prepared for today that I will save until next week. Today, the Lord has told me that there is someone here who needs to hear how to accept Christ."

The church was packed. When he finished, I was the only one who came forward. That day began my *Fit 2 Fight* journey! From the moment I heard and accepted Christ, I knew He had a battle plan for me.

Today, if you hear His voice, do not harden your hearts.
(Psalm 95:7-8 ESV)

> *Behold, now is the favorable time; behold,*
> *now is the day of salvation.*
> (Hebrews 4:7 ESV)

From that summer, I learned two very lasting lessons. First, the Lord has never left my side. Second, Christian homes have an authentic peace; I wanted that for my home one day.

I returned to campus one week after classes started with the self-confidence I had longed for. Every summer after that, I traveled to a different part of the country with whoever I could convince to join me. Four years later, I graduated from Furman University in the bottom ten percent of my class. However, I was in the top one percent of Southwestern student dealers, and our team finished in the top one percent of all teams.

But now I had become like a fiddler crab with one really big claw, but the rest of my appendages were tiny. While attending a retreat with Worldwide Discipleship Association (WDA), I was challenged to pray about becoming a part of their campus staff. Dismissively, I agreed to pray, not believing it would make a difference. The Lord shockingly changed my heart that night. I gave up my five-year plan of eventually becoming a sales manager with Southwestern. Instead, I joined WDA's campus staff at The University of Georgia, intending to skillfully communicate the gospel and recruit students to join my discipleship group. I was ready to take the fight to the enemy. However, he was also ready to fight, and I had some issues.

First, the adversary knew my weaknesses. For example, he knew of my then-flawed breastplate of righteousness. Our righteousness before the throne of God is what Jesus did for us on the cross. We exchange our deeply flawed "goodness" for His perfection when we accept His sacrifice for our sins. But the forces of darkness don't care about our theological standing. Basically,

I had it backward. Instead of fleeing youthful lust and resisting the devil (2 Timothy 2:22), I attempted to flee from the devil and resist lust.

Second, my confidence identity was based on my success at Southwestern, and my attention was more on myself than on God. All Satan had to do was trip me morally, keeping me mired in guilt, and laugh as I picked myself up by my bootstraps again. I stood strong in repentance for a while, sometimes for months, focusing on being with the guys in my small group, holding Bible studies, and evangelizing. Additionally, there were staff meetings and assignments from our campus director, like helping organize our large group meetings and programs. As I saw people come to the Lord, these activities were very rewarding. However, I was missing personal time in the Lord's Word and sitting quietly before Him. I was more Martha than Mary (Luke 10:38-42), and it rendered me less than effective.

After three years on WDA staff, and through no fault of their leadership, I became tired and discouraged, feeling as if the world had passed me by. The enemy had convinced me I had failed and was disqualified. Even though I was obedient to the Lord's call, *my expectations* were not met, and I quietly held a grudge against the Lord. I still attended church, but I drifted from the Lord. I left the battle, believing my adversary would leave me alone if I left the ministry. Yeah, right!

Can you relate to this? If so, let me share how you can regain your *Fit 2 Fight* prowess.

Know this: The Lord loves you no matter where you are, but He loves you too much to leave you there. When you seek Him, He will always show you the way forward.

> *Commit your way to the Lord, Trust also in Him,*
> *and He will do it.*
> (Psalm 37:5 NASB)

Eventually, I found myself back with Southwestern, and within a year, I was offered a sales manager position. Isn't that just like the Lord? However, He wasn't done yet! While recruiting students at the University of Vermont, I met Susan. I was presenting to about fifteen students, describing a summer with Southwestern, and I kept noticing this captivating young woman in the back row. The light seemed to gather around her. Six months later, with training responsibility pressure and leading over thirty student dealers in the book field, I asked the Lord to remove her distraction from me. Then, I thought to ask Him why I was so infatuated with her, since we had never even dated.

"You will marry her," was all He said.

I teared up and thought, "Lord, I'm not even walking with You now, and You're going to bless me with her? I am in no way worthy of her."

Would you believe that we have now been married for 37 years? It has taken me almost that long to become the man she thought she had married.

How does that progress work? I wander from God; He blesses me with the woman of my dreams *and* gives me the promotion I had hoped for to serve Him? It doesn't make sense, does it?

All I can say is: *If we are faithless, He remains faithful, for He cannot deny Himself* (2 Timothy 2:13 NASB).

By the end of that summer, my team diminished, and I lost my coveted sales manager position. It was very humbling but necessary so that I would come to the end of myself and return to the Lord. Why is that so often the case?

I applied and was accepted to both Dallas Theological Seminary and Trinity Theological Seminary, thinking that would be progress. Susan was now my fiancé, and she seemed happy with that direction. I had until the following August to decide which Masters of Divinity program to attend. Meanwhile,

I bought a diamond ring from McAlvany Precious Metals; when it arrived, a plane ticket to Colorado was included. The McAlvany Financial Group had been persistently recruiting me for several years. So, I finally thought to pray about it. Pulling out my Bible and Oswald Chambers devotional, I decided to get serious.

That day's reading was Genesis 22. God told Abraham; *Take now thy son... Isaac... and offer him for...a burnt offering* (Genesis 22:2 KJV). Chambers' point was that God chose the sacrifice and that self-determined sacrifice was almost a disease. This hit me hard because even though I was miserable on staff with WDA, I had made a public profession at my Baptist church to full-time Christian ministry. Having put myself on the altar, I wasn't crawling off now. I am convinced that the Lord anticipated my pride and stubbornness, and on the very day I decided to do business with Him, He and Oswald Chambers were waiting for me. I flew to Colorado and decided to give this new direction six months. If it was not where the Lord wanted me, I would be off to the book field for another summer and seminary by the fall. That was 38 years ago; I've been with McAlvany Precious Metals ever since. The McAlvany Financial Group has been an amazing Christian organization to work for.

> "For I know the plans I have for you," declares the Lord,
> "plans to prosper you and not to harm you,
> plans to give you hope and a future."
> (Jeremiah 29:11 NIV)

When asked what the kingdom of heaven was like, Jesus didn't describe its appearance, which I think the crowds had expected. Instead, He used parables like in Mark, chapter 4. Jesus described the kingdom's effect inside of us, explaining that a seed thrown to the ground is either snatched away, withers, choked out, or grows and bears fruit. (Mark 4:3-8 NIV). As a young believer, I was anxious not to be the third soil. As a mature believer, I now know that all four soils are in me. Also inside me is the Holy Spirit, and if I let it, the armor of God covers the outside. Why, then, do so many of us become discouraged or defeated? Because becoming *Fit 2 Fight* requires dealing with prideful sin's distraction.

Explaining what choked the fruit in the third soil, Jesus pointed to *the worries of this world, and the deceitfulness of wealth, and the desires for other things* (Mark 4:19 NASB).

Consider this perspective: I remember dealing with an infestation of skunks on our little farm. I was setting the skunk trap one evening for the umpteenth time when my little boy asked me, "Dad, when are you going to quit using peanut butter in the skunk trap?"

"When it quits working," I said.

I think our adversary must have a really boring job. We fall for the same things every time. It's all peanut butter.

Remember: *No temptation has overtaken you but is common to mankind. And God is faithful, he will...provide a way out* (1 Corinthians 10:13 NIV).

For me, battling anger, discouragement, alcoholism, anxiety, and porn temptation became a way of life for years. I was a man of integrity at work but not so much at home. John Eldredge's book *Wild at Heart* pointed the way out for me. Susan's respect for me had all but disappeared. I had kicked the bucket of trust over and had to refill it one drop at a time. One evening, she was in bed reading her Bible, and I spoke to the Lord, "Alright, Lord, you have her attention, so I need you to tell her to quit saying *that,* start saying *this,* and start doing *that.* "

He firmly retorted, "I only allow one person to stand before my throne and accuse my kids."

I wasn't expecting that and answered, "Well, I know Who that is, and I don't want His job, so I'll just fix me."

I began serving her every way I knew how, trying hard not to expect anything in return. The "Always/Never" talks became less and less frequent. For those who are not married, these go something like... "You're *always* this and *never* that." Now, our wives don't really believe we are always/never. However, when they aren't sure if we're listening, they want to make sure we get the point. During this marriage phase, I tried everything to make it stop. I'd listen for a while, but it seemed so one-sided. Then I'd argue defensively. At times, I'd become angry and walk away. Nothing worked. Now, my wife is very attractive, so I decided just to enjoy watching her talk. Even when she was running me down, I progressively chose to see her as Christ does, perfect before God. As such, I knew she had seen the change in me over the years; she's very perceptive. I just had to wait it out.

Sometimes, the fight is not to fight at all.

When that phase of our journey together was over, I thanked the Lord. Then it occurred to me that is how the Lord chooses to see us. He sees us as perfect. Not as we really are. I laughed, telling Him, "Wow, Lord, I wasn't even trying to be spiritual!"

I think I made Him smile.

Not long after, I was at a financial conference in Orlando with a co-worker I've known for over forty years. We've been friends since college. I was in his wedding, and he'd been in mine. He asked me, "Rob, what's your five-year plan?"

I knew he was thinking about business, but I wasn't. So, what was my five-year plan? It was to make Susan laugh every day for the next five years, and, at the end, she'd be crazy about me again, and when I stormed the castle, the gates would be open!

Would you believe that it didn't take five years? It didn't even take five months. We now live in near-constant laughter! As she was in my arms one night, I felt her weight and realized I would be carrying her for the rest of my life.

I then thought, *Can I do that? Can I carry her weight for the rest of my life?*

Darn right, I can! I said to myself.

I won her heart back; that ground was hard fought with the Lord. With Him, I will never surrender that territory again. Ever.

Friends, we fight a battle within. We also must fight for our marriages and families.

We fight against dark forces in this fallen world system. We fight these battles one at a time or all at once. *We can't do it alone.* We need our wives beside us just as we need each other.

Solomon reminds us, *As iron sharpens iron, so one person sharpens another* (Proverbs 27:17 NIV).

The Lord calls us to join the fight against the darkness in the unseen realm, not because He needs us but because He wants us to grow in Him. You don't sharpen a knife on a stick of butter.

Finally, we *must* follow the Lord into battle, or our battles will be lost. At the end of his Gospel, the Apostle John shares a conversation between Jesus and Peter. This was after Jesus was crucified and had risen from the dead and before He ascended to heaven to await His second coming. Jesus was describing how he, Peter, would die. Not an easy thing to hear. Peter saw John following and asked Jesus, *"What about him?"* Jesus answered, *"If I want him to remain until I return, what is that to you? You must follow me!"* (John 21:21-22 NIV). It's challenging to follow if you're not paying attention. Battling behind the Lord's lead ensures our fight fitness!

Central in my journey back to Jesus is the vision of stepping from this life to the next. I believe there will be a gathering waiting for me of friends and family who went before. During that joyous reunion, the crowd will part, and my Captain will come walking up to me. He will put His arm around my shoulders, look me in the eye, and say, "Well DONE! WELL done!!"

I don't want to be the guy looking at my shoes. I want to look back into His eyes, laugh, and say, "What do You mean, well done me? Well done You! I wouldn't be here if it weren't for You!"

I think I can get Him to laugh. We'll see.

Remember, it's not how we begin the fight that matters; it's how we finish in Christ.

Fit 2 Fight Insecurities

By Ken A. Hobbs II

Do not carry the weight of insecurity! The weight of insecurity comes in many forms. Most of the time, it was drilled into us in our youth, and as we grew, so did our insecurities. So, how do we now battle insecurity and find confidence and hope in our everyday lives?

First, we must understand how our insecurities can destroy who we are and how we see ourselves. The enemy will use our insecurities as his biggest weapon against us. Satan loves us to question who we are and how we measure up to others. His favorite words are, "You are not enough!" He lies and says you cannot overcome insecurity because you are not good enough.

Second, we must be *Fit 2 Fight* the battle against insecurity in our relationships. The devil wants us to feel insecure over the meaning and purpose of our lives. When we find and process the root of our insecurity, God provides us the grace, truth, and love to fight and overcome it.

Insecurity is not a stranger to most people, but we all deal with it differently. We can travel through the Bible to see examples of how others have dealt with insecurity. God spoke to each one in different ways, providing unique but always mighty ways for each individual to become an overcomer. We are not alone!

Insecurity can present itself through fear, worry, doubt, and so much uncertainty about tomorrow.

- The disciples were afraid on the boat in the storm.

- Jonah was worried about going to Nineveh and what people would think.

- Thomas doubted that Jesus rose from the dead.

- Moses was apprehensive about what to say to deliver Israel from Egypt.

- Gideon was uncertain how God would use him to lead with so few men as he was called to deliver Israel from the Midianites.

We grow through our relationship with God. We mature our faith by going through trials with God's help. We overcome hard things by trusting in Him. Our character develops, and we mature through facing our challenges. We can always trust God to hold us tight and give us refuge and strength while going through any struggle.

> *You are my hiding place; you will protect me from the trouble and surround me with songs of deliverance.*
> (Psalms 32:7 NIV)

It is easy to become distracted when trying to build up our own self-confidence. Instead, focus on turning your heart (and all the junk in your trunk) completely over to our loving Father. Then, you will grow and mature with peace, assurance, and strength that will not fade away when the battle rages. Simply put, you will gain a confidence that cannot be shaken.

Use love as a tool to battle your insecurities. Jesus left us the number one command and answer for everything life will toss at us: LOVE. Love in response to EVERYTHING! Jesus instructs us to *"Love the Lord your God with all your heart and with all your soul and with all your mind"* (Matthew 22:37 NIV). In other words, love God and love others. Insecurity can always be countered with love because, at its core, insecurity causes us to question our significance.

Focus on God and others. When we take our eyes off ourselves and put them on God and others, we become empowered to battle the war inside us. Love always wins the war in our minds. When we obsess about any unhealthy view we may hold of ourselves, we put ourselves, instead of others, first. When we constantly think of our perceived inadequacies, we look inward rather than outward. And the more we remain focused on ourselves, the more we get pulled into the tunnel of insecurity. So, intentionally focus on God, His truth, His promises, His love, and service to His people through love and compassion.

Again, the best remedy for insecurity is to trust in God. Trust who He is and who He says we are. Do not listen to the lies of the enemy. God will never leave or forsake us. You can trust Him!

> *Trust in the Lord with all of your heart, and lean not unto your own understanding; In all your ways acknowledge Him, and He shall direct your paths.*
> (Proverbs 3:5-6 NKJV)

> *In all these things we are more than conquerors through Him that loved us.*
> (Romans 8:37 KJV)

NICHOLAS TELLIS

Nicholas Tellis, a US Coast Guard Veteran, is an avid learner with diverse interests, including home cooking and devouring books. Currently taking a break from earning a master's degree in divinity at South Florida Bible College, he is a leadership team member for the Florida Band of Brothers, a role that showcases his strong leadership abilities.

A Florida-born native, Nicholas took time away to spend with family in New Hampshire while taking time with God and his walk in faith. With the current development of a YouTube channel, he has focused on teaching the Bible.

His passion for helping men is a driving force behind his ability to give back and help them find a new path through men's groups, men's Bible studies, and fellowship.

In his spare time, when he is not watching a new food video for recipes to try, he focuses on reading and learning more about Christianity and faith through podcasts, books, lectures, and discussions from different viewpoints.

You can follow him on Instagram: @nicholas_tellis.

DECIDED

By Nicholas Tellis

Life is a series of choices, and the decisions we make enhance or diminish our life's trajectory. That said, when I was twenty-four, I had a choice. Little did I know that decision would develop me into the man I am today.

To join or not to join the U.S. military was the question.

I was challenged—financially, emotionally, and physically, and I was burdened with uncertainty. I was an art museum teaching assistant and a part-time Uber and Lyft driver in South Florida, which was less than fulfilling. I was angry about life because I was neither doing what I wanted nor making enough money. So, after some reflective research into what to do next, I thought I could always join the military.

I researched the different branches and was fortunate to meet two retired naval officers who offered some candidly open insight. I shared what I knew about the Navy since my dad had been in the Navy. One officer offered the best advice I probably got at the time, asserting, "The biggest regret Navy personnel have shared with me is that they wish they had gone into the Coast Guard." I had completely forgotten that the Coast Guard even existed—her words gave me another option to consider. So, I researched the Coast Guard and saw they were a better option for me. After some additional thought, I ended up joining.

The journey to basic training was probably one of the most memorable experiences I'll ever have. For those of you who have been through military basic training, the first night is the most notable. If you know, then you know. I'm talking about the bus ride from the airport. Philadelphia was a few hours from Cape May, New Jersey's Coast Guard basic training location. Everyone on the bus was chatting—talking and joking about what was and what would be. Some were in it for the short run, while others were considering a long-haul career move. At that point, it was all speculation. Through the chatter, I sat in silence, smiling because everything leading here prepared me for what was about to happen over the next eight weeks.

I was fortunate enough to be in a recruiting office that cared about their potential recruits. They had us exercising twice a week at the recruiting office, helping us grow and strengthen our bodies and minds. They familiarized us with necessary knowledge and mannerisms, such as knowing how to speak, walk, behave, and the like. They were well known for producing high-quality recruits. In hindsight, I love and appreciate them for the proper caring preparation.

It was raining when we arrived at Cape May. We rounded the corner and saw the water tower that read "U.S. Coast Guard." The chatter swiftly shifted to dead silence. All we heard were the raindrops hitting the bus's roof. I'm certain some got a little stiff from sheer panic rising internally.

In contrast, I held back laughter and smiled because I knew what was about to happen. When we pulled up to the barracks, the lights came on, and the company commander entered the bus, shouting instructions with authority and telling us to be prepared! He exclaimed, "You have less than 30 seconds to get off the bus!" And so, we did.

We arrived around 9 PM. We received full instructions, went through our clothes and the paperwork, received our necessary gear for the next eight weeks, and called home to let our families know we made it safely. We finally went to bed at 2 AM.

That first night, we had to ensure we had the required clothing for the next few weeks. One specific item we needed was a plain white T-shirt, of which I had plenty! I had enough plain white Ts for the next eight weeks to three years and then some! I held onto those shirts even after I left the military. Every time I pulled one out, I remembered what those shirts stood for that night. They hold memories of the lessons, the blood, sweat, and tears of the camaraderie and fellowship during that time. I enjoy reflecting on those learning moments. Good times!

About four or five years later, another vital decision time was upon me. Stick with me here.

It had been raining all night and into the morning. As I got out of my car, the walk ahead of me to the beach looked gloomy. It was gray as far as the eye could see as people gathered to set up event tents. Over the next hour, the sun slowly rose and peeked through the gloom while the crews assembled the coffee and refreshment tents on the beach. I asked if anyone needed help setting up; they assured me they had it all covered. I was there to attend the event they were setting up. Music hit the air, letting me know it was all good with the event being prepared for me and others like me. "Well, alright," I thought. So there I was, enjoying the sunrise on the beach and pondering another decision that would change my life.

As I progressed through the sand, worship music permeated the air, intertwined with Scripture readings, reminding people why we were there. I called a friend who had been helping me through my journey to witness this moment with me. As soon as everyone arrived, we gathered for the event instructions. The team provided a clear rundown of the day's events and expectations. Once all was made clear, everyone, kids and adults alike, approached the water.

It had been raining all night, but the rising sun's brightness shone upon the clouds, and as the people lined up on the beach, the clouds parted to provide a moment of clarity over His people. The rain stopped all around us. This moment's memory stands at the forefront of this day. On our left were dark clouds. On our right were less dark but gloomy clouds as far as we could see. However, in our position, that moment was completely clear. The sun rose over the horizon as people entered the water to get baptized. His people were buried in the likeness of His death, only to rise as new creations in the likeness of His glorious resurrection! From death to life, we witnessed one burst of joy after the other. We embraced in tearful celebration as the SON took the horizon!

In grand anticipation, I patiently waited for my friend's arrival. He knew how important this was to me, and he didn't want to miss it. Did I mention that I was wearing that white T-shirt? It was much more than just a shirt to me because of the memories it held from basic training when I had ceased being a boy and became a man. It symbolizes my transition from childhood to manhood. The plain white T-shirt signified experiential learning and transformation and reminded me of what I had accomplished over the last several years. This moment was about to be another life-defining moment to add to the "white T memory lane."

My friend arrived, and we went down to the water together. I recalled everything leading to this moment, completely free of anxiety and fear. I entered the bobbing and weaving waves and publicly gave my life to Jesus Christ. Like so many others that day, my public actions were a physical display of me dying with Jesus in His death, only to rise with Him in His resurrection! As I came back up out of the surf, it was just as the Apostle Paul proclaimed in his second letter to the Corinthian church.

> *Therefore, if anyone is in Christ, the new creation has come:*
> *The old has gone, the new is here!*
> (2 Corinthians 5:17 NIV)

YES! My old life was gone, and I was made new in Christ! I am so grateful for Jesus' new beginnings! I will always recall this time as one of my most defining life moments. Accepting Jesus Christ as my Lord and Savior and being baptized on the beach on such a would-be gloomy day didn't make sense. However, when His people are ready and willing, He does make a way. Yes, He does! As everyone was baptized and the crowd started to leave the beach, the clouds returned and darkened the sun, and the rain came down once again. From that moment, I knew I would be on the next stage of my journey with the Lord.

My new journey was about more than just being a better man. It was about allowing the Lord's Spirit to change me from the inside out. It was time to go through basic training with Jesus Christ and learn how to prepare for the inevitable battles ahead. After all, Jesus never said that life would be perfect and challenge-free once we decide to walk with Him. He actually said the opposite. Our Savior Christ offers His peace to us as He declares, *"In this world, you will have trouble. But take heart! I have overcome the world"* (John 16:33 NIV). Other versions translate Jesus encouraging us to have courage, which is what I must do to face the challenges ahead. I must trust His will and way to strengthen a courageous heart within me.

The man who joined me on my baptism day was a writer in the 2022 book *United Men of Honor: Overcoming Adversity Through Faith.* Sean Loomis is a dear brother, but more so, an inspiring Brother in Christ! His story defines who the Lord calls us up to be as we discover His purpose through our painful challenges. His story is an inspiring read, to say the least, so check it out and be inspired as I was to embrace God's purpose so that we may be shored up in His lionhearted peace as we become *Fit 2 Fight!*

My baptism day was the next right move to becoming a warrior for Christ. That day, I declared war against the enemy's sinfully evil ways. I believe that Christ has already won the war, but I will never forget that day because I got substantially closer to Him as He equipped me to fight the enemy's maniacal attacks from the victory that He has already attained!

From my memories of the symbolic plain white T-shirt to being in godly company and brotherly fellowship and all my experiences en route to the beach, that day's experience was a culmination of several reflective moments. The greatest of these moments was included in a journal entry I sent to Sean in a message a week earlier. The entry included deep thoughts I had been processing concerning my past challenges. One specific unforgettable memory was from my time in the military. I was on a Polar Icebreaker down in Antarctica. Talk about going to the end of the Earth! Yeah, that's Antarctica; It's like an alien world, like nothing I had ever seen before or since. Yeah, that's right! Antarctica, I've been there!

Aside from a few research stations and our boat, there was no one for thousands of miles. I was standing alone on the ice shelf in pure silence. In deep reflection in the utter stillness, I experienced my first encounter with Jesus while thinking about my dad. Dad passed away when I was seven. I watched his burial; I still have his memorial flag to this day. The ice shelf revelation addressed a thought that I'd been alone my entire life. Then it hit me! I later journaled that as I was standing on that ice shelf in the piercing silence, two hands rested upon my shoulders. Jesus' hand was one, and Dad's hand was the other. Then, these assuring words were spoken through the silence: "I have never left you."

Some time later, I fully committed my life to Christ. Upon that revelatory reflection, I realized that the same week I gave my life, I was baptized. Honestly, to this day, I can't help but cry when I hear those words. The blessed assurance of hearing "I have never left you" means so much to me. From the sorrow and isolated loneliness to walking the platform at my basic training graduation, I longed for my dad to be there with me and Mom—for him to see me in uniform. What Jesus has clarified now, I had not ever realized before. My dad had never really left; he was always there with me. I had made him proud because I had what it took to be the man he never saw me grow up to be. And not only had Dad never left me, neither had God, my heavenly Father.

Friends, whether you believe in Jesus or not, He believes in you! I read my Bible nearly daily since I became a Christian, and there's one anchor verse that I hold dear to my heart. James, the half-brother of Jesus, scribes this inspiring truth. *Blessed is the one who perseveres under trial because, having stood the test, that person will receive the crown of life that the Lord has promised to those who love him* (James 1:12 NIV). James' inspired truth stands out to me concerning all that I have been through. All my experiences only prepared me for the next learning experience. Brothers, there is no triumph without a trial. Believe that!

I've met a lot of people who have persevered through challenges that I couldn't imagine going through myself. It's great to be there to listen to their testimonies derived from their tested perseverance. We all have our battles to fight. For me, the moments above stood out the most.

I return to James' passage as often as possible to remind me of who empowers my perseverance as we make our way forward together. The destination is always ahead of me. However, the journey is the best part when we decide to do the next right thing. As I reflect on the years that I've gone without Dad, I am reminded that he passed the day after his birthday. For the longest time, that day and week was tough. However, the one thing that kept me going was that I would outlive his dying age. At thirty-three, I have.

On my thirty-third birthday, in remembrance of Dad, I went to the movies. Since he informed me he has always been with me, I thought we could go together. The movie had a message that hit me hard and pushed me into prayer. I broke down and cried to God to let me meet someone who understood what I'd been going through. I knew many people who had lost a parent later in their life, but no one who had lost a parent as early as I had lost Dad. After the movie, I headed to a Bible study, where God swiftly answered that prayer.

She had also lost a parent at a young age, and when I met her, she was a few years older than her mom, who passed away when she was young. At that moment, it hit me that God answers prayers when our hearts are in the right place, and *for those who persevere, He presents the crown of life.* For too long, I lived not knowing how to pray with an open heart. So, for too long, I persevered alone.

Through my learning journey, I made a new friend. She gave me some solid advice on how to heal by not allowing the pain to hold me down. From that day, I started to let go. An applicable example is that I now celebrate Dad's birthday each year by reflecting on God, knowing that we will all three be together one day.

Dear friends, your struggles, the things you hold deep inside and refuse to discuss, and the whole isolating "No one understands the pain that I'm going through" thing only hold you back from the life you were created to live. Let me encourage you that *you are not alone.*

I encourage you to engage with God's Word and discover just how not alone you really are. Matthew's gospel is a great starting point. Start by reading a chapter a day until you finish the entire New Testament. Let Him show you a verse or passage that sticks out to you, and ask Him what He has to say to you about it.

Maybe you're challenged with believing in Jesus or God; I encourage you to take some time to consider the words that have stood time's test for over two millennia—the words written in the Bible. Find your verse, memorize it, and let it anchor you when you feel isolated or that no one understands your struggle. When you let the Word into you, you'll find God and Jesus are always with you. Just as He is for me, He is also for you.

All you must do is believe. If that is too difficult, come with an open heart and ask Him to help you believe. After God's words echoed His presence over me, He reminded me that I have never been alone. In Christ, I have what it takes, and so do you!

Friends, the Lord has what we need. Jesus calls us to Himself when He declares, *"Come to Me, all who are weary and heavy-laden, and I will give you rest. Take My yoke upon you and learn from Me, for I am gentle and humble in heart, and you will find rest for your souls"* (Matthew 11:28-29 NIV).

May the Lord Jesus Christ bless you, watch over you, and be with you always.

CHRISTIAN MAYBERRY

Christian Mayberry is undoubtedly one of the most outgoing and charismatic young men you could ever meet. He lives in Oklahoma, where ten years ago, he was the victim of a devastating ATV accident and suffered a severe traumatic brain injury. During that time, Christian died and went to heaven, where the Lord told him he was going to have a platform and help bring thousands to Him!

Now, Christian shares his testimony and the power of love and forgiveness in churches, schools, and literally everywhere he goes. And he could not love it more! He has a unique ability to make people feel loved and happy! One of the ways he does this is by giving them a great big smile and a Christian Mayberry hug!

Christian is a co-author in the number one best-selling book *Navigating Your Storm*.

If you would like Christian and his mom to come to your church, school. or group you can contact them on Facebook at Pray For Mayberry or www. prayformayberry.com

The Moment I Died

By Christian Mayberry

"Why did you come back from heaven?"

I have been asked that question more times than I can remember.

My answer can't be given in a single sentence. Instead, let me share with you my story of how I died and came back to life and, more importantly, how God chose me to be His vessel and what it has taken to meet the challenge of the mission He put me on.

What I needed to be *Fit 2 Fight!*

My name is Christian Mayberry. I was born and raised in Oklahoma and was just your typical 16-year-old beginning my junior year of high school when I died. I can't say I loved school, but I enjoyed the social aspect—including hanging out with my friends and playing football. I was a decent student and never got in trouble at home or school. I always tried to do the right thing and be the best Christian I could be, as I loved the Lord with all my heart. It's crazy how life can change in an instant. Well, it did for me on September 1, 2013.

In a single moment, my 16-year-old life was turned upside down and forever changed.

On what seemed like a typical day in September, I was invited to go down to the river to hang out with several of my football teammates. Little did I know when I walked out the door, I wouldn't return home for two years! What I thought was "a day at the river" was actually a party; I immediately knew I had no business being there. Everyone was drinking, but I chose not to drink. But I did agree to take a ride on a four-wheeler with the mother of one of my teammates. She was intoxicated, began driving erratically, and crashed the four-wheeler. I was immediately ejected from the ATV and thrown into a ditch, where I was left lying alone by the woman driving for several hours. My life changed in an instant.

I died in that ditch that night.

The beautiful part about those hours I was left dying is that although there was nobody to help me or tend to my physical needs, I wasn't alone. After all, we are never really alone—God is always with us. But in those moments, God wasn't just with me; He took me to heaven! I was in the presence of our Lord and Savior!

I met Jesus.

Jesus embraced me and told me to breathe because I wasn't going to stay with Him. He told me that I was to come back and have a platform. I would help Him bring thousands to Him. Jesus was making me a vessel!

While I was in heaven, I saw three of my grandparents and a sister I had never met. People ask me all the time what it was like. It's impossible to describe the absolute love and peace I felt in that moment. Everything was truly perfect! I felt so overwhelmed with love from the Lord that I still struggle to put it into words. It's like you need to feel it for yourself. This "feeling" has carried me through the hard times since that day.

I often ask myself, "Why did I come back?" My return has not been easy at all, but I know I have a mission.

My parents were told there was a very good chance I wouldn't survive. It was touch and go for quite some time.

Six days after the accident, I needed a double craniotomy. They said if they didn't have it, I would certainly die! So the doctors performed life-saving surgery to stop the swelling in my brain.

It was about a month after the accident before I opened my eyes, but even after I did, my parents told me I just wasn't in there. I wouldn't look at them. I wouldn't squeeze their hand if they asked. I just wasn't there.

The doctors soon told my parents there was nothing more they could do. It was time for me to go on to a rehabilitation facility. My parents couldn't believe that the hospital would discharge me in my current condition. I couldn't communicate verbally or even hold my own head or body up. The entire left side of my body was paralyzed. I was in diapers, and I couldn't eat.

My mom talks about the absolute nightmare that it was trying to find a facility that would take me. Her mother's instinct knew it was entirely too soon to leave the hospital, but the hospital staff was adamant there was nothing more they could do for me and that it was time for me to move on.

After leaving the hospital, I was admitted to the Children's Center in Bethany, Oklahoma, to start rehab treatment. The staff at Bethany tried to help me for two and a half months without improvement. I was still fully paralyzed on one side and not communicating at all. I can only imagine the agony that my parents were going through. How could this be happening to their youngest child? My mom shared with me that she and my dad would repeat a verse from 2 Corinthians, constantly reminding themselves that God was in control.

For we walk by faith, not by sight.
(2 Corinthians 5:7 NIV)

What my parents were seeing seemed nearly hopeless, nearly impossible! But God! They could not see with their eyes; they had to walk by faith, speaking and believing that they would get their son back.

During this time, my parents were told by more than one doctor in several different hospitals that I would never have a normal life again. They explained that I would never walk or talk again. My mom, with true belief, told the doctors, "No, not my boy! You remember his name is Christian Mayberry! We will get him back, he will walk, he will talk, and he will declare the works of the Lord!"

Another scripture my parents stood on is Psalm 118:17—*I shall not die, but live, And declare the works of the Lord* (NKJV).

My parents hung scripture on the walls of every hospital room, rehab facility, and nursing home I was in. They constantly played Christian music. They never allowed a doctor or anyone to speak negatively in my room or over me. My parents were always talking to me, believing I could hear and understand everything spoken to me. The miraculous part is that I could, at least, in part, at times, definitely hear what was being said. Countless people would come into my room and tell my parents there was something special about that room. That there was peace there. Nurses and cleaning staff would say, "I just want to hang out in this room." Nurses and aides were pushing to care for me because they wanted to be in the Mayberry room. That can only be the Holy Spirit! It had absolutely nothing to do with me!

At that point, I was still not saying a word. I wasn't charming anyone or making others laugh. It was simply the Holy Spirit.

My mom and grandma still talk about how so many people wanted to come and be in my room. They were also amazed at how many people were following our journey on Facebook—most of them were total strangers. My family understood the Lord was getting ready to show off. He was going to give my family and me a miracle. He wanted thousands to witness it, and I would be His vessel.

We all witnessed many miracles. The *greatest* miracle was that I had survived that first night. I was left purposely in the ditch for three hours before the intoxicated woman driving called for help. I died that night, but God brought me back.

Our pastor was Jake Gorham. In the first month after the accident, his wife, Karen, felt strongly led by the Holy Spirit to say out loud, "Wake up, Christian. Wake up." She started speaking this out loud and posted on Facebook, asking people to join her. Well, they did by the thousands. Yep, you guessed it. I woke up! After about a month, I woke up, and my eyes were open.

Then they all prayed, "Speak, Christian. Speak." So, after six months, I started slowly speaking.

The next prayer was, "Walk, Christian, Walk." After one year and four months, I was finally able to get up and take a step with complete assistance. I shouted and praised the Lord!!

The last prayer was, "See, Christian. See." The doctors told my parents that glasses were never going to help my vision, but my parents wouldn't settle for that! Praise God! They found a specialist in Florida who gave them hope for my vision. I now have 20/20 vision in my right eye and nearly that in my left eye. Thank you, Jesus! Thank you to all the people—my family, friends, and even strangers who shouted those prayers out loud.

My journey was full of praises and blessings, but not every part was easy. You might be thinking that everything fell back into place for me quite easily. But no, it didn't! After two years, we finally returned home. That is when my parents and I got a huge dose of reality. The friends I once had were gone. My hopes of graduating and dreams of playing football for the University of Oklahoma were gone. My dreams of having a special girl, a great job, and a cool truck seemed to be possibly gone forever. I wasn't able to do anything without help. I couldn't even make myself a meal. The basic everyday things were now a struggle at best! I couldn't get in my truck and go where I needed or wanted to go. My mom had to drive me and care for all my basic needs.

How did this happen? How could one foolish mistake and being with the wrong people create this much devastation? Why did this happen to me? I thought I was a good person. I found myself incredibly scared, angry, frustrated, and horribly depressed! I knew that if I were going to get through that battle, I would need to grab onto Jesus like never before.

I had been given a beautiful gift; I needed to decide what I would do with it. I had the opportunity to leave my body, leave this earth, and be in the presence of the Almighty King! I knew I'd better show God how grateful I was that He allowed me to survive. I was given a chance to continue this life and the privilege of returning to earth to share with everyone all that He had done for me. I knew I had to give Him all the praise and all the glory at all times!

I would be His *VESSEL!*

We gave God all the praise with every victory we experienced! My mom would video every step of this journey. I ended up at a rehab in Wauchula, Florida. It took my mom fighting with Oklahoma Medicaid to get me into this rehab facility. Eventually, she reached out to State Representative John Bennett and Senator Mark Allen. I ended up with an advocate, Miss Julie Weintraub of Hands Across the Bay in Tampa, Florida. They all went to battle to get me the rehab treatment I needed. God was with my parents. God sent amazing people to make this happen. I can never thank these beautiful people enough for what they did for me. It was a game-changer in my journey; there was no doubt God was in full control!

The facility in Florida helped me take the next steps in my rehab. It was in Florida that I learned to walk and so much more. In September 2014, one year after I was hurt, I flew on a medical flight to Wauchula on a gurney. One year later, I flew home on a commercial flight, leaving the wheelchair behind! Thank You, God, for this *MIRACLE!*

My mom documented everything, capturing videos of me learning to walk and giving all the praise and glory to God. Many people watched my journey and reached out to say how I inspired them to keep pushing through their own struggles. They saw my belief in God, my positive outlook, and how I always gave Him the glory. It was humbling to realize how many people I was able to help with the Holy Spirit guiding me. Despite the challenges I faced, God was using my story for His good and His glory. It was an incredible honor and blessing to be a part of something so meaningful.

While still in Wauchula, I was invited to share my testimony at two churches. With my mom by my side, we shared what the Lord had done in my life. I never imagined I would have the courage to speak in front of a crowd, but I felt only excitement and no fear. It was an amazing experience, and I realized this was my purpose. Now, my mom and I travel to churches, schools, and wherever we are invited to share our testimony together. I love this more than anything else!

One crucial aspect of surviving this journey and becoming *Fit 2 Fight* was the necessity of forgiving the woman who drove the ATV drunk and left me in a ditch to die for three hours. It was difficult to forgive someone for such a horrible thing, but as a Christian, I knew I had no choice but to forgive her. Just as God forgave me for all my wrongdoings, I had to extend forgiveness to others. Although forgiving was not easy for me or my parents, I understood the importance of forgiveness in the eyes of God. This journey was far from easy, but through it all, I held onto my faith. BUT GOD!

There were numerous beautiful moments and encounters with amazing people. We received incredible support, both financially and through gifts, which helped my parents tremendously during this difficult period. The blessings seemed endless, from financial assistance to treatments not covered by insurance being gifted to us. We were even gifted a wheelchair-accessible van and another vehicle. Despite these highs, there were also many hard times. It wasn't all smooth sailing, and there were moments when I questioned why I had returned. I want to emphasize that it was only by the grace of God that we were able to endure and overcome these hardships. I firmly believe that without the support of my heavenly Father, I would not have made it through this journey.

One of the toughest challenges during this period was the decline in the health of my father, John. Within a few months of my injury, he began experiencing heart attacks and strokes despite having been in good health before. In August 2022, we lost my dad, adding to the already difficult circumstances. However, once again, it was my faith in my heavenly Father that carried me through. Knowing that my dad was no longer suffering, confused, or confined to a nursing home brought me comfort. He was now free and at peace.

Through my story, I hope to inspire you with the words of Philippians 4:13, I can do all things through Christ, who strengthens me (NKJV). This *scripture has always been a favorite of mine. I pray that you w*ill look at your life and consider who you may need to forgive. Holding onto unforgiveness will hurt you more than the person you are withholding forgiveness from.

My hope is that my story will encourage you to find gratitude in every area of your life, appreciating even the smallest blessings. Do not take the simple joys for granted. I know that I did, but I have learned that every single day is a gift, and I want to share this gift with others.

Above all, I pray that my story will motivate you to prioritize God in all you do, offering Him praise and glory in every circumstance. Seek Him with your whole heart, knowing He is always there for you, ready to be your everything if you allow Him to be.

Forgive always!

Pray always!

Remember that you have the power over your tongue!

Always be unashamed to share with anyone, anywhere, and at any time!

Lastly, keep your eyes and heart ready for a *MIRACLE!*

Know that I love you, and I'm praying for you!

Armor Up with Restoration

By Allen L. Thorne

Regardless of who we are, we have all been through, are going through, or will go through challenges. Some might refer to such obstacles as "problems." However, as we navigate the challenges we face, it helps to understand that our words have power. Consider this, my friends: the word "problem" bears a negative connotation as a blockade from progress or something that cannot be overcome. In contrast, the word "challenge" holds a more positive implication as something that can be overcome. After all, in Christ, we are overcomers, right? Right! And as overcomers, no matter what challenges we encounter, we can trust God will bring us complete restoration, preparing us to battle on.

Remember, Jesus didn't ever say, "Come to Me, and everything will be flawless." He actually noted the opposite in John's Gospel. The Son of Man affirms, *"In the world you have tribulation, but take courage; I have overcome the world"* (John 16:33b NASB).

As we abide in Christ, we can trust He is in control and will always restore whatever the devil tries to take from us! Priceless! The Apostle Paul emphatically declares that we, in Christ, are most certainly NOT sheep to be slaughtered, but instead, *we are more than conquerors through Him who loved us* (Romans 8:36-37 NIV).

However, while these scriptural truths are excellent references to ponder, our real-time life experiences can sometimes distract and derail our faithful focus on His truth.

After all, didn't Jesus tell us that *"the thief (satan) comes to steal, kill, and destroy"?* Yes, He did mention that in John 10:10 (NIV). However, just after that, He reminded the religious leaders, *"I have come that they may have life, and have it to the full"* (John 10:10 NIV).

So, which half of the Savior King's statement will you choose to focus on?

In and through these challenging times, it's vital to recall that we are not the summation of our failures! The fall does not define us, but how we decide to get back up and move forward defines us. More so, though, it's *who* we allow to help us up and restore us that ultimately matters. We must make a conscious decision to receive the restoration our faith in Christ Jesus offers.

As it is written, my friends, he is *able to do immeasurably more than all we ask or imagine* (Ephesians 3:20a NIV), but His restoration is only *according to his power that is at work within us* (Ephesians 3:20b NIV). God is not one to barge into our lives and start fixing us up. We must voluntarily *receive* His restorative power and authority into our lives.

John confirms this in his revelatory vision when he records Jesus' declaration. He announces, *Here I am! I stand at the door and knock. If anyone hears my voice and opens the door, I will come in and eat with that person, and they with me* (Revelation 3:20 NIV).

In the middle of the storm, when everything seems to be fading to black, will you open the door to Jesus? Will you receive His Spirit's insight to guide you to better days?

When we recall how Jesus met the paralytic at the Bethesda pool in John, chapter 5, we observe that Jesus gave no ear to the man's excuses of how no one would help him. Jesus knew the man's challenge and how long he'd been in it. Jesus literally knew it all and only had one simple question for the man: *"Do you want to be made well?"* (John 5:6 NRSV)

The English word well is translated from the Greek adjective *hygies (hoog-ee-ace),* which means whole or true. So, Jesus was asking the man if he wanted to be restored to the person he was created to be. He was asking, "Do you want Me to restore your broken parts? Do you want Me to make you *whole* again?"

Do you want Jesus to restore your broken parts? Do you want Him to make *your* life situations well again? Are you ready to receive His restorative insight and healing? He's knocking. He's waiting for you to open the door. We encourage you to let Him in and receive His restoration, which truly is immeasurably more than you could ask or imagine.

Our faith experiences prove time and time again that no one restores the creation as well as the Creator.

You are not alone.

Armor up! Receive His restoration today and allow Him to prepare you to be *Fit 2 Fight!*

JJ MARIN

JJ Marin was born in Puerto Rico and came to South Florida at the age of six months. He settled in the Miami Lakes area, where he stayed through middle school, high school, college, and his law enforcement career.

After a great career in law enforcement, JJ became the CEO of his own private investigation firm. JJ continues to grow his business, always vowing to help give back to the community, especially to Christian organizations such as churches and the Band of Brothers.

JJ is on the leadership team for the Florida Band of Brothers, a men's ministry. His goal is to reach out to men to help them become warriors of Christ!

JJ is married to his beautiful wife, Lauren, and has two beautiful children, James and Jeremy. He loves to spend time with family and friends, whether in the woods or on a boat, always seeking to help them grow and succeed along with him.

Battling for Good with Jesus at My Side

By JJ Marin

When we think about all the lives that have had traumatic hardships and difficult woundedness, how can we summarize it? How can we explain how many times faithfully fighting in the power of Jesus has saved us? We don't realize our absolute salvific blessings from our mighty Lord and Savior's hand. Our fight bears a daily consistency while our goal is to keep fighting the good fight alongside Christ Jesus, our Lord!

My name is JJ Marin, and I've got some insight for you. I want to tell you a story about how I battled victoriously through my life guided by our Lord and Savior, Jesus Christ, and the Holy Spirit. I am an overcomer!

Like many, I endured difficult struggles growing up. I wanted a different life than the way I was raised and longed to leave my family's past painful dysfunction behind me. The past's generational curse must die! Only by following Christ was I willing to fight to live and be the wiser and stronger me God created!

I attained my bachelor's degree and set forth to begin my law enforcement career, determined to defeat the curse and become somebody who makes a helpful and protective difference in people's lives. I had been helplessly bound as a child and teen. However, as an adult, I felt equipped to make desired changes and be a difference maker!

I encountered constant battles but was determined to fight and be the best I could be. When attempting my career start, multiple police departments rejected me because of my driving record. Confident in my purpose, I remained focused on my goal.

With my faith tested, I didn't know which way to turn. So, I applied to the Coast Guard, which has a law enforcement division. After completing the paperwork, I received a call saying the Coast Guard was ready for me, but they couldn't guarantee that I'd stay in Florida. This caused some problems. I was concerned about leaving my mom, who had been through enough. I felt I needed to remain with her as her protective warrior. Likewise, I didn't want to leave my beautiful girlfriend (who's now my stunning wife). So, I asked the recruiter for a day to think over the offer.

As I considered my options, I thought about how I had been fighting relentlessly for my law enforcement goal but wasn't achieving it. Then, I remembered Mom's encouragement to have faith in Jesus. So, I prayed for God to help open my mind toward His plan. But though I thought and prayed, I couldn't discern the answer.

The following day, before contacting the recruiter, I GOT THE CALL! One of the police departments I had applied to asked if I was still interested in a law enforcement career. I excitedly said yes, completed the necessary paperwork, and set my start date. My desired career was finally within reach. I thanked God for the opportunity and had a renewed faith to fight with the persistent dedication to follow my dreams. Praise God, it was time to go to work!

I never thought my faith would be so challenged as it was when I was in law enforcement. The things I dealt with visually were tough. Because of the career's harsh nature, I saw the worst in everyone. I witnessed too much— from horrible criminals to abused and deceased youth to heinous physical and mental elder abuse. I saw a plethora of dreadful traffic incidents, leaving broken bodies strewn on the street. The career's vile debauchery left little space for a loving heart and soul. Without breaking confidentiality, I admit my involvement in many high-liability critical incidents with violent gang crimes. The street's necessary survival mode bore a serious mental strain between home and work.

Further, home now had my beautiful wife. She was a Registered Nurse (RN) at a hospital near the police station I worked out of. So, we both dealt with the dark side of the city's emergency situations. We were both young and thankful for our careers. We looked forward to starting our family; we didn't know we were about to face one of the toughest fights of our lives.

Things began to get rocky when my wife was pregnant with our first child. Between hormone shifts, wild work schedules, and taking on additional hours to save for our son's arrival, tensions were high. Concerned with the debilitating strain from my career, I wondered if I was making the right choices. My tested faith began to slip. The enemy threw continual blows at me as temptations surrounded me and my focus became dark and blurry. The dark drift began to affect my home life, which is what I always wanted to avoid. Since I was young, I so desired to avoid home and marital problems. I just wanted to be the best husband and father I could be so that my family would never experience abandonment woes. I had to stop, pray, and have faith that things would get better. I felt like the darkness was swallowing me, and I prayed faithfully for situational improvements. Jesus never said it would be easy. In fact, He warns, *The thief comes only to steal and kill and destroy; I have come that they may have life, and have it to the full* (John 10:10 NIV).

I valued my new family. I knew I had to make better decisions to enact change, and I trusted Jesus to help me. I fought against the world's lies and spiritual warfare through the power of ceaseless prayer. In His steps, Jesus empowered me as His faithful warrior. Together, we would win this battle!

As we held on to faith, our marriage's health improved greatly. The day that our son was born changed my life. A lifetime of thoughts raced through my mind as I held him for the first time. Holding him, I professed, "I will be the best dad I can be, and I will never leave you!" This moment's feeling was indescribable. Words fall short because it's something you must experience to know. It's as if the Holy Spirit provided His loving perspective. Such love for His blessed gift is priceless.

We were home for two weeks when terror struck. Our son stopped breathing. He was losing oxygen and turning blue. Fortunately, my wife was a critical care nurse. She administered oxygen while I drove us to the ER with great urgency. Once there, the nurse worked swiftly to raise our son's oxygen levels before they transported him to Joe DiMaggio Children's Hospital. He had a respiratory infection amid an underdeveloped airway from birth.

I couldn't help but wonder why this was happening. "Lord, I'm faithfully doing the right things. Please! Don't let our boy suffer like this," I prayed.

I called my mom; she encouraged further faithful, fervent prayer for our son's healing. I yielded to God, "Lord, please strengthen our son through this fight."

I prayed and believed God had already won the fight and our son would come through stronger!

After weeks in the NICU, our son recovered and we went home. The battle was intensely frightening, but prayer's power petitioned God, and He fought before us, so our son won!

Friends, the battles never stop. As I continued to fight the good fight of faith, I took on additional work while my wife took time off to care for our son at home. It was challenging covering her salary, but we do what we must for family. I pulled eighteen-hour days most weeks for months so she could provide the care he needed.

It wasn't long before she was pregnant again; it was Round Two time! Seemingly endless work hours, law enforcement's horror, and home hormone shifts took a toll on our souls. The devil's spiritual warfare hit us through resentment, ensuing divisive thoughts planted by other's skewed relationship advice. I became distant and worked even more so I wouldn't have to deal with the drama.

I knew I had to recenter and remember to fix my *eyes on Jesus, the pioneer and perfecter of faith* (Hebrews 12:2 NIV). Even through the drift, I prayed faithfully that my wife and I would return to our joy together. He fights our battles when we *take captive every thought to make it obedient to Christ* (2 Corinthians 10:5 NIV). I had to stand on my faith and trust the Lord! I knew what I had to do to please the Lord. So, I donned my big-boy pants and stopped allowing work to affect our home. I prayed, "Lord, guide me on Your chosen path so that I may be the man I must be for my family." He showed me that His *word is a lamp for my feet and a light on my path* (Psalm 119:105 NIV).

Jesus tells us in Mark 11:24 that when we believe for what we prayerfully ask, we will receive it. I did, and He rightfully restored our family only by His wisdom, peace, and power! We had tried on our own and failed. Our experience told us He is the only one who wins a focused warrior's battle.

When our second son was born, he stayed hospitalized longer than usual as a precaution based on our first son's challenges. Both boys were born a little early, but thank God they were strong and healthy. As we walked His path, the Lord blessed our growing family.

My heart always desired to live out Matthew 5:9, *Blessed are the peacemakers, for they will be called children of God* (NIV). My helpful and protective career was important to me for my family and society. I was extremely good at my career as a divinely blessed "peacemaker." They called me "Eagle Eyes" because of my detailed attention and ability to spot criminal activity. I helped put away many criminals and won several annual awards like the Law Enforcement Officer (LEO) award that recognized the county's best officers and investigators. As previously mentioned, I worked in a gang and financial fraud unit. Murder and money's toxic combination resulted in challenging warfare. The wars were seemingly endless. For example, when I was once working an investigation, I listened to a recorded jail call of a gang member I had arrested. He mentioned death threats toward me and my family. As I heard this, many wild thoughts ran through my head. Aside from initial thoughts of violently grabbing him by the neck, my warrior's perspective knew that I must protect my family. My goal became that the entire gang would be locked up, and my family would be safely relocated. THE FIGHT WAS ON!

In my young family's interest, I had to move fast for their safety. Honestly, my heightened alertness was through the roof, and life felt upside down for a moment. The department swapped my undercover car weekly, we moved every six months, and I lived on next to no sleep. I ran on adrenaline daily and did whatever it took to protect and serve my family well. Meanwhile, the city's heinous crime scene worsened with daily shootings and heightened criminal activity. Peaceful rest seemed unattainable.

I thought I could handle the strain myself, but I couldn't. I had to stop and give it to God. I prayed, "Jesus, I need You! I can't beat this alone. I'm drained, and I need Your strength, wisdom, and direction to protect my family." I needed His loving peace to see us through to His right decisions. It was time to get to church and discover what Jesus wanted from me and my family.

In 2013, I submitted my life to Jesus and felt like a twenty-ton truck came off my shoulders. When I decided to follow Jesus, answers came. He sent strength and clear vision as He went before me on life's path. We'd been through it, and He helped me understand that *I can do all things through Christ who strengthens me* (Philippians 4:13 ESV).

I needed to know how else I could support my family. I couldn't keep putting my family in harm's way, and I needed a change. I was dedicated to performing my career well to make a difference; however, my helping heart had a family now, and they were my first concern. Career change was a must, but how? Once I let go and let GOD, Jesus happily showed me the "how."

My private investigation and protection firm was His answer. It's a total win! I help people as a small business owner, enjoy more family time, and keep my loved ones out of a criminal's harmful eye. It's exciting that faith in the Lord led to the right decisions. As He answered the "how," I needed to know when to transition from the public to the private sector. As much as I prayed, He also had me waiting. Waiting elevates faith to fight through temporary challenges.

A prayerful year passed as I remained goal-focused. I prayed for clear divine guidance and patience through the process. However, His perspective isn't always instant. Often, patience is acquired through situational waiting. In the waiting, I knew God had brought us to it and He would bring us through it! So, we waited and consistently prayed for His next right move so I could passionately serve and protect without risking my life.

Time passed, and I was involved in a near-death shooting. Among all other shootings, vehicle incidents, and street violence, this was the worst. With the gun pointed at me, life passed before me. I saw through the barrel clearly; everything around was a peripheral blur. Thoughts of my family and home flashed through my mind. Faithful fortune found my partner and me shooting first to neutralize the threat. As the scene settled, I knew that if I kept this up, I would one day no longer be there for my family.

Not long after, my heart went into arrhythmia, and I was transported to the hospital. Rescue rapidly got me connected. My mind raced when my heart rate repeatedly fluctuated from eighty to 240 BPM. I prayed, "Jesus please help me! Heal me, Lord! I can't go down now; my family needs me!" I had to fight through it, *believing* that I would be alright. And that's what we did.

The hospital medical staff did all they could to help. Several hours later, my heart was stabilized, and my mind rested. Praise Jesus! My wife and Sergeant were at my bedside to check on my condition. After speaking with Sarge, I relinquished my department-owned firearm. After he left, I said to my wife, "I think this is how I start." She knew what I meant and quickly agreed.

The Lord told me to slow down, breathe, and listen to Him. He used this situation to sit me down long enough to *listen,* because it's so hard to hear Him in the noise. At that moment, He gave me this simple verse to lean on. Proverb 3:5-6 encourages us to *Trust in the Lord with all your heart and lean not on your own understanding, in all your ways submit to him, and he will make your paths straight* (NIV). What a grand idea! I'll do it!

Yeah, sure, we're tough guys! Know this, tough guy: our challenges are never-ending. We think we have all the answers, that "we got this," but we don't. God does. This fallen world tells us that we've got it handled. But Jesus says, *"Come to me all who are weary and burdened, and I will give you rest"* (Matthew 11:28 NIV). The world lies to us; Jesus is the Truth. It's okay to cry and ask for help. Real men cry and love Jesus! You are not alone! We are a Band of Brothers, and we must stick together and hold each other accountable so that we are *Fit 2 Fight* the good fight of faith!

We must guard our hearts and defend our families from this world. Our best effort is to believe in Jesus and allow the Holy Spirit to help us understand His loving truth. Regardless of our shortcomings, God's arms are wide open for us. Our goal seeks guiding truth and wisdom in His Word so that we minimize our mistakes through life's challenges. The Bible is our playbook. When we believe and absorb it, truth forges battle-ready warriors who are *Fit 2 Fight* His good fight. He calls us to *"Take My yoke upon you and learn from me"* (Matthew 11:29a NIV). So, let's put our big boy pants on, learn from Jesus, and defend ourselves and our families in Christ.

Always remember to "Armor up, Brothers!"

> *Finally, be strong in the Lord and in his mighty power. Put on the full armor of God, so that you can take your stand against the devil's schemes. For our struggle is not against flesh and blood, but against the rulers, against the authorities, against the powers of this dark world and against the spiritual forces of evil in the heavenly realms. Therefore, put on the full armor of God, so that when the day of evil comes, you may be able to stand your ground, and after you have done everything, to stand. Stand firm then, with the belt of truth buckled around your waist, with the breastplate of righteousness in place, and with your feet fitted with the readiness that comes from the gospel of peace. In addition to all this, take up the shield of faith, with which you can extinguish all the flaming arrows of the evil one. Take the helmet of salvation and the sword of the Spirit, which is the word of God. And pray in the Spirit on all occasions with all kinds of prayers and requests. With this in mind, be alert and always keep on praying for all the Lord's people.*
> (Ephesians 6:10-18 NIV)

Stay strong, my brothers and sisters, for the Lord has already won our battle. Let's fight from victory in the righteousness of our Lord and Savior, Jesus Christ!

ALEX GONZALEZ

Alejandro "Alex" Gonzalez graduated with honors from the University of Florida in 2002 with a Bachelors in Decision and Information Sciences. After, Alex worked as a database manager for the University of Florida Business Services Division. In 2008, he began a part-time career in financial services, then became a Regional Vice President and opened his first financial services office in 2012. Today, he continues to serve hundreds of clients, has a team of sixty-four licensed agents, and generates a six-figure income.

Alex has served on the Band of Brothers men's ministry leadership team since 2012. He is passionate about engaging men in pursuing their God-given purpose. Alex has been married to his beloved wife, Patty Gonzalez, since 2008 and has two sons, Sebastien and Adrian. He uses his business as marketplace ministry and currently leads the men's ministry at Victory Life Church in Plantation, Florida.

THE IMPORTANCE OF A FATHER LIKE JESUS

By Alex Gonzalez

God designed the family. It all began with His prize creations, man and woman, who were formed in His image (Genesis 1:27 NIV). He created the two for loving connections, as noted in the beginning: *A man leaves his father and mother and is united with his wife, and the two become one flesh* (Genesis 2:24 NIV). The Lord blessed them and encouraged them to be fruitful and increase in number—His will was for them to increase in number, fill the earth, and subdue it (Genesis 1:28a NIV). Here, in the beginning, God the Father's intended family unit was born.

I appreciate how Jesus reiterates His Father's intention in Matthew's Gospel. Our beloved Savior adds that as a married man and woman become one flesh, no man may separate what God has joined together (Matthew 19:5-6 NIV). Wow! That sounds great, doesn't it? Even better, the Word really points out how fathers should lead their families. For example, the Apostle Paul says that fathers are to encourage, comfort, and lead their children to live God-worthy lives (1 Thessalonians 2:11-12 NIV). What a great idea God has expressed through His Word! It all sounds just wonderful! However, there was a time when I just couldn't relate to His perfect plan.

Jesus asked what father would give his son a stone instead of bread or give him a snake instead of a fish to eat (Matthew 7:9-10 NIV); in my early life, I could relate to the stone and the snake. However, even as rough and tumble as my life has been, as left out in the cold as I have felt, and as out of control as I may have appeared, when I finally realized that our red-letter Savior was right there waiting for me to turn around, I found out that I was the one, I was the prodigal Jesus taught about in Luke 15 who received the Father's best robe, ring, and sandals. Our heavenly Father met me with open arms and showed me how to live for Him. My friends, I was lost, but today, in Jesus Christ, I am found (Luke 15:22-24 NIV). Through my experiences, I not only learned the importance of the biological family unit but also of the Christian family that we are all called to be part of. Buckle up. Let me tell you a story from the trough to the kingdom!

As you may have guessed, life started out pretty rough for me. I was born in 1978 in Cali, Colombia, to a 22-year-old woman who found out she would be a single mom the very day her first child was born. My father came to the hospital with his mistress to let my mother know that he had someone else and that he would not be with her any longer. This was the beginning of a child who would be raised without a father's continual presence. For the first five years of my life, my father would pick me up on weekends and spend time taking me to parks to fly kites and ride a bicycle.

My mother's business consisted of getting jewelry on credit and then selling it to her customers on credit. On one occasion, when I was five years old, a customer took a large order and disappeared, leaving my mother with significant debt. At that time in Colombia, if you owed money to someone and did not pay, you or your family could be killed. So, my mother left for the United States to work to pay off her debt so I could have a better future. As a result, I was left with my father, who lived with his mother, two sisters, and his sisters' three kids.

My father worked full-time for a corporation during the day and went to college full-time at night, so I was left to spend the day with my grandmother and three cousins. From the time I was five years old, I spent the majority of my time in the neighborhood without supervision. I learned how to fight and defend myself from street kids who would try to steal my bike or just have fun trying to bully me.

The first summer without my mother, my grandmother on my mother's side, who hated my father, took me from my father and moved me to Pereira, Colombia, to live with her and her husband, Rodrigo. In Pereira, I was the only small child. I spent time between my grandmother's house and her sister's house, who was like a second grandmother. Their message to me was, "Any man can be a father, but there is only one mother."

One evening when I was seven years old, Rodrigo said, "Tonight I'm gonna teach you how to be a man." He sat me down at a small table with a bottle of Aguardiente, which is a very strong Colombian alcohol. When I took my first shot, he said, "You gotta be a man and not make any faces."

That night was my first time getting drunk.

I continued getting drunk pretty frequently from that time on in my life. Rodrigo was a loving man to me; he was just doing the best he knew to teach me about manhood.

My mother brought me to America in 1985 when I was eight years old. She had remarried and brought me in on a Visa so we could all live in Miami, Florida. We lived in Kendall, Miami, with my stepfather, Francisco, and his mother and two brothers. Francisco taught me the importance of reading, while my mother taught me the values of discipline, integrity, and character. I felt like I finally had a normal home life. I played in the neighborhood, but my mother kept track of me. We lived in a decent neighborhood, and I was making some friends.

One summer in 1989, my stepfather bought a wave runner and took his nephew and me to a lake in Miami, where people took watercrafts for recreation. When we were wrapping up that afternoon, my stepfather took one last ride without his life vest. He hit a wave and drowned. I did not believe he was actually dead until I saw him for the last time at the funeral. It seemed every time there was a father figure in my life, he would leave somehow. At 12 years old, I began to see that I was the man who would take care of my mother.

My mother received a small life insurance payout and Social Security from my stepfather's death, so we moved to Plantation, Florida. As a fatherless child, I began associating with other fatherless boys and began to be mischievous. I learned manhood was about getting girls and having sex, making money, and winning fights. I started smoking weed at 14 and had sex for the first time in middle school.

In high school, I was in honor classes and on the honor roll. I felt proud of myself. I had plenty of friends, was sleeping with girls, and had a pretty lucrative part-time hustle. I managed to get a college scholarship because I did well in school and played on the high school soccer team.

Then, in my senior year in high school, I went to donate blood to get out of class and met Jodi, the phlebotomist who was 23 years old. I got her number, and soon, I was dating an attractive older woman.

I graduated high school, moved to Gainesville for college, and continued drinking and sleeping around, even though I was in a long-distance relationship. When I graduated from the University of Florida with honors, I proposed to Jodi.

She said, "If I am going to marry someone, he must be a believer."

So I said that I, of course, was a believer in Jesus.

That said, under the guise of my so-called belief, Jodi introduced me to Pastor Ron Bramos. Pastor Ron was her pastor who she intended to marry us, so it stood to reason that I should meet this fine fellow. Unlike myself, she was raised in church but fell away from her faith as she got older.

After a short conversation with Pastor Ron, he recognized that I was somewhat of an atheist. I remember thinking to myself, *What a typical Christian, judging me without even knowing me. Really, what does this guy know about me?*

I always believed in God. I just never had an opportunity to get to know Him. His Word encouraged parents to *Start their children off on the way they should go, and even when they are old, they will not turn away from it* (Proverbs 22:6 NIV). That's all fine and good, but I didn't get that proverbial "good head start." Because I had no godly men in my life, I had never read the Bible. So, I was just going on what I knew and hoping that would be enough.

Jodi and I got married in 2002 and lived together in Gainesville. My drinking continued, but I didn't allow it to affect my career or marriage, and I thought that I might like to believe. My wife and I tried having children but were not able to due to what they called infertility on my part. As time passed, the news kept spiraling downward when I found out my wife was cheating on me in 2006. Soon thereafter, we were divorced. Not that I knew this at the time, but it brings me some solace now that the only reason that Jesus advocates divorce is for sexual immorality. It was like He let me off the hook, and I didn't even know about it. Even in such dire straits, life was about to take a new turn.

I was twenty-seven when God's plan for me was about to take hold. I was single with no kids and had a carpet dying and cleaning business. My drinking habit was not getting any better, and as a bachelor, I was sleeping with many women. I was in business for myself and was pulling in a decent income. At the time, I thought I had it pretty good. I had a truck, a nice car, and a motorcycle. Life at this stage was me for me.

One evening, I ran into Patty, an ex-girlfriend I had dated in high school. We started dating; I told her I was previously married and could not have kids, so I was not family material. She said the same was true about her. She had also been married and tried having children but could not.

Six months later, one week after I almost lost my life in a devastating traffic incident in my company van, we found out that she was pregnant; we were going to be first-time parents! Did you read that right? I was going to be a father!

On the one hand, I was totally shocked because I thought I would be a bachelor for life. On the other hand, I was super excited about being a father. Our son, Sebastien, was born in January 2008, and Patty and I began attending Potential Church. I dug in and started reading the Bible and learning about God.

What a lifestyle shift! It was almost like a culture shock or something. We were rolling with it, but I must admit that change was a slow process for me. Look out! Here He comes! Enter THE HOLY SPIRIT! His obvious indwelling in Patty and I began strongly convicting us. We decided to get baptized and were married in late 2008. I had invested in several properties, but due to the 2008 market crash, I lost three homes. We struggled financially, and we both carried a lot of baggage from our past. We started a part-time business in financial services, and by 2012, I left my carpet business and opened my first office.

Later in 2012, I was invited to a Band of Brothers Bootcamp by a very successful person in my business named Guy Shashaty. At the time, we were financially strained. I had just spent $2000 fixing my car, not to mention that Christmas was coming, and I had no idea how I would get our family's Christmas presents. I told Guy that I wanted to hit up the Bootcamp, but I just couldn't afford it at the time. Guy is not one to take no for an answer, so he sponsored me so I could experience the Lord's next moves for this man who just needed a break. One break coming up!

The Bootcamp was transformational for me. I had never been on any type of spiritual retreat or spent a weekend examining my life. I had no idea what God was about to do. I was exposed to John 10:10, which informed me, *The thief comes only to steal, kill, and destroy* (NIV). Until that point, I had not realized I had an enemy my whole life. I finally realized that all these "sweet treat distractions" like alcohol, girls, and clubs were simply traps to kill my God-intended potential. I began to recognize that my first marriage had failed because the enemy of our souls wanted to destroy it. Likewise, if I didn't wake up NOW, he would destroy my second marriage.

For the first time, I heard God say, "I am your Father."

I understood that my self-destructive ways had come from a little boy's wounded heart. I was the boy who felt so drastically alone deep inside. Isaiah, the Lord's prophet, recognizes in his 63rd chapter that the Lord is our Father! Even as others fail to acknowledge Him, He is our Father!

> *You, Lord, are our Father, our Redeemer from of old is your name.*
> (Isaiah 63:16 NIV)

As I came to believe, the Holy Spirit taught me the truth that I have a Father who kept me alive when the enemy of my soul wanted me dead. My Lord, my God is my Father of several chances as He gives me a new opportunity to be a father to our two beloved young sons.

The Apostle Paul reckons in his letter to the Ephesians that *We are God's handiwork, created in Christ Jesus to do good works, which God prepared in advance for us to do* (Ephesians 2:10 NIV).

The time had come for me to surrender my life and begin living for Christ.

For the first time, I realized I had been playing on the wrong team. More than that, I didn't even realize that the wrong team's coach only ever played me with a desire for me to fail and die. The Lord revealed that I had been using the good gifts He had given me for the wrong things, and He had a Christian family prepared to show me how to use those gifts for His glory and the good of His people.

Sometime later, I joined the Band of Brothers leadership team. The Spirit was teaching me faithfully to understand that I needed to be the dad I never had for my children. Now I knew we must bring our children up in the way of the Lord.

In 2018, I was sitting in a client's home who lived with his parents. As we were discussing his financial plan, my client's parents arrived home. Guess who it was. Would you believe that it was Pastor Ron and his wife, Cheryl? God is so amazing that He would take me to the house of the same pastor who had called me an atheist just a few years earlier. I shared with him that I had remarried and how God had changed my life. I also told him I had been serving with Band of Brothers for five years as our magnificent Father God was preparing me to lead our church's men's ministry.

Today, I lead the men's ministry in Pastor Ron's Victory Life Church. As of March 2023, I am alcohol-free. I know that I could not have left drinking on my own. However, as Paul's tumultuous life declares in his letter to the Philippians, regardless of the circumstances, *I can do all this through him who gives me strength* (Philippians 4:13 NIV).

Today, I live a purpose-driven life, sharing with others that no matter who your biological father is, Jesus Christ is your true Father. The Apostle John's Gospel rivals the enemy's prowling when Jesus authoritatively declares, *"I have come that they may have life, and have it to the full"* (John 10:10b NIV).

I am so grateful that God used other men to introduce me to a life of following Jesus. Now, no matter what challenges arise, I confidently believe and know that *In all things God works for the good of those who love him, who have been called according to his purpose* (Romans 8:28 NIV).

I pray that my story can be used for God's glory. I hope that no matter what mistakes you have made, you discover that Jesus knew you would make them and that He already paid the price in full by His work on the cross and walking out of that tomb three days later.

Friends, just as our old person dies with Him at the cross, so has our new person been raised to life through His resurrection! I am a new creation in Christ. Similarly, as you believe, so are you!

God has the perfect plan for your life. One of His greatest creations is family, and I can guarantee that His plan for you includes surrounding you with family—HIS family. The family of Christian brotherhood who you can serve, learn from, and be accountable to. God designed us to establish loving connections with others. Will you step out and trust God, your Father, who has more for you than you can imagine?

> *Seek his kingdom, and these things will be given to you as well.*
> *Do not be afraid, little flock, for your Father has*
> *been pleased to give you the kingdom.*
> (Luke 12:31-32 NIV)

Fit 2 Fight from a Sound Identity

By Allen L. Thorne

In a world that seems to be in turmoil, it may appear that the idea of having a sound mind has gotten lost in the undertows. However, the craziness of the contemporary world isn't a new thing but a historical repeat of our fallibly finite human condition that surfaces when we remove God. The prophet Isaiah refers to such times in his fifth chapter, contending:

> *Woe to those who call evil good, and good evil; Who substitute darkness for light and light for darkness; Who substitute bitter for sweet and sweet for bitter! Woe to those who are wise in their own eyes and clever in their own sight! Woe to those who are heroes in drinking wine, And valiant men in mixing strong drink, Who justify the wicked for a bribe, and take away the rights of the ones who are in the right!*
> *(Isaiah 5:20-23 NASB)*

Wow! Is it just me, or does that sound frighteningly familiar? Investigate the next few verses for yourself, and you'll see that it doesn't end too well for those who decide to go their own way and find their identity somewhere out there in our created universe. When we conform to the world's pattern, we get what the world has to offer in the way of fear, anxiety, depression, and the like.

As created beings under the authority of our Creator Father God, our intended identity is found in Him. When we seek our identity in hollow pursuits like work, money, social status, and controlled substances, we operate in exhausting self-sufficiency. We tend to run a never-ending race for *more*, living in fear of what we'll lose if such is not attained. However, when we embrace being a creation who is under our divine Creator, we can *rest* in God's powerful strength and love with a disciplined, sound mind.

When preparing His disciples for His forthcoming departure, Jesus spoke of the Holy Spirit. Our Savior King declares, *"But when He, the Spirit of truth comes, He will guide you to all the truth; for He will not speak on His own, but whatever He hears, He will speak; and He will disclose to you what is to come"* (John 16:13 NASB).

Further, the Apostle Paul's declaration to his apprentice, Timothy, informs us of the Lord's baseline identity for us as His believing followers. Paul affirms, *For the Spirit God gave us does not make us timid, but gives us power, love, and self-discipline* (2 Timothy 1:7 NIV).

These three spiritual products—*power, love, and self-discipline*—translate from high-level Greek nouns. *Power* is translated from the Greek noun *dynamis,* which means mighty miraculous power. Likewise, the *love* provided by God's Spirit is translated from the Greek noun *agape,* which can best be defined as an unconditional feast of benevolent affection. Finally, self-discipline is translated from the Greek noun *sophronismos,* meaning *sound mind* or *self-control.* All three divine spiritual products are our intended identity components.

Notice that the Lord's provisions stand in stark contrast to the spirit of fear with which our satanic adversary clouds our judgment for as long as we allow. However, when we understand and believe that we are created in God's image, we trust that He always has our best interest in mind, and we begin to discover our *true identity.* Remember, it isn't basic finite power that the Lord's Spirit gives us; He provides *dynamis,* or *miraculous* power. He doesn't just provide love; His Spirit provides agape, the highest level of unconditional love available! And He does not just provide a sound mind;

He provides *sophronismos* or a divine calling to sound-mindedness.

By faith, we can trust that all the Lord provides is far greater than anything we could pursue in the world. Such is a firm foundation upon which we can build or rebuild our identity.

Our belief decisions today ultimately affect our future. If we choose to live in and of the world, its hollow deceptions will lead us astray toward fearful confusion and eventual victimhood. However, when we follow and trust God's infinite plan over our fallibly finite plan, He will encourage, enlighten, and empower us to be *Fit 2 Fight* satan's deceptions through His miraculous power and our God-given sound identity! Praise Him!

. . . .

AFTERWORD

Dearest fellow fighters, challenges are inevitable as we stride into life's arena. However, as the hands, feet, and body of Christ, we must know that we don't ever stride alone. As we bond together under and in the power and authority of Jesus Christ Himself, we become an army that is *Fit 2 Fight!*

We hope you have been inspired by how each *Fit 2 Fight* writer refused to let the darkness overcome them, instead choosing to embrace the Light of all mankind to guide their path back to His purpose for their lives. Fighters, the very same Light who is the way, truth, and life of all mankind is available for you! We are all welcome to come and faithfully believe *for* His truth through our circumstances. Embrace the Light, fighters! When we decide to learn from Him, His light fills us, pushes out darkness, and shines through us.

As He speaks life over His disciples, Jesus declares, *"You are the light of the world...Your light must shine before people in such a way that they may see your good works, and glorify your Father who is in heaven"* (Matthew 5:14a, 16 NASB).

Please know our prayers are with you and your families as you stride into and through the challenges together. We pray even more that as you embrace the journey, you believe that the Lord will go before you and direct you as you trust and follow His will and way over your own.

King David confirms, *Even before there was a word on my tongue, Behold, Lord, You know it all. You have encircled me behind and in front, and placed Your hand upon me* (Psalm 139:4-5 NASB).

Let us enter the arena together with confidence! Even though multiple trials will mount before us, we can trust they will all lead to triumph when we face them together, allowing God to lead us. Fighters, there is no triumph without a trial! There is no freedom without a fight! As we link arms, let's recognize that His Word does *not* declare that no weapon will be formed against you. Instead, Isaiah's prophetic word declares, *"No weapon that is formed against you will succeed; And you will condemn every tongue that accuses you in judgment. This is the heritage of the servants of the Lord, and their vindication is from Me," declares the Lord* (Isaiah 54:17 NASB).

When we stand on God's truth, the satanic accuser has no reign. Fighters, observe Isaiah's words just above once again. As creations under the one, true, and living God, He empowers us to condemn the accuser! Likewise, we are vindicated by God Himself; which means He defends us and secures us.

Wow! Such is the faithful belief that has gripped each writer in this book as they have strived toward their fighting fitness. Like them, we encourage you to embrace God's truth to empower you through your challenging arena!

Finally, our brotherhood's fighting fitness cannot be attributed to humanity's concepts but rather acquired through experiential learning opportunities. A wise man once said that sunny days are great, but if we only experience sunny days, then we won't know what to do in the rain. All sun and no rain destroys exposed life. Metaphorically speaking, authentic life growth requires rain. So, from that perspective, should we complain about or embrace the rain?

Fellow fighters, the rain is a blessing! The rain is where we learn from the Lord's teachable moments that empower our fighting fitness. Remember, there is no growth without life's challenging *rain*. Are you allowing the rain to bring anxiety and rob your peace and rest? If so, we encourage you to take some time to get quiet with the Lord and ask Him what He has to say about that. Remember also to take time to listen. Don't let the accuser weaken your fighting fitness. In Christ, you are emphatically better off when you decide to learn from Him.

Dear fighter, the Savior King is calling you. He invitingly proclaims, *"Come to Me, all who are weary and burdened, and I will give you rest. Take My yoke upon you and learn from Me, for I am gentle and humble in heart, and you will find rest for your souls"* (Matthew 11:28-29 NASB).

With Jesus, we are never alone.

Together in Christ, we have what it takes to be *Fit 2 Fight!*

MORE WPP ANTHOLOGIES!

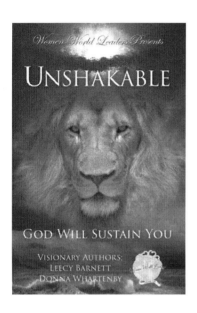

God longs for you to have ferocious faith grounded in His unwavering love. Get ready to be encouraged as you open the pages of *Unshakable: God Will Sustain You.* Through true stories written by faithful and resilient women, you will witness God's sustaining power available to those who rely on Him. Cast your cares on the Lord and he will sustain you; he will never let the righteous be shaken (Psalm 55:22 NIV).

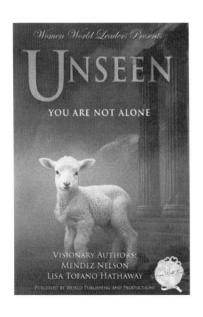

The authors of *Unseen: You Are Not Alone* share their struggles of feeling isolated and unnoticed and detail how our awesome God helped them overcome every obstacle to find what truly matters: Him. These stories and devotional teachings shed light on the truth of your significance and value. You are never alone!

Despite all the adversities we face throughout our lives, God is the source of our hope. As you read the pages of this book, you will see firsthand how God brings *Hope Alive* to every person who is yearning for a reason to go on. Like a broken tree in a dark place is primed for new growth, God can use the rich soil of your dark place to prepare a new life to sprout in you.

The authors of *Miracle Mindset: Finding Hope in the Chaos*, have experienced the wonders of God's provision, protection, and guidance. These stories and teachings will ignite a spark within you, propelling you to encounter the marvel of God's miracles, even in the chaos.

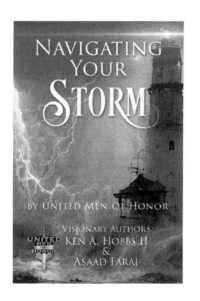

Life is full of storms and rough waters. The stories in *Navigating Your Storm: By United Men of Honor* will give you the ability to see the light of God and navigate your storm victoriously.

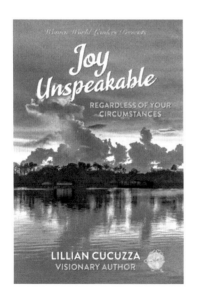

With *Joy Unspeakable: Regardless of Your Circumstances,* you will learn how joy and sorrow can dance together during adversity. The words in this book will encourage, inspire, motivate, and give you hope, joy, and peace.

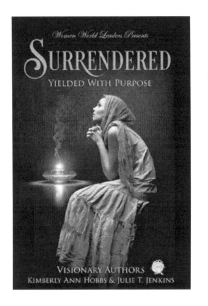

Surrendered: Yielded With Purpose will help you recognize with awe that surrendering to God is far more effective than striving alone. When we let go of our own attempts to earn God's favor and rely on Jesus Christ, we receive a deeper intimacy with Him and a greater power to serve Him.

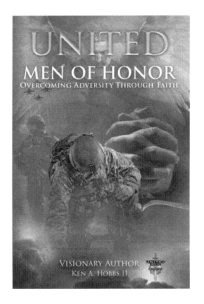

United Men of Honor: Overcoming Adversity Through Faith will help you armor up, become fit to fight, and move forward with what it takes to be an honorable leader. Over twenty authors in this book share their accounts of God's provision, care, and power as they proclaim His Word.

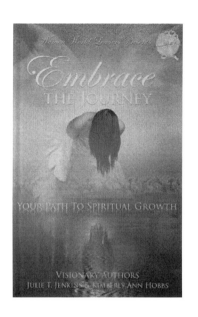

Embrace the Journey: Your Path to Spiritual Growth will strengthen and empower you to step boldly in faith. These stories, along with expertly placed expositional teachings will remind you that no matter what we encounter, we can always look to God, trusting HIS provision, strength, and direction.

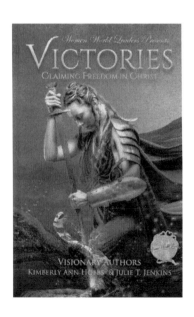

Victories: Claiming Freedom in Christ presents expository teaching coupled with individual stories that testify to battles conquered victoriously through the power of Jesus Christ. The words in this book will motivate and inspire you and give you hope as God awakens you to your victory!

WPP'S MISSION

World Publishing and Productions was birthed in obedience to God's call. Our mission is to empower writers to walk in their God-given purpose as they share their God story with the world. We offer one-on-one coaching and a complete publishing experience. To find out more about how we can help you become a published author or to purchase books written to share God's glory, please visit: **worldpublishingandproductions.com**

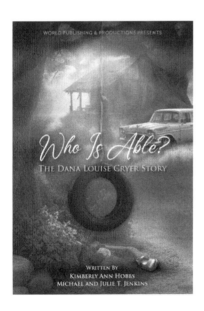

This phenomenal story of rescue, hope, healing, and forgiveness will captivate you. Dana Louise Cryer's tumultuous journey is filled with twists and turns as she learns that living in God's POWER can render ultimate forgiveness. God's incredible love transforms this true-life survival account into a miraculous outcome of total freedom. *Who Is Able?* will leave you breathless and in tears at what only God can do.

Heartbeat of a Survivor tells the story of Nita Tin, a Buddhist born and raised in an opulent lifestyle in Burma. As her country came under the control of a ruthless military dictator, Nita's whole life changed. Forced to flee her home, her soul was soon set free in a greater way than she ever dreamed possible.

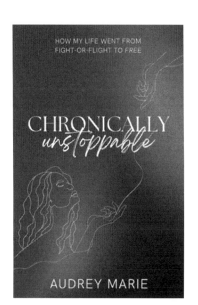

At seventeen, Audrey Marie experienced a sudden and relentless excruciating firestorm of pain. *Chronically Unstoppable* tells of her true-life journey as she faced pain, developed strength, and battled forward with hope.

The world has become a place where we don't have a millisecond to think for ourselves, often leaving us feeling lost or overwhelmed. That is why Max Gold wrote *Planestorming!*—a straightforward guide to help you evaluate and change your life for the better. It's time to get to work and make the rest of your life the BEST of your life.

THE BULLIED STUDENT
WHO CHANGED ALL THE RULES

A NOVEL BY
ROBERT M. FISHBEIN

Riley Rossey is not your everyday bullied student, but one who discovers how to utilize his talents to assist other shy and picked-on individuals. Journey with Riley as he meets bullying head-on and becomes a God-given blessing to so many in *The Bullied Student Who Changed All the Rules* by Robert M. Fishbein.